San Jacinto 1

San Jacinto 1

A Historical Ecological Approach to an Archaic Site in Colombia

AUGUSTO OYUELA-CAYCEDO
AND RENÉE M. BONZANI

THE UNIVERSITY OF ALABAMA PRESS
Tuscaloosa

Copyright © 2005
The University of Alabama Press
Tuscaloosa, Alabama 35487-0380
All rights reserved
Manufactured in the United States of America

Typeface: AGaramond

∞

The paper on which this book is printed meets the minimum requirements of American National Standard for Information Science—Permanence of Paper for Printed Library Materials, ANSI Z39.48–1984.

Library of Congress Cataloging-in-Publication Data

Oyuela-Caycedo, Augusto, 1961–
  San Jacinto 1 : a historical ecological approach to an archaic site in Colombia / Augusto Oyuela-Caycedo and Renée M. Bonzani.
     p. cm.
  Includes bibliographical references and index.
  ISBN 0-8173-1450-4 (cloth : alk. paper) — ISBN 0-8173-5184-1 (pbk. : alk. paper)
  1. San Jacinto 1 Site (Colombia) 2. Indians of South America—Colombia—Bolívar (Dept.)—Antiquities. 3. Indian pottery—Colombia—Bolívar (Dept.) 4. Excavations (Archaeology)—Colombia—Bolívar (Dept.) 5. Plant remains (Archaeology)—Colombia—Bolívar (Dept.) 6. Animal remains (Archaeology)—Colombia—Bolívar (Dept.) 7. Bolívar (Colombia : Dept.)—Antiquities. I. Title: San Jacinto One. II. Bonzani, Renee M., 1962– III. Title.
  F2269.1.B664O98 2005
  986.1′14—dc22

                                                                                         2004023855

To the people of San Jacinto

Contents

List of Figures   ix

List of Tables   xiii

Preface and Acknowledgments   xv

1. Introduction   1
2. The Theoretical Framework   33
3. The Strata and Features   50
4. The Pottery and Lithics   70
5. The Ecofactual Remains   108
6. San Jacinto 1 in Perspective   144

Appendix 1   165

Appendix 2   171

Notes   175

References Cited   179

Index   215

Figures

1.1. Location of the site of San Jacinto 1, Colombia, South America   3

1.2. Location of the study region and early Formative sites   4

1.3. Landscape of San Jacinto 1   4

1.4. Meander cut and profile view of site of San Jacinto 1   5

1.5. Profile of site of San Jacinto 1 from the San Jacinto stream   5

1.6. Mean annual precipitation and water deficiency in the Serranía de San Jacinto   19

1.7. Excavation of San Jacinto 1   30

1.8. Excavation of strata 9 and 10 at San Jacinto 1   30

1.9. Excavation of features from strata 9 through 20 at San Jacinto 1   31

3.1. Stream catchment and alluvial floodplains   51

3.2. Stratigraphic illustration of western and northern walls   53

3.3. Stratigraphy of the site as revealed in profile   54

3.4. Physical characteristics of strata and example of relationship with two augered perforations   54

3.5. Computer illustration of the spatial distribution of the site based on the extrapolation of the stratigraphy obtained during coring   55

3.6. Excavation revealing features recovered at San Jacinto 1   57

3.7. Example of excavation of earth oven: Feature 57   58

3.8. Detail of excavation of Feature 57 showing variation in the fire-cracked rocks employed   58

3.9. Example of variation in feature sizes and volume of fire-cracked rocks   59

3.10. Example of feature sizes and thermally altered walls after the excavation of the anthropic soils   60

3.11. Mollusk concentration recovered from San Jacinto 1   61

3.12. Distribution of fire-pits in strata 9, 10, and 12   66

4.1. Vessel from Puerto Chacho, dating around 5000 B.P.   72

4.2. Zoomorphic lugs from San Jacinto 1   73

4.3. Lug from San Jacinto 1 with representation of bird   74

4.4. Lug from San Jacinto 1 with representation of bird   75

4.5. Lug from San Jacinto 1 with unidentified representation   76

4.6. Typical decoration of top part of vessels   77

4.7. Edge decoration of vessel   77

4.8. Impressions of grasses (Poaceae) in the fiber-tempered paste   78

4.9. Block metate found cached in situ in Feature 63   78

4.10. Basin-shaped metate from Feature 76   79

4.11. Examples of flake technology at San Jacinto 1   88

4.12. Slab metate Pl #1   91

4.13. Handstones from San Jacinto 1   92

4.14. Handstones from San Jacinto 1   93

4.15. Handstone showing grinding edge   94

4.16. Mortar or nutcracker   95

4.17. Nutcracker   95

4.18. Mortar   96

4.19. Hammerstone   97

4.20. Distribution of pottery and fire-cracked rocks in stratum 9   104

5.1. Botanical fragment from San Jacinto 1 and maize cupule fragment from the Highbee Tavern site in Fayette County, Kentucky   120

5.2. Seed fragment from stratum 10 and modern carbonized maize kernel showing the scar of the abscission layer   121

5.3. SEM photograph showing secondary layer or aleurone of modern carbonized maize kernel   122

Figures

5.4. SEM photograph showing secondary layer or aleurone of modern carbonized northern teosinte kernel   123

5.5. SEM photograph showing secondary layer or aleurone of archaeological carbonized parenchyma fragment from San Jacinto 1   124

5.6. Close-up SEM photographs showing secondary layer or aleurone of modern carbonized northern teosinte kernel and archaeological carbonized parenchyma fragment from San Jacinto 1   125

5.7. Beads made from the opercula of *Neocyclotus*   139

5.8. Distribution of *Pomacea* spp. and *Neocyclotus* cfr. *dysoni* in stratum 9   141

6.1. Anthropomorphic representation in fiber-tempered pottery from San Jacinto 1   159

6.2. Anthropomorphic representation in fiber-tempered pottery from San Jacinto 2   159

6.3. Anthropomorphic representation in fiber-tempered pottery from Puerto Hormiga   160

6.4. Lug fragment from a bowl from San Jacinto 1   160

6.5. Fragment of a fiber-tempered pottery lug from a surface collection at San Jacinto 2   161

6.6. Fragment of a fiber-tempered pottery zoomorphic lug from a surface collection at San Jacinto 2   162

Tables

1.1. Radiocarbon dates from strata 9 through 20   6

1.2. Plant species in reserves in the region of San Juan de Nepomuceno, Bolívar, Colombia   8

1.3. Plants collected in the vicinity of San Jacinto 1 and at the marketplaces of San Jacinto and Cartagena de Los Indios in 1991–1992   10

1.4. Radiocarbon dates from other sites in northern Colombia with early pottery   23

3.1. Soil formation sequence of San Jacinto 1   56

3.2. Relationship between mobility strategy, variation between sites, seasonal reoccupation, and assemblage redundancy   62

3.3. Feature redundancy and mobility   64

4.1. Pottery fragments recovered by type and stratum   71

4.2. Cross-section form of slab, block, and basin-shaped metates   79

4.3. Total number of complete metates recovered by stratum   79

4.4. Total number of fragments of metates recovered by stratum   80

4.5. Direction of use-wear and type of metates   80

4.6. Raw material types selected for metates   80

4.7. Stratigraphic distribution of handstones (manos), mortars, and hammerstones   81

4.8. Raw material types selected for handstones (manos)   81

4.9. Use-wear patterns on mortars   81

4.10. Raw material type of fire-cracked rocks by number and total weight in stratum 9   82

4.11. Stratigraphic distribution of fire-cracked rocks by sedimentary raw material type and weight   82

4.12. Stratigraphic distribution of fire-cracked rocks by igneous raw material type and weight   83

4.13. Basic general rules of technology   85

4.14. Basic statistics of pottery and fire-cracked rocks by weight   103

4.15. Pottery fragments from stratum 9   103

4.16. Total weight and number of fire-cracked rocks in stratum 9   105

5.1. Stratigraphic distribution of carbonized botanical remains   117

5.2. Grasses collected near the site in 1991–1992   128

5.3. Stratigraphic distribution of mollusks   136

5.4. Percentage of *Pomacea cornucopia* and *Pomacea elegans* in relation to *Neocyclotus* cfr. *dysoni* by stratum   138

5.5. Basic statistics of the freshwater snails *Pomacea* and *Neocyclotus* by number of individuals   140

Preface and Acknowledgments

To do archaeology is more than to have a research problem, economic support, excavations, and a presentation of results. Any archaeological project takes place in a social, economic, and political context that influences its development. This fact is especially true of the current work, which took place in one of the most violent democracies in the world: Colombia. It seems to be contradictory to have the two terms *democracy* and *violence* joined together, but that is the case. Colombia is a Latin American county with the distinction of having had only one dictatorial government (1953–1957) in its history. However, it also has one of the worst records in the hemisphere of human rights violations and of violence committed with impunity.

Colombia is fast becoming a symbolic democracy and one of the oldest on the continent. The scope of the problem is complex and beyond the primary purpose of this book. However, this work took place in that context and it cannot be ignored. I grew up close to the area where the research took place (Sincelejo, capital of the Department of Sucre). The project started in 1986 when I was sent to San Jacinto with a commission to evaluate whether it would be possible to help a local cultural organization of high school students create a cultural center (Comite Cultural y Civico de San Jacinto). The student organization and later Oyuela-Caycedo requested assistance from the Museo de Oro of the Banco de la Republica to help organize a museum. The Museo de Oro supported the project, and a small museum was developed with artifactual materials that the students had collected from the surface. Among the material were fragments of pottery that employed fiber temper in the manufacturing process. It is well known that this technique is associated with early forms of pottery manufacturing. The report of a site called Puerto Hormiga elaborated by G. Reichel-Dolmatoff (1965b) clearly demonstrated that by at least 3000 B.C. some of the oldest pottery in the American continents was being made on the north coast of Colombia.

With the collaboration of a teacher from the high school and the enthusiastic students, we located two of the sites. However, during the year after the inauguration of the small museum, all of the students who collaborated on the project had to abandon the town; one of them was even exiled. They had become a target of the paramilitary organizations that are controlled by one of the landlords of the town and a major political boss of the area. We became aware of what had happened to the students only when I returned with Renée M. Bonzani to San Jacinto in 1991. None of the people whom he met in the previous years were there. The deterioration of the town was visible in the infrastructure and it was as if we were in a totally different place. The friendly town had been transformed into a town being choked by the high tension of a war.

This book has been in the planning for more than 12 years. Initially we hoped to excavate other sites that correspond to different seasonal stages of human occupation in the area in order to gain a more complete vision, and we found other sites that seemed to make possible such a reconstruction. These dreams of being able to continue fieldwork in the region of San Jacinto, or even in Colombia, however, seem each year to be less and less attainable because of the increased violence. For this reason we decided to publish the book now. There is no hope for the next 10 years of returning to the area. At the time of the excavation of San Jacinto 1, we thought that the situation was very difficult, but things have gotten even worse. The guerrillas attacked the town on several occasions and the army's constant presence and the paramilitary activity have made the area into a war zone. With massive killings and the displacement of people to the major cities such as Cartagena, the escalation of the war has reached a level that we never could have imagined.

The period from 1991–1992 was one of the driest in many years. It only rained once from the end of November to the end of April. Peasants lost their crops. There was not even water for drinking; one had to pay up to $60 for 55 gallons of untreated water. The only real employer was the bankrupted town administration, which never received resources and had not paid its employees for more than a year. Unemployment was very high. People survived by growing food in home gardens and by taking any occasional jobs they could. Even the local landlords experienced economic crisis because of the low prices of cotton, tobacco, and meat in the national market. The situation of the town was desperate. Some time after our arrival our neighbor's son was kidnapped. He owned a cattle ranch nearby and was wealthy by San Jacinto standards. He was released several months later, a few weeks after we completed the project, and the family had paid a large ransom. Every night we heard them gathered in prayer.

In this context it was common to run into all kinds of problems. People did not understand what we were doing in the town and why we would spend money to make a hole in the ground. They called it the "*piscina*" or swimming pool. We tried to educate people on what archaeology was. We worked with all the schools of the nearby towns (Carmen de Bolívar and San Juan de Nepomuceno) and even schools in the capital cities of Cartagena, Barranquilla, and Santa Marta. However, we failed in working with the adult population and that created all kinds of rumors about what we were doing. To make things worse, we were excavating on property that had been part of one of the first haciendas in northern Colombia invaded by a peasant organization in the early 1970s. The land is now managed by a peasant organization (Organización de Campesinos "Hacienda Cataluña"). Later, some politician or politicians, who usually are absent landlords, classified us as sympathizers of the left organizations. After all, we had been working on the land of a hacienda that was now run by a communal group. Our relations with the peasant organization in charge of the hacienda were always good. We employed these people in our activities and even made them an integral part of the project. We dreamed of making a local museum at the site. However, this was impossible.

Four months after we left, an irresponsible television journalist concocted the story that we had been excavating a gold treasure and that we escaped with eight tons of gold. This story made one of the national news programs on prime time. The story shared the headlines with news on the adventures of the cocaine drug lord Pablo Escobar. Rapidly, the Instituto Colombiano de Antropología and the Banco de la Republica Museo de Oro gave statements on the stupidity and irresponsibility of the story. We still wonder why such a tale was fabricated. The explanation, we think, is related to the horrible torture and killing of the Spanish Catholic priest of San Jacinto that occurred just a week before the story about excavating gold was made up. This was one of the most brutal murders on the north coast of Colombia at the time and followed numerous other killings that occurred there unreported while we were excavating the site. We think that the news was created to distract attention from these events.

During the time that we lived in San Jacinto, it was normal each week to see the mourning of families of peasants who were killed because of their ideas or for being part of x or y organization. We feel terrible that we were unable to do anything to stop the killings. One aspect that strikes us is that none of these killings made the regional news or the national news; we even began to think that there was a complicity to not report the murders by the local police, the local landlords, and the paramilitary organization. After we left, the violence escalated, and now the area is under the administrative control of the army. However, the violation of human rights continues unabated.

Today, at the beginning of the twenty-first century, the killings continue in the area and conflict has expanded in Colombia. We moved to work in the Amazon for the past few years, and we have seen the same process beginning there as in San Jacinto—a gradual increase in the violation of human rights (see Human Rights Watch 1998; Oyuela-Caycedo 2001). Expanding relationships between the army and the paramilitary groups, police inefficiency in finding any killer or even common criminal, inefficiency in the judicial system and the massive corruption of the local government, and the disappearance of homeless people all are occurring in the Amazon region. All of this makes Colombia one of the most dangerous places to work and live. Most Colombians think that the solution to the problem lies outside of Colombia. We think that Colombian history is characterized by bloody conflicts that go back to the nineteenth century when the country became independent. The basis of the problem is inbred in a corrupt elite that has controlled the country for the past 100 years without an interest in dealing with the problems of social and economic inequality. The generalized violence is the product of the marginalization that the north coast of Colombia has been subjected to by a centralized economy. The lack of employment opportunities and education has favored daily violence and deterioration of the living standard in towns such as San Jacinto. The intolerance to ideas and poverty have created violence in the region between peasants, landlords (*terratenientes*), police, army, *guerrilla*, *narcotrafico*, paramilitary groups, and politicians from the left to extreme right as well as common delinquents. In this environment an archaeological excavation of people who lived in the area more than 5,000 years ago is something that is very difficult to justify. It is in this horrible context that this research took place.

ACKNOWLEDGMENTS

We would like to thank the excavators of the project: Don Anillo, Dionisio Castellar, Jaime Castro, Victor Castro, Tomas Contreras, Esperanza Duarte, Cesar Estrada, Juan Fonzeca, Luis Garcia, Moises Herrera, Umberto Herrera Lora, Santander Ibañes, Benjamin Landero, Francisco Landero, Manual Martinez, Pedro Medina, Rosmery Moreno, Elkin Navarro, Hernando Olivera, Pascale Olivera, Victor Pacheco, Janneth Panche, Rodrigo Ramirez, Carlos Ramirez Yepes, Diogenes Reyes, Felipe Rueda, Mary Santana, Saul Serrano, and María Angélica Suaza. Field support was given by my late grandmother, Emma Gonzales de Caycedo, and by Gustavo Mazuera and family. For their hospitality in Cartagena, thanks are given to Edgar Fernandez, María Pia Mogollon, and Pilar Falla and our friend Santiago Madriñan.

Identification of the mollusks was done by Juan Parodiz (Carnegie Museum). The identifications of the modern-day plant collections were done by Hermes Cuadros Villalobos, Daniel Debouck, and Alba Marina Torres. Dr. Jaime Aguirre C. also assisted with permissions and information concerning the collection of the modern-day plant specimens. Dr. Wilma Wetterstrom provided access to the Margaret M. Trowle Collection of Ethnobotani-

Acknowledgments

cal and Archaeological Plant Specimens at the Peabody Museum, Harvard University. Dr. Walton C. Galinat, Dr. C. C. Chinnappa, Dr. Paul M. Peterson, the late Dr. Frances King, and Dr. Hugh Iltis offered comments in 1994–1995 on the macrobotanical remains. Thanks also go to Ed Buckler, who attempted to extract DNA from the botanical remains for more precise determinations. We also thank Dr. Dolores Piperno for the phytolith determinations from Feature 63, stratum 12. Thanks go to Dr. Betty Meggers for sponsoring the trip that enabled the photography of the artifacts illustrated in this book, work that was done by the generosity of Vic Krantz.

We especially thank the late Dr. Gerardo Reichel-Dolmatoff and Alicia Dussan de Reichel, who inspired this work and for their support and continual encouragement. We are also particularly grateful to Dr. Tom Dillehay of Vanderbilt University, who has helped us in recent years to find the time and support to publish the results of our work on the excavation of San Jacinto 1 during our time at the University of Kentucky (2001–2004). We are also extremely grateful to Dr. J. Scott Raymond of the University of Calgary, who helped us as a friend and colleague in creating great conditions to advance the analysis of the site at the University of Calgary as a University Post Doctoral Fellow (1994–1996) and for Bonzani to complete the botanical analysis and writing of her dissertation. Thanks are also extended to Oyuela-Caycedo's advisor, friend, and *mecenas,* Dr. Robert D. Drennan (University of Pittsburgh), who made possible the work of San Jacinto, and to Bonzani's advisor, Dr. Jeremy A. Sabloff (University of Pennsylvania), for various types of assistance and research associate affiliations to the University of Pennsylvania Museum of Archaeology and Anthropology, American Section.

We also thank Dr. Jack Donahue for visiting the site in 1991 and helping us solve the problems of the stratigraphy. Thanks also to Dr. Lee Newsom for her recent assistance in reviewing the botanical remains and for funding for the AMS dating. Dr. Lewis Binford also has greatly aided in the final drafts of this volume with his comments and suggestions to stick to the scientifically generated facts in the interpretations of the site. Thanks are also extended to Drs. Jim Adovasio, the late Miriam Balmuth, Ofer Bar-Yosef, Marc Bermann, Ana María Boada, Angela Close, George Crothers, Christine Hastorf, John Hoopes, Dick Jefferies, Jane Kelley, Peter Little, Allan McPherron, Carl Partanen, Tanya Peres, Chris Pool, Steve Randall, James Richardson, Tom Rocek, Jack Rossen, Patty Jo Watson, and Robert Tykot.

Furthermore, thanks are extended to Ana María Falchetti, Luisa F. Herrera de Turbay, and Clemencia Plazas for visiting the site during the excavation and to Rodolfo Arango, María Elvira Bonilla, Gonzalo Correal, the late Luis Duque Gomez, Roberto Pineda, Camilio Rodríguez, Monica Therrier, Carlos A. Uribe, Consuelo Vengoechea, and Hildur Zea for their help in

Bogotá. Thanks also go to members of the Fulbright Commission in Bogotá for much assistance during the year of excavation in Colombia.

We thank our parents, the late Augusto Oyuela-Mazuera, Mabel Caycedo, and James S. and Rogene O. Bonzani, for all their support and patience for many years.

Funding for the project came from Dissertation Improvement grants to both authors from the National Science Foundation; the Center for Latin American Studies, University of Pittsburgh; the Heinz Foundation; the Fulbright Commission; a Grants-in-Aid of Research from Sigma Xi, The Scientific Research Society; and the Fundacion de Investigaciones Arqueológicas del Banco de la Republica. This project was conducted with the permission of the Instituto Colombiano de Antropología e Historia. Appreciation is also extended to Judith Knight, for her enthusiasm in publishing this work, and to Kathy Cummins and Joanna Jacobs for their fine editorial skills.

San Jacinto 1

1 Introduction

Few topics in the development of humans have prompted as much interest and perhaps debate as that of the origins of pottery and food production. The first appearance of pottery in any area of the world is heralded as a new stage in the progress of humans toward a more complex arrangement of thought and society. Cultures are defined and divided by the occurrence of pottery types, and the association of pottery with mobility and food production has driven and continues to drive research in anthropology. In this volume, a site is examined that has the earliest fiber-tempered pottery in the New World in association with intensive processing of plants and mobility. The use of the term *fiber tempered* is important, as pottery types with other tempers date earlier than the remains found at San Jacinto 1. These pottery types have been recovered in Santarem, Brazil (Roosevelt et al. 1991).[1] However, in all other instances of the earliest recovered pottery types throughout the world, the temper has been initially of fiber and it is with this group of sites that San Jacinto 1 can be placed (see Meggers 1997 and Rice 1999 for a discussion of early pottery). In Colombia, later sites with mixed sand-, grog-, and fiber-tempered pottery types include Puerto Hormiga, Puerto Chacho, and San Jacinto 2 (Legros 1990; Reichel-Dolmatoff 1965b, 1971; also see Marcos 1988; Meggers et al. 1965; Raymond et al. 1998). The other part of the Americas where fiber-tempered pottery has been recovered in early contexts is the southeastern United States (3,500 to 4,500 years ago) (Sassaman 1993, 1998).

In relation to food production, the exact identification of the majority of the macrobotanical remains recovered from San Jacinto 1 remains elusive mainly because of their highly fragmented nature. Tentative suppositions that these remains represent maize kernel and cupule fragments were explored without success using DNA, isotope, and lipid analyses and scanning electron microscopy photography (see Chapter 5). The majority of the plant remains appear to be from C_3 plants (plants that metabolize carbon dioxide photosynthetically through a 3-carbon [Calvin] pathway; Vogel and van der Merwe 1977).

Besides trying to answer what and when, the true questions of importance focus on why pottery was invented and in what contexts (Barnett and Hoopes 1995; Hoopes 1994; Rice 1999). Why were seed-producing plants intensively utilized during this period and in what contexts? To this corpus of information, the data recovered from the excavation of San Jacinto 1 can add substantially. The site of San Jacinto 1 was determined to have unique characteristics that open a window on the understanding of a complex structure of adaptation to the landscape from the perspective of historical ecology. The people who occupied the site were hunter-gatherers who moved logistically from base camps to special-purpose camps. San Jacinto 1 yielded evidence of being just such a special-purpose site that was utilized to collect and process plants possibly for making a fermented beverage and for cooking in earth ovens. Mollusks were also collected for food and to make prestige items of beads with the operculum. The seed resources would have been intensively collected and processed at their time of abundance prior to the full onset of the dry season. Pottery in this context appears to be a serving item and potential means of marking identity for groups who had gathered to perform social and economically labor-intensive activities necessary for their survival in a highly seasonal savanna environment.

The following chapters present an analysis based on the data from the excavation of the site. After the evidence is presented, little doubt should remain about the context of the origins of ceramic technology in the tropics and how the technology is tied to a reduction in mobility and an increase in territorial control. The observed link between the intensive use of seed resources and pottery may also be that both provide a social means of coping with a changing, highly seasonal environment between groups who were becoming more territorial and were becoming a major selective force in the evolution of the environment.

SITE DISCOVERY

In 1986, Augusto Oyuela-Caycedo was contacted by the Museo de Oro in Bogotá to go to a small town called San Jacinto on the Caribbean coast to look at the feasibility of developing a museum in the town (Figures 1.1 and 1.2). On arrival, it was noticed that a number of the pieces to be included in the museum were fragments of pottery made with fiber temper. When it was asked where these fragments came from, the local teachers, residents, and mayor took Oyuela-Caycedo to a stream embankment out of which the ceramic fragments were eroding. Oyuela-Caycedo returned to Bogotá and informed the Museo de Oro about the good possibility of establishing a museum at San Jacinto. It was also realized that pottery made with fiber temper was usually associated with the earliest pottery in the New World. This pottery type had been found at Puerto Hormiga by Reichel-Dolmatoff (1965b). Puerto Hormiga was also located on the north coast of Colombia near Car-

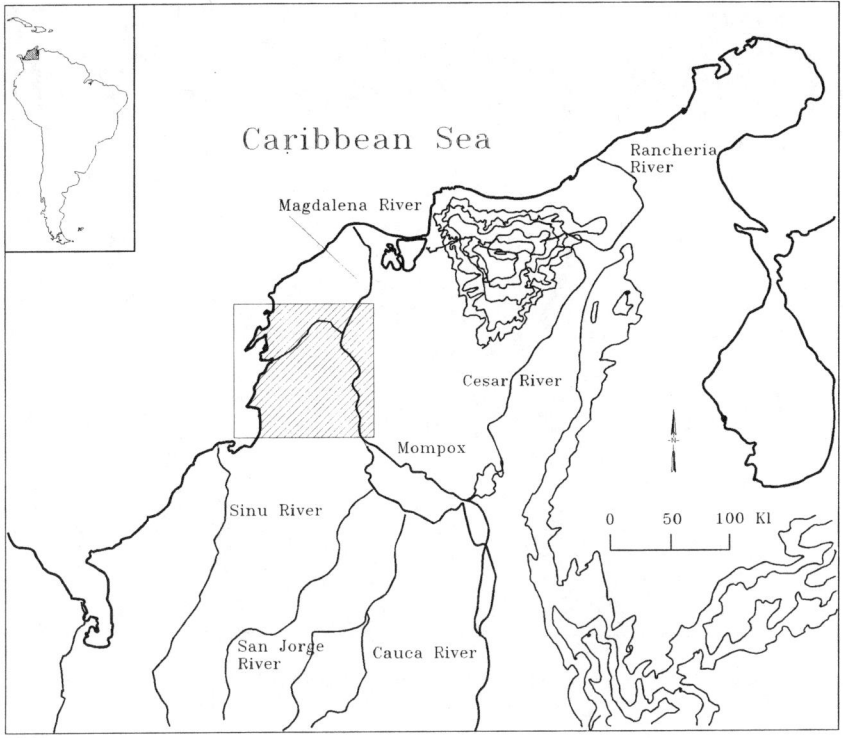

Figure 1.1. Location of the site of San Jacinto 1, Colombia, South America.

tagena and was at the time one of the sites with the earliest pottery known in the New World, along with the Valdivia sites of Ecuador (Meggers et al. 1965). What was unique about the material from San Jacinto was the highly decorative nature of the fragments with modeling, incision, excision, and other manufacturing techniques clearly visible. Realizing the possibility of discovering another such site, it was determined that it was necessary to evaluate the site better, and Oyuela-Caycedo returned to Cartagena and San Jacinto within the week.

After arriving at San Jacinto, Oyuela-Caycedo returned to the stream embankment out of which the pieces of fiber-tempered pottery were being eroded. The profile of the embankment was cleaned with a trowel and it revealed a complex stratigraphy of charcoal layer upon charcoal layer being separated by what appeared to be sterile yellow clay layers (Figures 1.3, 1.4, and 1.5). Pottery was eroding from all of these strata and samples were collected for radiocarbon dating, which confirmed the early development of this pottery technology (Table 1.1) (Oyuela-Caycedo 1987). That was the good news. The bad news was that the layers of charcoal that indicated where the site was

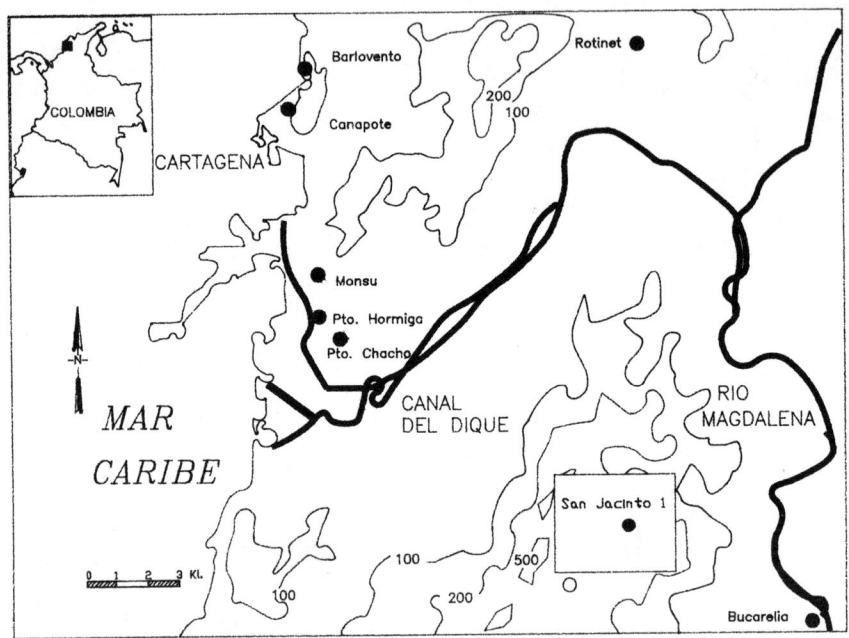

Figure 1.2. Location of the study region and early Formative sites.

Figure 1.3. Landscape of San Jacinto 1.

Figure 1.4. Meander cut and profile view of site of San Jacinto 1.

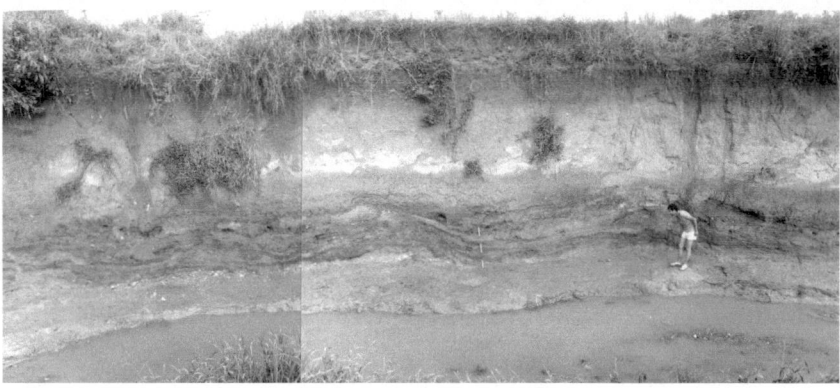

Figure 1.5. Profile of site of San Jacinto 1 from the San Jacinto stream. First field season 1986.

located were buried under 4 m (15 feet) of sterile overburden or soils that had been deposited over the site since its use. Obviously, no quick excavation would suffice here.

After attending graduate school at the University of Pittsburgh and obtaining enough funding to conduct a year-long excavation of the site, Oyuela-Caycedo and Bonzani returned to San Jacinto in 1991 and 1992 to excavate the site for their dissertations. Since the archaeological site was located just outside of this town, the name San Jacinto 1 was given to it. The following year

Table 1.1. Radiocarbon dates from strata 9 through 20

Stratum	Feature	Lab. No.	Material	Date B.P. (uncalibrated)	$^{13}C/^{12}C$ Ratio
5	1	Beta-79781	Charcoal	2120 ± 90	–25.0*
5-6	2	Beta-78619	Charcoal	1750 ± 80	–25.0*
10	31	GX-20353	Charcoal	5300 ± 75	–28.4
10	15	GX-20352	Charcoal	5315 ± 80	–27.4
10	45	GX-20354	Charcoal	5325 ± 80	–27.4
10	57	Beta-77407	Charcoal	5330 ± 80	–25.0*
10	53	Beta-77405	Charcoal	5510 ± 70	–25.0*
12	151	GX-20355	Charcoal	5530 ± 80	–28.5
12	Profile	Pitt-0154	Charcoal	5665 ± 75	–25.0*
12	Profile	Beta-20352	Charcoal	5700 ± 430	–25.0*
12	63	Beta-77406	Charcoal	5730 ± 110	–25.0*
16?	Profile	Pitt-0155	Charcoal	5940 ± 60	–25.0*
20	AMS	Beta-183290	Charcoal	5400 ± 40	–26.1
20	AMS	Beta-183291	Charcoal	5190 ± 40	–25.3
20	AMS	Arizona-AA57882	Charcoal**	5208 ± 28	–23.6

*Calculated relative to the PDB-1 international standard.
**AMS-dated sample illustrated in Figure 5.1a.

led to the discovery of nine cultural strata buried under the soils that were radiocarbon dated to between 5940 ± 60 years B.P. and 5190 ± 40 years B.P. (Table 1.1). A more recent occupation layer was also discovered that dated to 2120 ± 90 years B.P. and 1750 ± 80 years B.P. with ceramic kilns (which are not discussed in this volume because of the different cultural nature of these features). Out of the earliest occupation layers came many pottery fragments, some of which showed strange zoomorphic configurations. Earth oven features overlapped one upon another and metates and manos were found throughout the strata, one metate even being inverted and stored within a feature. In short, the site was astounding for the unfamiliar features and material remains that were unearthed in the tropical lowlands.

Five kilometers south of San Jacinto 1 another archaeological site, known as San Jacinto 2, was also identified. A preliminary excavation was conducted at the site. However, since the site is not located in a depositional environment, the stratigraphy was compressed or reduced to a few centimeters and most of the cultural material was subject to erosion. In general, the recovered artifacts from San Jacinto 2 are similar to those from San Jacinto 1, but they are more elaborate in their appearance. The stone or lithic artifacts consist of

Introduction

metates, hand mills, ground stone axes, ground "nutcracker" stones, and hundreds of pieces of flaked stone debitage specimens. Pottery was also recovered, but unlike at San Jacinto 1 where all of the pottery is fiber tempered, at San Jacinto 2 only 69 percent of the surface-collected material is fiber tempered. The rest of the pottery is sand tempered. San Jacinto 2 has been dated to approximately 4565 ± 85 years B.P. (Oyuela-Caycedo 1987, 1998).

THE NATURAL ENVIRONMENT

The town of San Jacinto is located in the municipality of San Jacinto, Department of Bolívar of Colombia, on the edge of the Serranía de San Jacinto, also known as the Montes de Maria (site location is at latitude N 9° 50', longitude W 75° 7') (Figures 1.1 and 1.2). The Serranía de San Jacinto is a series of foothills that rise to the west of the site to heights of up to 700 m above sea level. The town and the site of San Jacinto are located at approximately 210 to 250 m above sea level. The general region around San Jacinto and the surrounding lower-lying areas are defined as savanna and given the name the Savannas of Bolívar (Instituto Geografico "Agustín Codazzí" 1975). To the east and north this savanna area is surrounded by what is known as the Depresíon Momposina (Mompos Depression) located approximately 80 km to the east and by the Canal del Dique to the north. Some regions of this depression lie below sea level and are exposed to frequent seasonal flooding episodes from the San Jorge and Cauca Rivers that flow in a northerly direction into the Magdalena River. This is the region where numerous archaeological canal remains and platform mounds have been associated with the Sinú culture (Plazas and Falchetti 1981). These constructions were built over a period of two thousand years in a gradual process beginning before the ninth century B.C. and continuing until the tenth and twelfth centuries A.D. (Plazas et al. 1993).

Perhaps the most important environmental aspect of San Jacinto's location is that it is in a savanna. Sarmiento (1984:6) defines a savanna as a "type of tropical vegetation where certain forms of grasses dominate and where seasonal droughts and frequent fires are normal ecological factors." The two key parts of this definition are the abundance of grasses and the seasonal nature of the environment.

When one looks around the area, it is easy to see that grasses predominate, with trees mainly located near the stream embankments. Only about 6 percent of the vegetative cover of the area is of tree-level height (Bonzani 1995), placing the area into the wooded savanna type (Sarmiento 1983) (Tables 1.2 and 1.3). Changes in the relative abundance of trees in the area in the past are expected to have occurred, but grasses appear to have always formed a signifi-

Table 1.2. Plant species in reserves in the region of San Juan de Nepomuceno, Bolívar, Colombia

English Common Name	Spanish Common Name	Scientific Name
	Ornamentals	
Orchids	Orquideas	*Phalaenopsis* sp.
		Cymbidium sp.
Ferns	Helechos	*Camptosorus* sp.
		Adiatum sp.
	Fruit Species	
Papayo	Papayos	*Carica papaya*
Sour sop	Guanabanos	*Anona muricata*
Citrus	Citricos	*Citrus* sp.
Guava	Guayabos	*Psidium* sp.
Avocado	Aguacates	*Persea americana*
	Tree Species	
	Abarco	*Cariniana pyriformis*
Mahogany (*Swietenia* spp.)	Caoba	*Swietenia minuscula*
	Cativo	*Prioria copaifera*
Spanish cedar	Cedro	*Cedrela odorata*
		Cedrela mejicana
Cashew (*A. occidentale*)	Caracolí	*Anacardium excelsum*
	Carreto	*Aspidosperma dugandii*
Jacaranda	Guayacan	*Jacaranda* sp.
Trumpet tree	Roble	*Tabebuia rosea*
Clammy cherry	Vara de humo	*Cordia alliodra*
	Brasil	*Hematoxylon brasiletto*
	Balsamo	*Heliocarpus popayanesis*
	Ceiba Tolua	*Bombacopsis quinatum*
	Canalete	*Cordia gerascanthus*
	Camajon	*Sterculia apetala*
	Campano	*Samanea saman*
	Agricultural Products	
	Fruit Species	
Papaya	Papaya	*Carica papaya*
Granadilla	Maracuya	*Passiflora edulis*

Table 1.2. *Continued*

English Common Name	Spanish Common Name	Scientific Name
Cultivars		
Common bean	Frijol	*Phaseolus* spp.
Colored bean	Frijol cabecita	*Vigna unguiculata*
Black bean	Frijol negra	*Vigna unguiculata*
Yuca	Yuca	*Manihot esculenta*
Sorghum	Mijo	*Sorghum vulgare*
Sweet potato	Batata	*Ipomoea* sp.
Yams	Ñame	*Dioscorea* sp.
Horticultural Products		
Tomato	Tomate	*Lycopersicum esculenta*
Onion	Cebolla de rama	*Allium fistulosum*
Eggplant	Berejena	*Solanum melongena*
Lettuce	Lechuga	*Lactuca sativa*
Pepper	Ají	*Capsicum annum*
Squash	Ahuyama	*Cucurbita* sp.
Cucumber	Pepinos	*Cucumis sativus*
Grasses and Fodder		
King grass	Kikuyo	*Pennisetum* sp.
Canavalia	Canavalia	*Canavalia ensifirmis*
Kunzu	Kunzu tropical	*Puveraria faseolodes*

cant part of the vegetation in the area back to the Pleistocene (Le Roy Gordon 1983). Resources from grasses are integral parts of the adaptive strategies of groups who reside in savannas around the world (DeWet 1975, 1981) and grasses have also played an important role in the past on all of the continents (Harlan 1989, 1992a, 1992b, 1993, 1999).

The second aspect of great importance for this area is the seasonality of rainfall. Wet and dry periods of the year in the tropics are climatic changes similar to cold and warm periods in the temperate latitudes. The importance of the changes that occur are just as great. As indicated, the present-day climate of northwest Colombia and the Serranía de San Jacinto is noted to be marked by "sharply contrasting wet and dry seasons" (Parsons 1980:284) and is characterized by a bimodal pattern of precipitation (Figure 1.6) (Oyuela-Caycedo 1993). Based on palynological evidence for the region, this same pattern of seasonality would have existed in the past and may even have been more pronounced (Markgraf 1989; Van der Hammen 1974, 1983, 1991). Currently, the first dry season lasts for approximately (*text continued on page 18*)

Table 1.3. Plants collected in the vicinity of San Jacinto 1 and at the marketplaces of San Jacinto and Cartagena de Indias in 1991–1992

Scientific Name		Common Name	Ref. No.
Family	Genus and species		
ACANTHACEAE			RB* 260, 262
ACANTHACEAE		Arroyero	RB 261
ACANTHACEAE	*Aphelandra*	Arroyero (Col.)	RB 257
ACANTHACEAE	*Elytraria*	Verbena (Col.)	RB 183
ACANTHACEAE	*Ruellia* L.	Oreja de mula (Col.) Arroyero (Col.)	RB 253, 258, 268
ACANTHACEAE	*Ruellia tuberosa* L.	Oreja de mula (Col.)	RB 146
AMARANTHACEAE	*Achyranthes aspera* L.	Cadillo (Col.)	RB 130
AMARANTHACEAE	*Alternanthera polygonoides* (L.) Brown	Siempre viva (Col.)	RB 328
AMARANTHACEAE	*Amaranthus*	Bleo (Col.)	RB 143
AMARANTHACEAE	*Amaranthus dubius* Mart.	Bleo floral (Col.)	RB 330
AMARANTHACEAE	*Celosia cristata* L.	Cresta de gallo (Col.)	RB 312
AMARANTHACEAE	*Iresine diffusa* Humb. & Bonpl. ex Willd.		RB 273
ANACARDIACEAE	*Anacardium excelsum* (Ber. et Balb.) Skeels	Caracolí (Col.)	RB 343
ANACARDIACEAE	*Anacardium occidentale* L.	Marañón (Col.) Cashew (English)	RB 361
ANACARDIACEAE	*Spondias* L.	Jobo (Col.)	RB 122
ANNONACEAE	*Annona muricata* L.	Guanábana (Col.)	RB 134, 367
ANNONACEAE	*Annona reticulata* L.	Mamón (Col.)	RB 164, 192
ANNONACEAE	*Annona squamosa* L.	Anón (Col.)	RB 101, 290
APOCYNACEAE	*Rauvolfia tetraphylla* L.	Cerecillo (Col.) Fruta de pava Pepa de culebra	RB 152, 245, 246
ASTERACEAE		San Antonio (Col.) Siuso (Col.)	RB 125, 191
ASTERACEAE	*Artemisia absynthium* L.	Ajenjo (Col.)	RB 319, 322
ASTERACEAE	*Baccharis trinervis* var. *rhexioides* (HBK.) Baker.	Mansanillo (Col.)	RB 151

Table 1.3. Continued

Scientific Name		Common Name	Ref. No.
Family	Genus and species		
ASTERACEAE	*Bidens pilosa* L.	Cadillo (Col.)	RB 267
ASTERACEAE	*Delilia biflora* (L.) Kuntze	Escobilla (Col.)	RB 141, 153
ASTERACEAE	*Eupatorium*	Valdivia (Col.)	RB 197
ASTERACEAE	*Melampodium*	Co (Col.)	RB 186
ASTERACEAE	*Melanthera*	Siuso (Col.) Co (Col.)	RB 169, 195
ASTERACEAE	*Verbesina*	Manito Dios (Col.)	RB 171
ASTERACEAE	*Wedelia latifolia*	Valdivia (Col.)	RB 270
BIGNONIACEAE	*Crescentia* L.	Totumo (Col.)	RB 105, 355
BIGNONIACEAE	*Memora patula* Miers.	Trébol (Col.)	RB 259
BIGNONIACEAE	*Tabebuia* Gomes ex DeCandolle	Roble (Col.)	RB 347
BIGNONIACEAE	*Tabebuia chrysea* Blake	Cañaguate (Col.)	RB 294
BIXACEAE	*Bixa orellana* L.	Achiote (Col.)	RB 168, 225, 226, 336
BOMBACACEAE	*Ceiba pentandra* (L.) Gaertn.	Ceiba (Col.)	RB 353
BORAGINACEAE	*Cordia* L.	Uva de monti (Col.)	RB 317
BORAGINACEAE	*Cordia lutea* Lam.	Uvito (Col.)	RB 118
BORAGINACEAE	*Heliotropium angiospermum* Murray	Verbena (Col.) Verbena criolla (Col.) Verbena si (Col.)	RB 109, 142, 185
BROMELIACEAE	*Aechmea veitchii* Bak.	Piñuela (Col.)	RB 277
BROMELIACEAE	*Tillandsia usneoides*	Palbamico (Col.) Spanish moss (English)	RB 282
CACTACEAE	*Lemaireocereus griseus* (Haworth) Britton et Rose.	Cardón (Col.)	RB 232
CAESALPINIACEAE		Cuchillito (Col.) Tienda de la ropa (Col.)	RB 231
CAESALPINIACEAE	*Bauhinia* L.	Pata de vaca (Col.)	RB 107, 211
CAESALPINIACEAE	*Cassia* L.		RB 103

Continued on the next page

Table 1.3. *Continued*

Scientific Name		Common Name	Ref. No.
Family	Genus and species		
CAESALPINIACEAE	*Cassia emarginata* L.	Cuchillito (Col.) Tienda de las ropas (Col.)	RB 236
CAESALPINIACEAE	*Cassia grandis* L.f.	Cañandonga (Col.) Grano de oro (Col.) Cañafístula (Col.)	RB 359, 360
CAESALPINIACEAE	*Cassia odoratissima* Jacq.	Reuma (Col.)	RB 106
CAESALPINIACEAE	*Cassia reticulata* (Willd.) I. & B.	Bajagua (Col.)	RB 274
CAESALPINIACEAE	*Cassioidea*	Vicho (Col.)	RB 177, 182
CAESALPINIACEAE	*Retusa*	Muñequito (Col.)	RB 227
CAESALPINIACEAE	*Tamarindus indica* L.	Tamarindo (Col.)	RB 137
CAPPARIDACEAE	*Capparis odoratissima* Jacq.	Olivo (Col.)	RB 104, 354
CAPPARIDACEAE	*Crataeva tapia* L.		RB 346
CARICACEAE	*Carica papaya* L.	Papaya (Col.)	RB 298
CHENOPODIACEAE	*Chenopodium* L.	Yierba santa (Col.)	RB 309, 331
COMMELINACEAE	*Commelina diffusa* Burm.	Ojito de Santa Lucia (Col.)	RB 159, 224
CONVOLVULACEAE	*Evolvulos*	Sabe secunda (Col.)	RB 326
CONVOLVULACEAE	*Ipomoea*	Variety of campanilla (Col.) Yierba de arroz? (Col.) Batatilla (Col.)	RB 271, 311
CONVOLVULACEAE	*Ipomoea hirta*	Campanilla (Col.)	RB 167
CONVOLVULACEAE	*Ipomoea coccinea* L.		RB 265
CONVOLVULACEAE	*Ipomoea tiliacea* (Willd.) Choisy	Campanilla (Col.)	RB 207
CONVOLVULACEAE	*Ipomoea tubiflora*	Papuche (Col.)	RB 263
CONVOLVULACEAE	*Jacquemontia*	Campania (Col.)	RB 287
CUCURBITACEAE	*Cucurbita*	Ahuyama (Col.) Squash (English)	RB 111, 254, 289, 296, 297, 301

Table 1.3. Continued

Scientific Name		Common Name	Ref. No.
Family	Genus and species		
CUCURBITACEAE	*Cucurbita maxima* S. Am.	Ahuyama criolla (Col.)	RB 222
CUCURBITACEAE	*Lagenaria*	Calabazo (Col.) Gourd (English)	RB 239
CUCURBITACEAE	*Luffa cylindrica* (L.) Roem.	Lavaplato (Col.)	RB 278
CUCURBITACEAE	*Melothria pendula* L.	Toporotopo (Col.)	RB 266
CUCURBITACEAE	*Momordica charantia* L.	Balsamina (Col.)	RB 172, 179, 252
CUCURBITACEAE	*Sicana odorifera*	Pepino morado (Col.)	RB 338
CYPERACEAE	*Cyperus odoratus* L.	Flor de la viabilla (Col.) Coquito (Col.)	RB 176, 269
CYPERACEAE	*Cyperus rotundus* L.	Coquito (Col.)	RB 160, 201
DIOSCOREACEAE	*Dioscorea*	Type of ñame? (Col.) Yam (English)	RB 235
DIOSCOREACEAE	*Dioscorea alata* L.	Ñame criollo (Col.) Yam (English)	RB 113
DIOSCOREACEAE	*Dioscorea bulbifera* L.	Ñame espina (Col.) Ñame congo, ñame de mata (Venezuela) Batata de rama, cará del aire (Brazil) Yam (English)	RB 112
EUPHORBIACEAE	*Euphorbia heterophylla*	Verdolaga (Col.)	RB 150
EUPHORBIACEAE	*Jatropha* L.	Corazón herido (Col.)	RB 357
EUPHORBIACEAE	*Manihot* Miller	Yuca venezolana (Bol.) Yuca amarilla (Bol.) Yuca (Col.) Manioc, cassava (English)	RB 221, 315, 352
EUPHORBIACEAE	*Phyllanthus acidus* (L.) Skeels	Grossella (Col.)	RB 293
EUPHORBIACEAE	*Ricinus communis* L.	Higuereto (Col.)	RB 124

Continued on the next page

Table 1.3. *Continued*

Scientific Name		Common Name	Ref. No.
Family	Genus and species		
FABACEAE		Salsa espinosa (Col.) Carachua (Col.) Changarita (Col.)	RB 166, 170, 286
FABACEAE	*Aeschynomene*	Sieva pie (Col.)	RB 148
FABACEAE	*Aeschynomene sensitiva* Sw.	Escovillita (Col.)	RB 190
FABACEAE	*Cajanus*	Guandul (Col.) Wandul (Col.)	RB 116
FABACEAE	*Cajanus indicus* (L.) Spreng.	Wandul (Col.) Wandul pintada (Col.)	RB 223, 313, 368
FABACEAE	*Calopogonium caeruleum* (Benth.) Sauvelle	Platonita (Col.)	RB 288
FABACEAE	*Centrosema plumieri* (Turp.) Benth.	Pitillo (Col.) Flor de mula (Col.)	RB 145, 204, 205
FABACEAE	*Gliricidia sepium* (Jacq.) Steud.	Mata-ratón (Col.) Circa viva (Col.)	RB 126, 283
FABACEAE	*Indigofera mucronata* Spreng.	Añil (Col.)	RB 178
FABACEAE	*Phaseolus*	Caraota (Col.)	RB 110, 220, 373
FABACEAE	*Phaseolus lunatus* L.	Caraota (Col.) Cabeza de Santo (Col.) Garbanzo frijoles (Col.)	RB 138, 194, 255, 256
FABACEAE	*Phaseolus vulgaris* L.	Frijol (Col.)	RB 372
FABACEAE	*Rhynchosia pittieri*	Buyuco candera	RB 198
FABACEAE	*Stizolobium*	Pika pika, terciopelo (Col.)	RB 316
FABACEAE	*Teramnus volubilis*	Cadillo (Col.)	RB 144
FABACEAE	*Vigna unguiculata* (L.) Walpers. subspecies *unguiculata*	Frijol soya (Col.) Frijol blanca (Col.) Frijol negra (Col.) Frijol (Col.) Also known as coupi, cowpea, bendija	RB 216, 314, 366, 369

Table 1.3. *Continued*

Scientific Name		Common Name	Ref. No.
Family	Genus and species		
GUTTIFERAE	*Mammea americana* L.	Mamey (Col.)	RB 350
HERNANDIACEAE	*Gyrocarpus americanus*	Papayate (Col.)	RB 280
LAMIACEAE (LABIATAE)	*Hyptis capitata* Jacq.		RB 275
LAMIACEAE (LABIATAE)	*Mentha*	Hierba buena (Col.) Mint, peppermint, spearmint (English)	RB 303
LAMIACEAE (LABIATAE)	*Ocimum* L.	Torrangil (Col.) Albaquita (Col.) Cañelon (Col.) Basil (English)	RB 300, 305, 320, 323, 332, 335
LAMIACEAE (LABIATAE)	*Ocimum americanus*	Torrangil (Col.)	RB 333
LAMIACEAE (LABIATAE)	*Origanum vulgare* L.	Marjoram, oregano (English)	RB 308
LAMIACEAE (LABIATAE)	*Salvia*	Salvia (Col.) Sage (English)	RB 310
LAURACEAE	*Ocotea* Aublet	Avocado (Col.)	RB 241
LECYTHIDACEAE		Cocuelo (Col.) Coca de mico (Col.)	RB 121, 131
LECYTHIDACEAE	*Eschweilera* Martius	Cocuelo (Col.) Coco de mico (Col.)	RB 238
MALVACEAE	*Bastardia viscolor*	Escobillom (Col.)	RB 147
MALVACEAE	*Gossypium* L.	Algodón (Col.) Cotton (English)	RB 212
MALVACEAE	*Malachra rudis* Benth.	Malva (Col.)	RB 114, 206
MALVACEAE	*Pavonia*		RB 264
MALVACEAE	*Sida rhombifolia* L.	Escobilla la platonita (Col.) Escovia (Col.)	RB 129, 244
MELIACEAE	*Melia*	Paradisio (Col.)	RB 292
MIMOSACEAE		Aramo (Col.) Salsa cororor (Col.)	RB 209, 229, 230

Continued on the next page

Table 1.3. *Continued*

Scientific Name		Common Name	Ref. No.
Family	Genus and species		
MIMOSACEAE	*Acacia*	Chicho (Col.)	RB 119, 228, 339
MIMOSACEAE	*Calliandra*		RB 285
MIMOSACEAE	*Desmanthus*	Escobilla (Col.)	RB 149
MIMOSACEAE	*Inga densiflora* Benth.	Guamo (Col.)	RB 363
MIMOSACEAE	*Mimosa pudica* L.	Sierras (Col.)	RB 181
MYRTACEAE	*Psidium guajaba* (L.) Radd.	Guayaba (Col.) Guava (English)	RB 136, 341
PALMAE	*Elaeis melanococca*	Corozo (Col.)	RB 165
PALMAE	*Phoenix dactylifera* L.	Datil (Col.) Dates (English)	RB 362
PASSIFLORACEAE	*Passiflora edulis* var. *flavicarpa*	Maracuya (Col.)	RB 219
	Passiflora quadrangularis L.	Badea (Col.)	RB 351
PHYTOLACCACEAE	*Petiveria alliacea* L.	Amamú (Col.)	RB 173
PIPERACEAE	*Peperomia* Ruiz et Pavón	Benturosa (Col.) Canelón (Col.)	RB 276, 323
PLANTAGINACEAE	*Plantago mayor* L.	Yenten, llantén (Col.)	RB 329
POACEAE	*Axonopus*	Pajita azul (Col.)	RB 203
POACEAE	*Cenchrus*	Cadillo (Col.)	RB 249
POACEAE	*Dichanthium aristatum* (Poir) C. Hubb	Name unknown but two possibilities were given: cochito, hanglito (Col.)	RB 156
POACEAE	*Dichanthium pertusa*	Yerba zorrio (Col.)	RB 175, 199
POACEAE	*Digitaria insularis*	Yerba de zorra (Col.) Yerba zorro (Col.)	RB 157, 189
POACEAE	*Hyparrhenia rufa* (Nees) Stapf	Faragua (Col.)	RB 161
POACEAE	*Lasiacis sorghoidea* (Desv.) Hitch.	Bambu (Col.) Granadiya (Col).	RB 162, 217
POACEAE	*Panicum maximum* Jacq.	Guinea (Col.) Mirable (Col.)	RB 155, 158

Table 1.3. *Continued*

Scientific Name		Common Name	Ref. No.
Family	Genus and species		
POACEAE	*Paspalum plicatum* var. *villosisimum*	Yerba de zorra (Col.)	RB 188
POACEAE	*Paspalum virgatum* L.	Pajon (Col.)	RB 210
POACEAE	*Sorghum halapense* (L.) Pers.	Pasto gigante (Col.) Sorgo, yerba vero	RB 139, 208
POACEAE	*Sorghum sudanense* (Piper) Stapf.	Sorgo migo (Col.)	RB 251
POACEAE	*Sporobolus indicus* (L.) R. Br.	Yerba estrella (Col.)	RB 187
POACEAE	*Zea mays*	Maíz (Col.) Maize, corn (English)	RB 218
POLYGALACEAE	*Securidaca*		RB 345
POLYGONACEAE	*Antigonon leptopus* Hook.	Bellisima (Col.)	RB 248
POLYGONACEAE	*Coccoloba uvifera* (L.) Jacq.	Uvero (Col.)	RB 117
POLYGONACEAE	*Triplaris* Loefling	Guacamayo (Col.)	RB 123
PORTULACACEAE	*Portulaca meracioides*	Verdolaga (Col.)	RB 337
PORTULACACEAE	*Talinum triangulara* (Jacq.) Willd.	Bleo (Col.)	RB 233
PUNICACEAE	*Punica granatum* L.	Granada (Col.)	RB 304
ROSACEAE	*Chrysobalanus icaco*	Icaco (Col.)	RB 163
RUBIACEAE	*Chomelia spinosa*	Fruta de pava (Col.)	RB 108
RUBIACEAE	*Mitracarpus turnis* (L.) DC.	Escovillan (Col.)	RB 184
RUTACEAE	*Citrus* L.	Naranje (Col.) Azahares de la India (Col.) Limón mandarina (Col.)	RB 135, 324, 325
RUTACEAE	*Ruta*	Ruda (Col.)	RB 364
SAPINDACEAE	*Serjania* Miller	Salsa dulce (Col.)	RB 344
SAPOTACEAE	*Chrysophyllum cainito* L.	Caimito (Col.)	RB 348

Continued on the next page

Table 1.3. *Continued*

Scientific Name		Common Name	Ref. No.
Family	Genus and species		
SAPOTACEAE	*Manilkara zapota* (L.) P. von Royen. Syn: *Achras zapota* L.	Níspero (Col.) Sapodilla (English)	RB 102, 295
SCROPHULARIACEAE	*Scoparia dulcis* L.	Yerba anni (Col.)	RB 180, 240
SOLANACEAE	*Brugmansia* Persoon	Borrachero (Col.)	RB 306
SOLANACEAE	*Capsicum* L.	Ají (Col.) Ají dulce (Col.) Ají silvestre, guagua (Col.)	RB 340, 370, 374
SOLANACEAE	*Nicotiana tabacum* L.	Tabacco (Col.)	RB 237
SOLANACEAE	*Solanum ovalifolium* Dunal.	Tabacco macho (Col.)	RB 247
STERCULIACEAE	*Guazuma ulmifolia* Lam.	Guasimo (Col.)	RB 120, 318
STERCULIACEAE	*Matisia cordata* H. et B.	Zapote (Col.)	RB 327
STERCULIACEAE	*Melochia pyramidata* L.	Escovillon (Col.)	RB 215
STERCULIACEAE	*Theobroma*	Cacao (Col.) (English)	RB 284
TILIACEAE	*Corchorus orinocensis*	Escovilla de platonita (Col.)	RB 243
VERBENACEAE	*Bouchea prismatica*	Granavi (Col.)	RB 196
VERBENACEAE	*Lantana* L.	Malvita (Col.) Mejorana (Col.)	RB 140, 321
ZINGIBERACEAE	*Zingiber officinale* Rosc.	Jenjibre (Col.) Ginger (English)	RB 279
ZYGOPHYLLACEAE	*Tribulus cistoides* L.	Tripa de pollo (Col.)	RB 299

*Designates reference turned in to the herbaria at JBGP and COL in Colombia.

four months and occurs from December to March. A small *veranillo* or "little summer" occurs in July and August. Annual precipitation is 1,030 mm as recorded for a 46-year period from 1931 to 1941 and 1953 to 1987 at the weather station in Carmen de Bolívar, located approximately 12 km south of the town of San Jacinto. Annual mean temperature as measured at this station is 27.5 degrees Celsius with little yearly variation.

The significance of the bimodal precipitation pattern means that it can

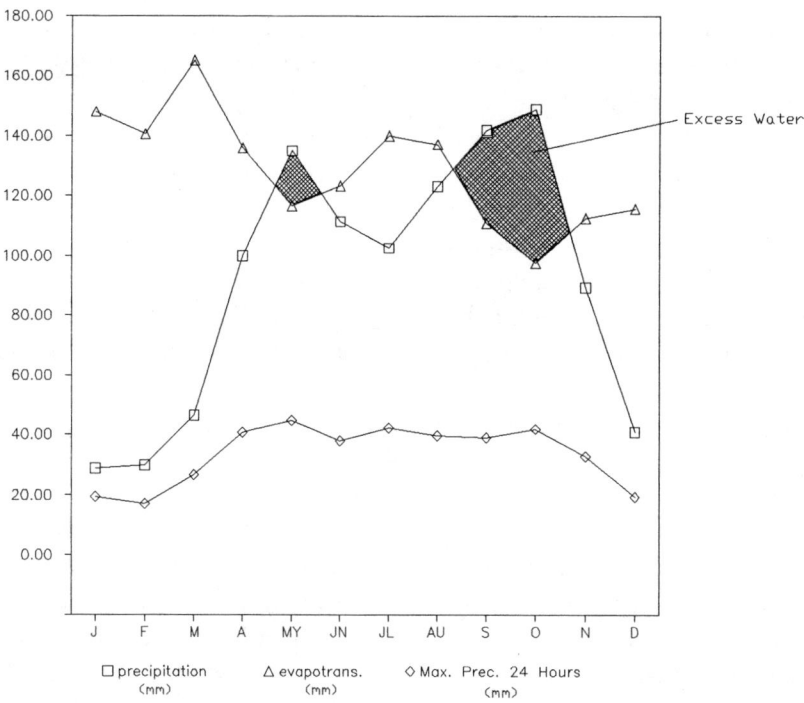

Figure 1.6. Mean annual precipitation and water deficiency in the Serranía de San Jacinto.

stop raining in November and not rain again until April. This is five months without rain and clearly an environmental stress that inhabitants of the area have always had to deal with. Indeed, palynological evidence indicates that the area around San Jacinto 1 about 6,000 years ago was probably even drier than it currently is, with precipitation around 500 mm per year and a dry season that could last up to seven months or more. For instance, Van der Hammen (1984) has done palynological work in the area of the Sierra Nevada of Santa Marta and the Cienaga Grande of Santa Marta located on the Caribbean coast ca. 150 km from San Jacinto. His work indicates that the area around Santa Marta had effectively less precipitation and higher temperatures in the mountains between 6000 and 5500 B.P. Van der Hammen (1974, 1983, 1991) and Van der Hammen et al. (1991) have also done palynological and sediment studies in the Llanos of Colombia, in the savanna of Bogotá, and in the Colombian Amazon, which have information about the Holocene. Their work indicates that a dry period occurred at 5500 B.P. and again at 4700 B.P. Other information based on pollen analysis and changes in lake levels from the Peten, Panama Canal, Lake Valencia of Venezuela, and Lake Moriru of Brazil all lead to paleoenvironmental reconstructions of a drier period after 8000 B.P. until 5500 B.P. or 3500 B.P. (Lake Moriru). In all of these instances the seasonally dry interval would have become more prominent (Markgraf 1989:8).

Oyuela-Caycedo (1996) further indicates that at about 5800–5400 B.P. a climatic dry period occurred that resulted in a lowering of sea level correlated with lower river and water table levels. The lower river and water table levels point to down cutting of stream channels and possible increases in the occurrence of savannas as a consequence of the fall of the water table. These data indicate that the climate during the occupation of San Jacinto 1 was drier than today and this conclusion is supported by the recovery of mollusks from the site (see Chapter 5).

In general these lines of evidence indicate shifting climatic and vegetative regimes for San Jacinto and the region of the Savannas of Bolívar. Vegetation can be envisioned as changing between savanna woodland and drier grass savanna elements depending on climatic and human influences. Given the increase in aridity, longer dry seasons for the area were also most likely occurring. In that case, the Savannas of Bolívar would best be characterized as a subhumid savanna with 500–1,000 mm of precipitation per year and with a medium dry season (5.0 to 7.5 months) or a semiarid savanna with 250–500 mm of precipitation per year and with long dry seasons (7.5 to 10.0 months) (see Harris 1980 for concepts related to the lengths of dry seasons).

HISTORY OF RESEARCH IN THE AREA

Research in the northwestern coastal regions of South America and lower Central America (Bruhns 1994; Dillehay 2000; Lavallée 1995; Raymond and Burger 2003; Scheinsohn 2003) has led to some of the most significant discoveries in the New World of archaeological sites with early pottery and evidence of domesticated plants. The research, however, has tended to focus on the questions of when and where as opposed to why. Questions related to the processes of adaptive change and to the relationship between pottery, sedentism, and plant domestication are relatively new ones for research in this part of the world. However, a great deal of information has been gathered and a brief review of the history of research in this region is presented in terms of its relevance to the issues of adaptation and historical ecology.

What occurred during the preceramic of northern Colombia is just starting to be known. Evidence includes only some surface material collections of preceramic sites (Correal 1986; Lopez 1998) that do not permit the reconstruction of how people used to live before the invention of pottery. However, recent research in the middle Magdalena Valley of Colombia has indicated that people were living in the area at the time of the late Pleistocene/Holocene boundary. They resided in small campsites of mobile populations with a tendency for more permanent sites on terraces with open vegetation (La Palestina, San Juan de Bedout, and Peñones del Río) and in small resource-specific camps (Puerto Nare T-46, Barranca T-408). In these sites projectile points occurred at least from 10,500 B.P. to 6000 B.P. (there is a more recent date, but this does not seem to correlate with the point typologies to support an overlapping with pottery producers from the lower Magdalena Valley populations; Lopez 1998:8–9).

Around 6000 B.P., pottery was invented (Oyuela-Caycedo 1993, 1995b) in this area and is characterized by the initial use of plant fibers as temper and firing in reduced conditions, possibly in earth ovens. Fiber-tempered pottery seems to be manufactured mainly by direct shaping and was produced by the household for the household (Raymond et al. 1994, 1998). Its distribution in northern Colombia is restricted to the lowlands of the Magdalena River basin, especially along the Dique canal branch and the low mountains of the Serranía de San Jacinto.

As mentioned previously, 5 km south of San Jacinto 1, at an altitude of 250 m above sea level, is the hilltop site of San Jacinto 2. Unlike San Jacinto 1, this site has no nearby perennial stream. Oriented on a north-to-south axis, the site is oval in plan and covers an area of about 2,340 m^2. A round depression, similar to a pithouse, as yet unexplored, dominates the extreme southern portion of the site. In general, the archaeological remains from San Jacinto 2 are similar to those from San Jacinto 1, but they are more elaborate in their appearance. The stone or lithic artifacts consist of metates, hand mills, ground stone axes, ground "nutcracker" stones, and hundreds of examples of an expedient core technology.

The ceramic assemblage from San Jacinto 2 reveals some interesting differences, however, when contrasted with that from San Jacinto 1. Only 69 percent (n = 419) of the 607 sherds recovered at San Jacinto 2 are fiber tempered. The remaining 31 percent (n = 188) are sand tempered and appear to have their closest technological and stylistic affiliations with the pottery from the Puerto Chacho (Rodríguez 1995) and Puerto Hormiga sites and with later pottery from the earliest phase of Monsú. Unlike Puerto Hormiga but similar to Monsú, San Jacinto 2 is not a shell mound site, though it does appear to represent an upland version of the same cultural adaptations seen at San Jacinto 1. In addition, the pottery from San Jacinto 2 is very similar to that collected from the undated Bucarelia site (Reichel–Dolmatoff 1991). Recently, other sites with similar assemblages have been found in the vicinity of El Guamo (Municipio de San Juan de Nepomuceno) and in El Bongal (Municipio de Zambrano).

The radiocarbon dates for San Jacinto 2 were obtained from the fiber temper of the pottery. The laboratory analysis used 100 g of this pottery. The dated material came from an excavated midden of redeposited material located on the hillside of the site. The oldest date of 4565 ± 80 B.P. came from sherds from one vessel found at the 10–20-cm level. The youngest date is believed to be too young and is possibly the product of dating sherds from different vessels (see Atley 1980). On the basis of the radiocarbon dates and comparison with other Formative sites, the chronological positioning of San Jacinto 2 most likely falls between the dates of 5250 ± 90 B.P. obtained for Puerto Chacho and 4565 ± 80 B.P. obtained for the site itself.

Fiber-tempered assemblages were later completely replaced by more heat-resistant and thermally conductive pottery with sand, grog, and shell temper (see Wagner et al. 1994; Wippern 1988). One aspect that seems not to have changed was the firing condition: a neutron activation analysis on material from Canapote indicates strongly reduced firing conditions, which was also inferred for the San Jacinto 1 pottery (Gebhard et al. 1988/1989). The new technological innovation in temper type replaced the older tradition around 4600 B.P. and led to the development of ceramic sequences represented by such sites as Monsú, Guajaro, Canapote, and Barlovento. The work carried out at all of these sites has been very useful for the development of ceramic and chronological sequences for the area (Table 1.4) (see Hoopes 1992), but what do we know of the northern lowlands of Colombia besides their chronology and cultural sequences?

Changes across time that have been proposed are from gatherers with fishing stations that depended on seasonal variation to groups that depended on root crops such as manioc (*Manihot esculenta*) (Reichel-Dolmatoff 1954, 1965a, 1982). Groups that depend on resources with seasonal variation tend to be more highly mobile. These changes are represented by sites close to the sea, such as the shell midden sites of Puerto Hormiga (5000 B.P.), Barlovento, and Canapote, and by riverine sites, such as Malambo (3000 B.P.), that are indicative of sedentary life (Wippern 1988). These populations used a broad spectrum of resources from the diverse microenvironments that characterize the area, such as lagoon-estuary, savanna, and dry forest systems (Reichel-Dolmatoff 1971:344). In all of these processes of change pottery was present in large quantities in relation to the lithic material. The lithic material represents mainly a plant food processing technology to supplement the diet of fish. This plant processing technology reflects gathering of nuts and grinding or mashing of roots (Reichel-Dolmatoff 1965a:53–59).

Changes in diet (manioc to maize) have also been indicated at the site of Momil around 2150 B.P., as well as at the Malambo site around 3000 B.P. (Angulo 1978, 1981; Reichel-Dolmatoff 1986:75–76). At the excavations of the

Table 1.4. Radiocarbon dates from other sites in northern Colombia with early pottery

Site	Lab. No.	Material	Date B.P. (uncalibrated)
Puerto Chacho	Beta-26200	Charcoal	5220 ± 90
Puerto Hormiga	SI-153	Shell	5040 ± 70
	SI-152	Shell	4970 ± 70
	I-445	Shell	4875 ± 170
	SI-151	Charcoal	4820 ± 100
	I-1123	Charcoal	4502 ± 250
San Jacinto 2	Pitt-0362	Temper	4565 ± 80
	Pitt-0361	Temper	3505 ± 85
San Marcos	Beta-16125	Charcoal	3650 ± 60
Monsú	UCLA-2149c	Shell	5300 ± 80
	UCLA-2149a	Shell	5000 ± 80
	UCLA-2149b	Shell	4200 ± 80
	UCLA-2565g		4270 ± 80
	UCLA-2568a		4175 ± 70
	UCLA-2568f	Bone	4170 ± 300
	TK-625a	Shell	3240 ± 60
	TK-625b	Shell	3230 ± 90
Guajaro			
Cut 7	Beta-13347	Charcoal?	4190 ± 120
Cut 6	SI-13347	Charcoal?	3800 ± 110
Canapote	Y-1317	Charcoal	3890 ± 100
	Y-1760	Charcoal	3730 ± 120
Barlovento	Y-1318	Charcoal	3510 ± 100
	W-739	Shell	3470 ± 120
	W-743	Shell	3140 ± 120
	W-741	Shell	2980 ± 120

Sources: Angulo 1988; Bischof 1966; Oyuela-Caycedo 1987; Plazas and Falchetti 1986; Reichel-Dolmatoff 1965b, 1985, 1986; Reichel-Dolmatoff and Dussan 1955; Rodríguez 1988.

sites of Barlovento and Monsú (Barlovento Period), shell hoes have been reported that are interpreted as indicators of some kind of root horticulture with a mixed strategy of gathering and hunting (Reichel-Dolmatoff 1985; Reichel-Dolmatoff and Dussan 1955).

In the interior of Colombia, dispersed sources of data tentatively indicate that agriculture may have been present very early in the northwestern Andes in preceramic contexts. This is evident in the results from the Calima project in which maize pollen has been reported from approximately 7000 B.P. (Monsalve 1985; Pearsall and Piperno 1990; Piperno and Pearsall 1998:261–262). Similarly, data from preceramic sites at El Pital dated approximately 6500 B.P. (Salgado 1987) suggest that some kind of plant processing and cutting of forests was occurring. In the lowlands of the Colombian and Ecuadorian Amazon an early maize subsistence base at 4645 ± 40 B.P. (pollen evidence, Herrera et al. 1992) has been suggested for the region of Araracuara and at approximately 5300 B.P. (phytolith evidence, Piperno 1990; Piperno and Pearsall 1998:262–265) for Lake Ayauch. No other evidence corroborates these findings yet.

In Venezuela, research findings in relation to the change from foragers to agriculturalists are very similar to those in Colombia. Sanoja (1989) proposed a close relationship between the relatively sedentary way of life found in estuaries and that involved in the initial stages of agricultural food production. The earliest evidence of corn in Venezuela comes from the Middle Orinoco. There, maize was introduced after 3000 B.P. According to Roosevelt (1980), the introduction of maize produced a major shift toward social complexity as a result of the increased carrying capacity of this crop and concurrent population growth (cf. Sanoja and Vargas 1983). This perspective agrees with evidence presented from Panama.

Other studies in progress on this matter in the lower Amazon in Brazil have advanced further data for consideration (Roosevelt 1989). At the site of Taperinha, the early sedentary population placed emphasis on a broad spectrum of resources and showed increasing sedentism defined by the early presence of pottery. This is the earliest sand-tempered pottery in the New World and dates to approximately 8000 B.P. (see Roosevelt et al. 1991; Simoes 1981; cf. Brochado 1984; Räsänen et al. 1991) (see Note 1). The subsistence base used by this early pottery-producing population was focused on riverine foraging (Roosevelt et al. 1991). Not until 4000 B.P. does the early horticultural village in this area begin to appear, when an increasing dependency on starchy root crops seems to occur (Roosevelt 1989:45). This scenario, however, is hypothetical, as no data on subsistence have been provided for the site.

On the coast of Ecuador, the research conducted sheds some light on the process of change from preceramic to ceramic times (see the volume on the

Ecuadorian Formative edited by Raymond and Burger [2003]). Research at the preceramic sites of the Las Vegas tradition (10,000–7000 B.P.) on the Santa Elena Peninsula of Ecuador concludes that there were sedentary populations living in a rich environment. The evidence from Las Vegas suggests that the diet of the early population was basically typical of broad-spectrum hunters and gatherers (Stothert 1985, 1988:237–260; Ubelaker 1984:509–511). In relation to the lithic material, edge-grinding tools and small grinder tools as well as ground stone axes were recovered, suggesting some sort of plant food processing; it is important to note that no metate/mano technology was recovered. The lithic tradition is considered to be part of the so-called edge-trimmed tool tradition (Hurt 1977) typical of a northwestern South American tradition of people adapted to a tropical forest area (Stothert 1985:633). Information on the subsistence base suggests the presence of maize cultivation around 8000–7000 B.P. (based on phytoliths) (Stothert 1985, 1988:217–219) and possibly the early use of domesticated species of *Cucurbita* around 10,100 to 9300 B.P. (based on phytoliths) (Piperno and Stothert 2003).

The next group of sites with important botanical remains from Ecuador is found in the southwest Guayas and southern Manabí provinces and dates to the early Valdivia Period (5500–4400 B.P.) (Pearsall 2003). The early Valdivia ceramic site of Real Alto (5150 B.P.) has yielded phytoliths and starch granules of maize. These recoveries suggest that maize was in production at the site (Pearsall and Piperno 1990; Pearsall et al. 2004; Piperno and Pearsall 1998:250). Also recovered from early Valdivia contexts were macrobotanical remains of *Canavalia* sp. (jack bean), which was found also in preceramic contexts at Huaca Prieta in Peru (Bird et al. 1985:233), sedge, and cotton (*Gossypium barbadense*). In addition, possible phytoliths of achira (*Canna* sp.), the Cucurbitaceae, and arrowroot (*Maranta* sp.) (Damp et al. 1981; Pearsall 1988; Piperno and Pearsall 1998:250) have been recovered. Botanical remains recovered from the early Valdivia site of Loma Alta include members of the Sapotaceae and Palmae, a root of *Scirpus/Cyperus,* and fragments of *Canavalia* beans (Piperno and Pearsall 1998:249–250; Raymond 1988). An impression of a kernel fragment was also recovered from a ceramic vessel in deposits with later dates of 3900 to 3800 B.P. at the San Pablo site in Ecuador (Zevallos et al. 1977). In the highlands, macrobotanical remains, pollen, and phytoliths of maize and beans have been recovered at the Formative village of Cotocollao, dating around 3450 B.P. (Villalba 1988).

The ceramic sites of the Valdivia tradition in Ecuador have a different artifactual assemblage from those of the preceramic sites discussed. The lithic material is characterized by the presence of a ground stone technology such as metates/manos and stone axes. Other new technologies also present include earth ovens and storage pits that are interpreted as being used to store maize (cf. Gregg 1991:211). In the highlands at the Cotocollao site, a diverse ground stone technology is characterized by metates and manos as well as by a diverse technology of chipped-stone tools. Storage pits and earth ovens with fire-cracked rocks associated with rectangular houses in what was a large village are reported for a time period around 3500–3000 B.P. (Villalba 1988).

The settlements of the ceramic Valdivia tradition also differ from the adaptation and subsistence system of Las Vegas. It is argued that the way of life centered on large villages developed around a floodplain farming system (Raymond et al. 1980). This research in Ecuador was the first to recover data on house forms. Real Alto was characterized as a village that started to develop very early on (Valdivia I). It became more complex through time until the development of mounds, ceremonial areas with temples, and charnel houses occurred (Marcos 1988; Raymond 1993). The form of the houses from Valdivia I (5300–4300 B.P.) was small, elliptical one-room dwellings with diameters between 2.3 and 4.53 m at the site of Loma Alta (Damp 1984a, 1984b). Similar structures are also reported for Real Alto for the same time (Damp 1988). In Valdivia III the size of the dwellings shifted to diameters around 8 to 12 m in elliptical forms that have been interpreted to be similar to "malocas." Furthermore, such structures seem to have internal divisions (Marcos 1988:137–140).

Evidence of population growth is available from the settlement pattern study conducted in the area, which suggests a strong change at the end of Valdivia and Machalilla times (3500–3000 B.P.) (Zeidler 1986). The change is so drastic during the Machalilla Period that the population doubles compared to previous late Valdivia phases. For the first time a hierarchy in settlement size is also observed (Raymond 1993, 2003). If the interpretation on subsistence is correct, the population growth in the area occurred after agriculture was already in place. This would be contrary to what some of the models on agriculture and population growth predict. For instance, a skeletal remains analysis conducted with samples from Santa Elena and more recent sites such as Cotocollao and Guandala (3500–2000 B.P.) confirms that people relied on agriculture around 2000 B.P. (Ubelaker 1984:510; also see Staller 2001; Staller and Thompson 2002). If this interpretation is correct, then the effect of agriculture on population growth or vice versa still is not clear for the area (for a critique of early evidence of maize subsistence see Lippi et al. 1984:118–119). In synthesis, the transition from preceramic sites to ceramic settlements on the coast as well as in the highlands of Ecuador is still not very well understood. The role of maize and food production also remains questionable as differing lines of evidence indicate both the importance of maize and its secondary role in the development of agriculture and social hierarchies in this area.

In the case of the research conducted in Panama, the results show a more balanced and systematic research approach. Differences of adaptation through time and space depending on the ecological setting are demonstrated. For example, the populations of the Caribbean slopes of western Panama depended on root and tree crops for food (Linares et al. 1975; Linares and Ranere 1980) while those in the Parita region during later periods depended on seed crops. For the preceramic period (10,000–4500 B.P.) it has been suggested that the diet was concentrated around the exploitation of palm and other wild plants and on root crops of some kind. Palynological studies as well as phytoliths (microbotanic analyses) from various places in Panama indicate the existence of maize as early as 7000 B.P. (Bartlett et al. 1969; Cooke 1984; Piperno and Clarie 1984; Piperno and Pearsall 1998:221–227). Furthermore, the use of root crops including manioc (*Manihot esculenta*), yams (*Dioscorea* sp.), and arrowroot (*Maranta arundinacea*) has been identified from starch grains on assemblages of milling stones at Aguadulce Shelter in Panama in contexts dating to 7000 to 5000 B.P. (Piperno et al. 2000). It seems, however, that maize consumption was very low at this time and only started to have a major impact on the diet around 2500–1500 B.P. (Cooke and Ranere 1992a, 1992b). The earliest macrobotanical remains of maize are dated around 2015 B.P. Studies on human remains from the preceramic period (Cerro Mangote) to the later ceramic periods (Sitio Sierra) corroborate a gradual process of specialization in food production from a broad, varied diet to one more concentrated on maize. Major shifts are observed only in a decrease in the quality of nutrition for later populations in the Pacific region of Panama (Norr 1984).

In terms of lithics and food production, the preceramic site of Cerro Mangote has a different assemblage reported from that of preceramic sites in Ecuador. Unshaped boulders similar to metates are reported, as are other ground stone technologies, indicating heavy reliance on plant processing with grinding, pounding, and mashing tools (McGimsey 1956; McGimsey et al. 1986–1987). One of the diagnostic artifacts from this early stage of plant-processing technology is the "edge-ground cobble." This artifact was used to produce a grinding or mashing action on roots (Ranere 1975, 1980). Edge-ground cobbles have been found in the Chiriquí region, where a heavy reliance on nut palm harvesting occurs. They have also been found in the preceramic and ceramic sites of Cerro Mangote and Monagrillo, respectively, where the food staple seems to be more oriented to shore-based fishing activities (Cooke 1992a; McGimsey 1956; Willey and McGimsey 1954:73). Evidence of stone tools interpreted as useful in maize processing like metates and manos only appears in the archaeological record in contexts dated to 2500–2000 B.P. with polished axes and adzes.

In the context summarized above, the appearance of pottery in Panama seems not to be related to agricultural production even when it is present in large quantities, as at the Monagrillo site (20,301 fragments), which has a contrastingly low quantity of lithic artifacts (230 artifacts). It can be stated that in this part of the continent pottery appears to be linked to fish and mammal hunting and plant-food processing from gathering (Norr 1984; Willey and McGimsey 1954).

In summary, the information available for this region of Central America and northwestern South America on the processes of change from mobile hunting-gathering to sedentism as well as to food production is expanding but still limited. The exception to this would be the long-term research conducted in Panama, where the data and interpretations are richer in this regard. The process reconstructed for Panama shows a gradual shift from semisedentary seasonal fisher-folk and populations of collectors to food-producing populations, a process that depended for its development on an environmental diversity that was not the same for inland and coastal populations. In this process, pottery does not have a direct impact. Also proposed is a later change from subsistence based on root crops to one based on maize with direct effects on population growth and village development (for a comparative discussion on this issue in Colombia, Ecuador, and Panama, see Raymond 1998).

In the case of Colombia and Venezuela the evidence indicates an early sedentism focused around rich and diverse environments where a gradual process to horticulture or root crop use took place and where later the introduction of maize had a major impact on population growth and formation of villages. In the case of Ecuador, good data are available for the preceramic period on the coast (Raymond and Burger 2003). Sedentary populations seem to be the norm and later give rise to villages and food producers. Here the presence of pottery correlates with food production. In this frame of reference, the process leading from mobile hunting-gathering to sedentism is unknown. The appearance of villages and food production is a punctual change or "revolution" (see Marcos 1988) accompanied by changes in the site structure from small family dwellings to long houses of possible extended families with internal separation of space. Besides the information on dwelling form, practically no information on site structure is in existence. The research conducted at San Jacinto 1 contributes to the understanding of this regional context.

THE EXCAVATION

Because there was so much overburden over the cultural strata of the site, prior to excavation and to better define where to excavate, subsurface probing was utilized to identify the boundaries of the site. The instrument used to auger San Jacinto 1 was a soil-recovering auger that allowed for the recovery of the soils in plastic liners and for storing the recovered soil sample. This instrument is not a coring device because the head of the perforator cuts the soils in a helical motion. To make the perforations, 20 feet (6.096 m) of quick-connecting extensions were used. These elements permitted perforations to 6.48 m deep. The placement of cores was based on initial establishment of a base point and grid of the terrain in squares of 25 × 25 m. Each point was located on a Cartesian metric system of coordinates east (E) and north (N). By a trial-and-error procedure of finding or not finding evidence of anthropic soils or paleosols, the area to be perforated was reduced until the borders of the anthropic soils were delimited.

On the basis of the augering results, the site is estimated to be 346 m^2, of which 75 m^2 was excavated. Based on the form of the site, it was also possible to calculate the area lost by the current meander cutoff of the stream. The minimum activity area destroyed was 35 m^2, thus a majority of the site was intact at the time of excavation. The excavation of 5 × 15 m (75 m^2) with a northern orientation was determined to be appropriate for uncovering the expected area of human occupation. The excavation was divided into three quadrangles, each of 5 × 5 m (Figures 1.7 and 1.8). The augering results also indicated a total of 26 strata, the first eight of which were mainly overburden with strata 9 through 20 yielding the cultural material of interest. The excavation, therefore, was conducted in two stages. The first stage was a fast removal of strata 1 through 8 in order to open the area and start excavating the lower strata. The second stage was a careful excavation of strata 9 through 26.

Of the first eight strata, only stratum 5 was excavated in detail. A total of five features were identified within this anthropic soil. All of the features were excavated using trowels and detailed information on the content of each feature was recovered, which indicated possible uses as kilns (see Pool 2000 for other examples). The collected material from Features 1 and 2 corresponded to a period dated between 2120 ± 90 years B.P. and 1750 ± 80 years B.P.

The second stage of the excavation involved horizontal stratigraphic excavation in which each stratum was completely excavated before passing to the next one. A reference of three quadrangles of 5 × 5 m was maintained. This space was then divided into square meters with excavation proceeding in a chessboard pattern (Figures 1.7 and 1.8). The excavation of strata 9 and 10 went smoothly with both present in the total area excavated. The difference between these two strata was marked by an abrupt change in color, stratum 10 being a dark soil. Strata 9 and 10 evidently witnessed the major spatial occupation of the site. The next anthropic soil, stratum 12, had a very different spatial distribution and joined with stratum 10 to the north. As was expected from the augering of the site, stratum 11, a light-colored sterile soil layer, was

Figure 1.7. Excavation of San Jacinto 1; view from south (bottom) to north (top). Bottom section (5 × 5 m) (south) unexcavated. Middle section (5 × 5 m) in process of removal of strata using chessboard pattern and exposure of features from stratum 10. Cultural strata have been removed in top 5 × 5 m (north).

Figure 1.8. Excavation of strata 9 and 10 at San Jacinto 1; view from north (bottom) to south (top). Note unexcavated features in bottom section; however, borders of earth oven features and other features are exposed.

Figure 1.9. Excavation of features from strata 9 through 20 at San Jacinto 1. Southern (bottom) section (5 × 5 m) in process of excavation.

deposited in two-thirds of the excavated area, leading to the differentiation of stratum 12 from stratum 10. This differentiation occurred toward the south and can be explained in relation to the alluvial setting of the site: flooding episodes were depositing sterile soil layers between the human occupation layers and a point bar was growing toward the north. The same phenomenon is recognized for stratum 13 and the anthropic soil of stratum 14. These flooding episodes led to the formation of strata 11 and 13, which cover the lower part of the point bar. The other flood markers are the inclined sterile deposits of strata 15, 17, and 19. These flooding episodes allowed for the differentiation of dumped garbage material from strata 14, 16, 18, and 20.

Features were excavated following their internal stratigraphy. When a feature did not have a clear stratigraphy, it was excavated in arbitrary levels until it was possible to differentiate the context associated to the feature (Figure 1.9). One hundred seventy-four features were encountered and carefully recorded (Oyuela-Caycedo 1993). Material for flotation was recovered from both floors and all types of features encountered. In total 875.66 kg of material were floated from 267 samples. Of the floated material, 67 random samples of the features and floors and 10 nonrandom samples of ^{14}C-dated features were analyzed for their macrobotanical content (Bonzani 1995, 1997). Additionally, information on uses and seasonality of plants in the area was collected from local informants (Bonzani 1998, 1999).

CONCLUSION

The discovery of the site of San Jacinto 1 gives us a rare opportunity to view part of the lifeways of groups of hunter-gatherers living 5,000 to 6,000 years ago in northwestern South America. The environmental setting was one of a savanna region mainly composed of grasses and probably somewhat drier than today (less than 1,000 mm of rain per year). Strong seasonal changes occurred between wet and dry periods with a dry season from four to possibly more than seven months of the year. Early pottery has been found in this area at the sites of Puerto Hormiga and Puerto Chacho in Colombia and at the Valdivia culture sites in Ecuador. The fiber-tempered pottery recovered from San Jacinto 1 adds to the evidence of early pottery in the New World, and its association with metates, manos, and earth oven features helps to yield information on adaptive strategies employed by hunter-gatherers. The site of San Jacinto 1 gives us a chance to look into the issues of the relationship between the invention of pottery, the mobility patterns of these groups, and their use of the resources available to them in an environment that was probably drier than today and highly seasonal.

2 The Theoretical Framework

The importance of theory in archaeology and other sciences lies in its ability to ask questions that direct data collection. Once a preliminary evaluation of San Jacinto 1 was done in 1986 and the dates confirmed the early evidence of fiber-tempered pottery, an excavation of the site was needed to approach the theoretical problems concerning the issues of the origins of pottery and food production and the relationship of these to sedentism and landscape dynamics. The research design for the excavation in 1991–1992 was planned according to the questions generated in the disputed explanations on these issues. In this chapter are presented the approaches developed and the research questions that were considered and that continue to be valuable for studying these issues.

MOBILITY STRATEGIES AND THE ORIGINS OF SEDENTISM

In a review of the literature related to sedentism it is not surprising to find that most arguments are built around how to identify or recognize sedentism and that little effort has been made in explaining why a population becomes sedentary (Kesarwani 1987; Rafferty 1985). Mobility and sedentism involve factors per se that require a more careful analysis than that generally expressed (Close 2000; Kelly 1995). Keeping in mind that most of the models related to the origins of agriculture consider mobility or sedentism as a major factor in this process, it is considered here to be necessary to evaluate sedentism on its own terms. This means that another set of questions must be addressed. Prior questions have included the following: If sedentism is confirmed, does it occur before agricultural dependency, does agriculture occur before sedentism, or do both co-occur in a gradual manner? More probing questions ask why and how sedentism develops: What caused people to change from being mobile to becoming less mobile or even the other way around (there are some archaeological and ethnographic cases that seem to show this alternative)? What does it mean in terms of adaptation to be mobile instead of sedentary or vice versa? The answers to these questions become as complex as the explanations of the origin of food production itself. It is interesting to note that models that explain the reduction of mobility are still scarce as a result of the normative view that relates sedentism with agriculture (see Rocek and Bar-Yosef 1998).

A revision of the data on the mobility of agricultural populations leads to the questioning even of the whole concept of sedentism as being useful for understanding the variations in subsistence changes or processes of intensification (Hard and Merrill 1992; Preucel 1990). Horticultural populations, for example, expend significant time on hunting and gathering activities that require monitoring of resources and mobility (Descola 1996:221–269; Gorecki 1991; Healey 1990; Johnson 2003:38–39; Rival 2002:68–93). Another example is in relation to shifting cultivation, which is commonly believed to be an adaptive response to low soil productivity, but it is very likely to be more related to the interactions of mobility in maintaining the productivity of hunting (Cabrera et al. 1999:221–312; Moran 1983). It seems that sedentism of human populations may be more imagined than real. In the case of agricultural populations a solution to the problem is the understanding of daily, periodic, seasonal, and long-term movements (Cabrera et al. 1999:108–129; Gonçalves 2001:77–134; Preucel 1990).

In this volume the concept of sedentism is used more in a general form to mean reduction of mobility and increase of territorial control by the constant presence of a group in the same spot. As with any classificatory concept, sedentism allows one to get a general idea of what kinds of populations are being talked about. Variations in mobility strategies are developed to put, in one form or another, people and resources together in space and time. The social implications of sedentism, of course, can be diverse and complex and initially involve the development of and reliance on extended kinship networks for access to resources such as food. A related occurrence is the development of territorial kinship hierarchies to control important land and water resources.

In a model proposed by Testart (1982; also see Ingold 1983; Pollock 1985), the variation of hunter-gatherers observed in the world led to the consideration that there are societies of hunter-gatherers that differ in their economic bases. One type is the nomadic hunter-gatherer with a practice of immediate use of foods (Bushmen and Australian aboriginals). The other type practiced large-scale seasonal storage (California and Northwest Coast Indians). Testart (1982) considered this difference the magic key in understanding the causes of sedentism, population density, and inequality. The role of storage as a key component has also been used to explain the development of complex societies. This model can be considered to be very similar to that dealing with immediate- and delayed-return systems (Woodburn 1982, 1991). The difference is that it views the variation of hunter-gatherers not just by subsistence

The Theoretical Framework

and technology but also by adding the environment as a significant factor that conditions hunter-gatherers.

In relation to hunter-gatherers, if one asks which societies would become sedentary, the answer by Testart (1982) would be those societies that had the possibility of having an economy based on storage. In order for this to occur the following conditions must be fulfilled:

Ecological Conditions:
  Abundance of resources
  Seasonality of resources
Technical Conditions:
  Efficient food getting
  Food-storage techniques

A hunter-gatherer group that fulfills these conditions is expected to be sedentary on the grounds that large bulk reserves of food are incompatible with mobility and, in addition, accumulations of stocks urge people to settle. In relation to the first condition, in order for groups to settle in a base camp the resource must be concentrated in the same geographical area as the camp and must be abundant at least in one season (Binford 2001:396–398). In relation to the second, the resource has to be able to be stored in order to be consumed during a time of scarcity and risk (Binford 2001:35–40; Halstead and O'Shea 1989; O'Shea 1981; Wiessner 1982). In sum, it is storage that inhibits the possibility of residential mobility as well as suppresses its necessity.

Other models also incorporate the environment as an important factor in the mobility strategies of hunter-gatherer groups. In this sense, mobility strategies are responses by human populations to cope with environmental fluctuations. On the basis of previous observations on resource variations and fluctuations of settlement patterns by diverse groups, it has been considered that there is a close relation between variations in space and time of resources and variations in mobility patterns (see Ebert 1992; Steward 1938; Thomas 1983). It has also been argued that a correlation exists between storage and social hierarchy (Binford 2001:401).

Binford (1978, 1980) differentiates two forms of subsistence strategies using the environment as a major determining factor (see Bettinger 1991:100–103; Ebert 1992; Humphreys 1987; Kelly 1995; Preucel 1990:12–13; Price and Brown 1985; Thomas 1983 for further discussions).[1] The two forms are foraging and collecting. These two strategies correlate with two strategies of mobility in a continuum. At the extremes of the continuum are residential and logistic mobility. By examining the extreme cases (the G/wi San and the Inuit), Binford proposes a clear difference between foragers and collectors as well as between residential and logistic mobility that can look very similar to the model defined by Testart (1982). Foragers are seen to use strategies equivalent to those of immediate-return systems while collectors can be associated to immediate- and/or delayed-return systems. One difference, however, is that both strategies can be found in the same group.

Foragers are characterized by a group that "maps onto" resources by moving consumers to resources, resulting in frequent movements of the base camps. On the other hand, *collectors* move resources to consumers and residential movement is less frequent. These two strategies produce different patterns of assemblages. In the case of foragers, it is expected that the patterns of the archaeological record would correspond to two kinds of sites: residential camps and locations. *Residential camps* would be characterized by evidence of most of the processing, manufacturing, and maintenance activities. These camps can be expected to have low accumulations of debris and low visibility, with the exception of camps located near critical resources such as water sources in a desert. A *location* is a place where extraction of resources is carried out. These sites or nonsites would have very low visibility. As a result of the high mobility of foragers and more regular daily food procurement, low-bulk inputs are expected. The variability between camps is likely to be related to the seasonal scheduling of activities.

Collectors are characterized by storage of food during part of the year and logistically organized food procurement parties. Collectors' activities are more visible and show more variability in the interassemblages of sites. In collector groups, the two kinds of sites described for foragers plus other kinds of sites such as field camps, stations, and caches are expected to exist. The *field camp* or *special-purpose location* is a provisional camp of a task group and as a result should reflect the nature of the target of the group. *Stations* are places such as observation sites. *Caches* are temporary storage places for bulk food that are utilized in the process of moving the food to the base camp.

Binford (1978, 1980, 2001) structures the model by asking why some populations choose as a strategy residential mobility whereas others prefer logistic mobility and by explaining that such variation in strategy is related to variation of the environment. The mobility strategies or combinations of strategies that hunter-gatherers develop are selected to cope with the structure of food resources in a defined environment (see Aldenderfer 1998:276–307, 1999:388–390; Bettinger 1991:83–111; Gifford-Gonzalez et al. 1999:405–408; Kelly 1995; Marean 1997). The basis of the argument lies in considering humans as energy-capturing systems that leave different types of patterns in the landscape ("grain sizes"). The grain size of the archaeological record is understood as the resolution of events that take place at a site: the higher the resolution

The Theoretical Framework

in recognizing an event, the finer the grain of the archaeological assemblage at a site. Binford (1980, 1983) argues that the factor that regulates the assemblage grain size at a site is mobility. He defines mobility in terms of distance of movement in a year between residences, where these movements are products of the structure of the habitat and the pressure on resources and the strategies to cope with these aspects (Binford 2001:255). The higher the mobility (residential) at a site, the finer grained the archaeological assemblage would be as well as the higher the interassemblage variability at the site. Between-site interassemblage variability would be less for highly mobile groups.

The organization of technology, then, is invented to solve problems of coping with the energy-entropy structure. This implies that an extreme foraging strategy will be more successful in certain environmental conditions than in others. Such foraging strategies generally involve social organizations of groups made up of few individuals, often referred to as bands. By using cross-cultural analysis of ethnographic groups, Binford concludes that high mobility is more frequently developed in very productive or in extremely low productive environments. The data show that in fully equatorial environments, 75 percent of the cases show high mobility. In the semitropics, 64.2 percent of the cases show high mobility; in warm settings the figure is reduced to 9.3 percent and in cool environments it is reduced drastically to 7.5 percent, but in boreal environments it increases to 41.6 percent of the cases (see Binford 2001:276). This variation led to the proposition that under conditions of *spatial incongruity* a logistic strategy is more likely to be selected for. This allows the group to move the residential camp to the bulky resources and permits the extraction of other resources by task-group movement. Such strategies could result in social organizations with higher populations, as more labor would be needed to perform the required special-purpose tasks. Storage would be very useful in the cases of *temporal incongruity*, but it increases the problem of coping with spatial incongruity (Binford 2001:256–262, 303). Another expectation is that logistic mobility covaries in relation to the length of the growing season. Binford (2001:260) argues that storage among hunter-gatherers is uncommon below 35 degrees latitude as storage correlates with a decrease in the length of the growing season. The shorter the length of the season, the more the response is in the form of logistic mobility. In summary, Binford convincingly argues that the greater the seasonal variability, the greater the expected role of logistic mobility as well as the greater the interassemblage variability between archaeological sites.

Binford (1980) recognizes that other factors can restrict residential mobility, such as an increase in population density. Social or economic constraints also would favor logistic strategies over the "maps onto" strategy of moving consumers to resources. An aspect that is significant in Binford's model is that it does not deal with the relation of mobility strategies and, for example, intensification of food production and sedentism. It is in this context that we ask what the relationship is between the level of mobility and food production or how this variability in mobility explains sedentism. For Binford (2001:438), "Sedentism is a response to intensificational pressures, as are such strategies as an increased investment of labor in rendering plants edible, an expansion of the temporal usefulness of food resources by means of storage techniques, the cultivation of plants themselves, and the selection of a limited number of domesticated plants for cultivation. At some scale, all of these strategies result from the same determinant processes; one is not the cause of the other." Here one sees the importance of the relationship between mobility strategies and food production. As the need for logistic mobility strategies increases (i.e., as mobility decreases), strategies to intensify food production in the form initially of collection and processing and later of cultivation will also increase. The origins of food production then lie in changing mobility strategies and the reasons for such changes.

THE ORIGINS OF FOOD PRODUCTION IN TRANSITIONAL SAVANNA ENVIRONMENTS

What are the reasons for changing mobility strategies and the origins of food production? Most of the studies on the origins of food production and agriculture have agreed that there appears to be no single explanation for the changes involved in the shift to sedentism and/or to food producing. One must keep in mind that the process of domestication of a plant species can occur long before societies adopt full-scale agriculture (Ford 1985; Harris 1996a, 1996b; Hart 1999; Rindos 1984; Smith 2001; Terrell et al. 2003; Zohary 1989; Zohary and Hopf 1988; Zvelebil and Rowley-Conwy 1986). Domestication is a process that results in genetic changes to the plant species that make it dependent on humans for reproduction and that can occur during the tending and cultivation of a plant (Ford 1985). These changes are often found in archaeological plant remains long before a society practiced agriculture and used the plant as a staple food source. It is clear that various plant species were cultivated before agriculture occurred and even before the invention or innovation of pottery. It is also clear that the contribution of cultivars to the diet was low for foraging populations (Bar-Yosef and Belfer-Cohen 1992; Belfer-Cohen and Bar-Yosef 2000; Dillehay and Rossen 2002; Flannery 1986; Gil 2003; Hastorf 1994, 1999a; Henry 1992; King 1987a; Lynch et al. 1985; MacNeish 1992; Pearsall 1989; Pickersgill and Heiser 1978).

The problem remains that few studies have established the proportion of cultivated plants in the diet (Roosevelt 1984) and, likewise, what the degree of sedentism was in these cases. Three hypothetical positions have been advanced to outline the process. First, sedentism is viewed as occurring before agriculture, as in the case of Peru and southeastern Asia (Bar-Yosef and Belfer-Cohen 1989, 1991; Bird et al. 1985; Flannery 1973; Kuijt 2000; Moseley 1975; Rossen and Dillehay 2000). Second, transhumance is seen as the basis for incipient agricultural development that later led to sedentism (Flannery 1986; Lynch 1973; MacNeish et al. 1983; Sanoja 1989). Third, the process toward agriculture and sedentism is seen as parallel and gradual until radical phenotypic change in one or more cultigens favored intensification and human dependency, as for example with maize (Flannery 1973; Reichel-Dolmatoff 1961; Rindos 1984; Smith 1987). A fourth position has been advanced that considers the three previous propositions (called the trilinear theory). In this fourth position all of these strategies (called routes) are likely and depend mainly on the ecological setting (MacNeish 1992; cf. Oyuela-Caycedo 1995a). These models are discussed and reviewed by Flannery (1973), Ford (1985), MacNeish (1992), Smith (1995), Stark (1986), Terrell et al. (2003), and Watson (1991).

For the site of San Jacinto 1, the fourth position is considered most relevant because it views the ecological or environmental setting to be of major importance in defining the food-getting strategies that the groups who occupied the site 6,000 years ago would have used. Further, the use of risk-management theories beyond simple foraging models is important. The idea of "dealing with risk" helps to explain why certain strategies are used over others depending on the types of environments (Bettinger 1991; Binford 2001:26–29; Cashdan 1983, 1990, 1992; Cashdan, ed. 1990; Cruz-Uribe 1988; Gremillion 2002, 2004:228–229; Hawkes et al. 1982; Neusius 1986; Wiessner 1982; Winterhalder 1986, 1990).

A number of anthropologists have dealt with the importance of the environment when dealing with the issues surrounding the origins of food production. Two of these models were specifically addressed during the research at San Jacinto 1. These included Harris's (1972) and Binford's (1968) theories on the relationship between the origins of food production and transitional or marginal areas. Based on population pressure, but with a more ecologically minded approach, Binford (1968) hypothesizes that the earliest evidence of plant domestication would be in areas of marginal environments or "recipient" zones. Harris (1972) has also called for "transitional" areas between major ecotonal regions as the most likely areas for early plant domestication. In general, he equates transitional areas with tropical savanna. In particular, however, he more specifically indicates that agriculture probably first originated in those regions with long dry seasons (7.5 to 10.0 months) and was later introduced into short dry season savanna regions. From this Harris thus predicts that grassland or tree/shrub savannas should first have indications of plant cultivation and domestication.

Although both of these hypotheses are early examples of the interest in the origins of agriculture, they are still important in that they outline the environmental characteristics of the areas where the origins of food production most likely occurred. These areas are savanna environments with strong seasonality. Why would such environmental conditions lead to the need to intensify food gathering and collection, which ultimately results in plant species domestication and agriculture? The answer to this appears to lie in risk-management theories, which indicate that humans will adopt strategies that even out risk over time and space (Cashdan 1992; Winterhalder 1990, 1996, 2001; see also Fitzhugh 2001). In seasonal environments, to avoid a shortfall of food during the dry season, for instance, groups must intensively collect and process the available food resources before such resources die off as a result of the dry weather. Intensified collecting and processing of plants, as evidenced by processing technology and potentially macrobotanical remains, is expected. This strategy of risk reduction also fits in nicely with Binford's (1978, 1980, 2001) ideas on mobility strategies since logistic mobility is expected to occur when resources are patchy in space and, we can add, in time as well. This form of spatial-temporal territoriality explains how groups monitor food resources both in space and time. When plant resources such as grasses become available, groups can map onto these seasonal markers and schedule activities to collect and process enough of the resources to allow for the group's survival over a seasonally stressful period.

It is in the reduction of mobility in both time and space that one finds the common denominator between the origins of pottery, the increase in sedentism, and the beginnings of food production (Flannery 1986). A strategy of reduced mobility can occur during environmental changes and leads to an increase in social or economic interactions (Rowley-Conwy 2001). Intensifications in social and economic interactions are strategies selected to average out resources in space and time by reducing the risk of unpredictability (Cashdan 1992). Intensification of social activities could involve, for instance, an expansion of social or kin networks through activities such as drinking and raiding parties and the collection and processing of seasonal plant resources to obtain the necessary ingredients for these activities (Braidwood 1953; Cauvin 2000a, 2000b; Hastorf 1994, 1999a; Hayden 1990, 1995, 2001). Binford (2001:371) refers to this with the concept of social storage, which relates to Mauss's (1967) explanation of the importance and meaning of the gift. Archaeological evidence of artifacts with symbolic ornamentation is expected and pottery can play a significant role as a symbolic item in food serving or food preparation (e.g., fermentation vessels) during activities that may occur when larger than normal groups of people are gathered to complete a specific task. In this case a need for labor could be one reason for such group activities. Other reasons might include competition or a reduction in conflict.

In the intensification of economic activities, a shift in focus to one or a few abundant seasonal food resources is expected as are new forms of processing that enhance the nutritional quality of previously exploited resources. Examples of this sort of enhancement are fermentation and detoxification. This intensification could be expressed in repetitive activities related to the processing of such food resources (Stahl 1989) such as the archaeological recovery of similar (redundant) features at one location. An increase in artifacts used for processing (i.e., ground stones and/or pottery) is also expected, as is the recovery of macrobotanical remains focused on only a few species at specific site locations. This economic intensification can be considered an initial stage in the origins of food production, which would occur prior to signs of cultivation (i.e., planting) and potentially, though not necessarily, domestication (Bar-Yosef and Belfer-Cohen 1992; Bonzani 1995, 1997; Flannery 1986; Henry 1992; King 1987a; Lynch et al. 1985; MacNeish 1992).

In summary, then, one would expect to find signs of logistic mobility practices in savanna environments with strong seasonality. Such practices are the result of a need to map onto resources both in space and time (scheduling) to ensure that enough food is available to the group during the season of scarcity. The risk of not having food necessitates these mobility strategies and an increase in the intensification of collection and processing. This intensification is also expected to result in the need to obtain additional labor for the processing of food resources. It is therefore in such seasonal savanna environments that the conditions leading toward reduced mobility and the intensification of food production are expected to occur.

THE ORIGINS OF POTTERY PRODUCTION

The origin of pottery production among hunter-gatherers can also be seen as an adaptive strategy brought about by changing external conditions (Armit and Finlayson 1995; Arnold 2003; Bonner 1980; Brown 1986, 1989; Cashdan 1992; Cashdan, ed. 1990; Dawkins 1976:203–215; Fitzhugh 2001; Nelson 1991; Oyuela-Caycedo 1995b; Rambo 1991; Reid 1984a, 1984b, 1989; Rice 1999). The most active of these external changes is the productivity of environmental resources, which is affected by such things as climatic change toward a more arid environment or prolonged dry seasons and concomitant changes such as a shift from homogeneous distribution of resources to patchiness of resources. In other words, changes toward less predictable seasonality of higher ranked resources would have important consequences for hunter-gatherer adaptations. In order to cope with these changing conditions, the territoriality and mobility strategies of the population can change. The population has several alternatives: (1) move to a more predictable environment not occupied by another group, (2) increase the size of its territory with residential mobility, or (3) be more territorial by controlling different patchy resources through constant monitoring. Such territoriality would favor a more logistic strategy of mobility. It is expected that this last alternative will be the preferred one, considering that these kinds of environmental changes are gradual and populations can map the distribution of resources as well as practice a spatial-temporal territoriality over the resources. The next part of this continuum would be the permanent residence of groups referred to as sedentism.

Since the early development of archaeology, a relationship between the origins of pottery production and sedentism has been assumed. In only a few cases has this not been accepted as fact (Eerkens et al. 2002). Therefore, one must ask whether the presence of pottery necessarily indicates sedentism. Part of the problem is based on a strong ethnographic correlation between mobility and a lack of pottery and between sedentism and the occurrence of pottery, as well as the influence of V. Gordon Childe's interpretation of the origins of agriculture (Sassaman 1993:1–3, 1995). The relationship between pottery and sedentism and the reasons for pottery's innovation cannot be explained by looking at the ethnographic information alone, however. One must explore the evidence from the archaeological record (see Barnett and Hoopes 1995; Bollong et al. 1997; Meggers 1997; Oyuela-Caycedo 1995b). Looking at most of the archaeological areas where early fiber-tempered pottery innovation and production occurred in the Americas makes it clear that the origin of fiber-tempered pottery production has a strong relationship with non-sedentary populations. Only in a few cases is it associated with sedentary populations. To answer our first question, then, let us examine in more detail the context of this early fiber-tempered pottery in the Americas, specifically that from the Southeast and Midwest of the United States (also see Heidke and Habicht-Mauche 1998), with other examples from Latin America. This comparison should help us examine the meaning of the fiber-tempered pottery at San Jacinto 1 in a broader context than that described in Chapter 1.

Pottery of the Gulf Coastal Plain in the southeastern United States was made with fiber temper and first recovered from the shell middens of Stallings Island on the Savannah River. Four series are recognized in the U.S. Southeast (Sassaman 1993, 1995, 1998). These are the Stallings series, the Thom's Creek series, the Orange series, and the Wheeler series. The oldest pottery is the Stallings series, which may have been manufactured as early as 4500 B.P. The distribution of this pottery is from the Atlantic coast to the piedmont of the Savannah River (Stoltman 1972) and from the Atlantic coast of the Santee River in South Carolina to the Altamaha River in Georgia. Sand-tempered vessels, by contrast, characterize the Thom's Creek series. This series overlaps in spatial distribution with the coastal Stallings series. The geographic distribution extends from the mouth of the Savannah River valley to the coastal area of South Carolina. The chronology of this series also has some overlap with the Stallings series, Thom's Creek being more recent in time. The Orange series has a distribution in peninsular Florida. Numerous Archaic sites of the Orange period have been located and excavated; all of them are shell middens (Bullen 1972; Widmer 1988:67–73, 2002). The Wheeler series is a fiber-tempered pottery whose distribution is in the middle Tennessee Valley and in the central and upper Tombigbee Valley in the states of Alabama and Mississippi. In general, this pottery is found in very low frequency. It is interesting to note that pottery from this area greatly emphasizes decoration. In a manner similar to that of Colombia, a high proportion of the pottery is decorated, with ratios from 4.6 plain sherds to 1 decorated sherd in the early assemblages (Stoltman 1972:45). The decoration is mainly punctated, incised, or stamped.

In the past it had been suggested that this pottery originated from the Puerto Hormiga complex in northwestern Colombia, but this now seems totally unlikely, considering the chronological differences between the two areas. When fiber-tempered pottery was innovated in the Savannah River drainage, in Colombia the people were using sand temper and coiling in pottery manufacture. If long-distance diffusion did occur, what would be expected would be the introduction of material similar to that fabricated at the sites of Monsú or Canapote in Colombia (see Wippern 1988), but this was not the case. In general, the interpretations of the origin of this pottery are mainly of a diffusionist or functional character (for a detailed discussion and critique of past interpretations, see Sassaman 1993:23–31).

Fiber-tempered pottery spread to other areas after 3200 B.P., such as to the Tennessee Valley (Griffin 1972) and western Gulf Coastal Plain (Jenkins et al. 1986). Most of the sites of this region where pottery has been found have a common aspect: pottery appears in a variety of forms, creating problems in relation to the function of early pottery. Logistic mobility seems to be the norm for these populations. Most of the sites indicate populations of shellfish collectors. Few sites have been studied on the floodplain, nor have riverine sites in the piedmont or upland interriverine zones been studied that would clarify the settlement pattern or subsistence base of these early pottery groups (Sassaman 1993). It is interesting to note that sedentism occurred much later in the Tennessee Valley and western Gulf Coastal Plain than in other parts of the United States and seems to go in hand with sand-, shell-, and grog-tempered pottery. Sedentism did not occur until the rise of villages on the southwestern coast of Florida around 1720 B.P., and in some areas the agricultural way of life never developed at all, although social and political complexity did (Widmer 1988).

Fiber-tempered pottery in the Midwest is found in some early contexts such as at the Nebo Hill site in the lower Missouri River drainage. In excavation at this site only 85 fragments of fiber-tempered pottery were recovered (Mehrer 1998; Reid 1984b). Part of the problem with the scarcity of fiber-tempered pottery is considered to be the result of taphonomic problems such as ground frost that affect its conservation and that may explain why pottery is rare above 35 degrees north latitude (Reid 1984a; Skibo et al. 1989).

One of the most interesting problems in relation to the late appearance of pottery in the Midwest at the end of the Archaic and start of the Early Woodland period is that it is not clear what other changes occurred in the lifeways besides the enrichment of a technological system. As with the other regions described for the southeastern United States, a definite pattern of a slow and progressive wave of adoption of pottery manufacture is observed, but no clear understanding of the purpose of pottery use in its early stages is indicated. One of the hypotheses suggested was that the function of pottery was related to the processing of nuts to extract oils, but this hypothesis has been refuted on the grounds that such processing took place without the involvement of pottery at all (Brown 1986). Another line of thought considered pottery to be a very sensitive tool for reflecting changes in cooking practices and noted that a close relationship existed with seed food processing (Braun 1983, 1987; Reid 1989). What is clear is that in all of the sites where early fiber-tempered pottery is present, only small amounts of pottery are found in comparison to those found for later periods and the pottery is always associated with mobile hunter-gatherers.

The next question that is necessary to ask is, what changed with the introduction or innovation of pottery? Does pottery have a radical impact on lifestyle as is always presented in the scenario of "before and after pottery"? Clearly, human populations knew how to cook without pots for thousands of years, but for some reason cooking with pots is in general considered a "revolution" in the same sense as once considered for the origins of agriculture, that is, as a rapid, all-encompassing change. Is such an abrupt change logical when viewed with the theories of technological invention, innovation, or adoption? The answer to this seems to be no. In general, from the examples given, such changes are gradual and even can take centuries or generations to occur (Brown 1989:220).

Another aspect to consider is the assumption that pottery was invented primarily for cooking daily meals. Is this true? Is it necessary to demonstrate this assumption? Yes, it is necessary to demonstrate such a relationship, and, in fact, in a gradual process of cultural evolutionary change what we should expect is totally the contrary. Pottery initially must play a secondary role in cooking or in other kinds of activities, such as acting as serving vessels with specialized functions (Brown 1989; Vitelli 1989; see chapters in Barnett and Hoopes 1995).

In addressing some of these questions, Sassaman (1993:111–188) identifies four major innovations in cooking technology for the U.S. Southeast: (1) the use of soapstone slabs or cooking stones between 5000 B.P. and 4400 B.P., (2) the use of ceramic vessels with indirect firing or stone cooking between 4500 and 4000 B.P. and continued use of soapstone slabs, (3) a change from subterranean fire-clay pits to ceramic containers, and (4) direct use of pottery over fire in cooking until the later part of the sequence, around 3500 B.P.

A model utilizing social interactions as the reason for the variation in the early pottery in time and space has been proposed for the U.S. Southeast (Sassaman 1993, 1998; also see Crown and Wills 1995). Basically, the model argues that pottery was innovated in a context of mobile hunter-gatherers, where two factors inhibited the development and spread of pottery. The first factor was demand for kinship labor. As Sassaman (1993:35) explains, "Pottery is related to social production, that is, to the strategies of cooperation, appropriation, and reciprocation that define hunter-gatherers social life." This has a direct effect in that as long as a group was able to avoid kinship demands on labor, pottery was not incorporated into the assemblage.

The second factor that constrained the innovation of pottery was the production and use of a soapstone cooking technology. The production and exchange of soapstone for cooking was important as a result of the restricted distribution of the raw material. Soapstone maintained a network of exchange. In this context, pottery was a threat to the traditional exchange networks by changing the social rules of exchange. As the model predicts, the inland groups that had direct access to soapstone did not accept the innovation of pottery. The first groups to adopt pottery were located on the coast at the end of the distribution line of soapstone. Fiber-tempered pottery was adopted for use as containers exposed to indirect heat. The major innovations in the technology also took place on the coast, such as direct cooking pot techniques. The model is appealing in regard to the evidence and variations in space and time. It explains well what happened in this area but does not explain the delay in the adoption in areas outside the soapstone network (see Ingold et al. 1991).

To summarize, the origin of fiber-tempered pottery in the Gulf Coastal Plain has been best approached by understanding its variability in space and time through the use of anthropological models that deal with the innovation of technology in a social and economic context (Arnold 2003). One cannot just rely on the traditional perspective of diffusionism (Meggers 1997; Meggers et al. 1965) or the functionalist approach of technological advantages. In this case even if pottery represented a technological advantage in cooking, it required social acceptance to become popular, and as this case reveals, this was a process that could take hundreds of years and was not an abrupt change or revolution.

Although in many of the other cases cited the earliest recovered pottery is fiber-tempered, the pottery of the littoral of Salgado (Pará) in Brazil is characterized mainly by the use of shell as temper.[2] The area of distribution is not well known but seems to encompass the northeast of Pará and the lower Amazon River up to Santarem in Brazil (Roosevelt 1995; Roosevelt et al. 1991; Simoes 1981). The pottery complex for this region is known as the Mina phase. The activities of fisher-people and collectors of the littoral (see Simoes 1981) formed 43 shell middens. The diet of the population concentrated mainly on mollusks, crustaceans, and fish. The radiocarbon dates for the sequence are between 5000 and 4600 B.P. The lithic material is characterized by trapezoidal plates for smashing and includes rudimentary axes, anvils, hammers, nutcrackers, flakes, and other bone and shell artifacts (Simoes 1981). One site, Taperinha, with early pottery is characterized as part of the Mina phase and dated to approximately 8000 B.P. (Roosevelt 1995; Roosevelt et al. 1991). The evidence from this site as well as others of the Mina phase seems to indicate a semisedentary association of fisher-people and collectors with early sand and shell–tempered pottery.

In the research conducted in Panama, the appearance of pottery seems to have a relationship with mobile hunter-gatherers (Norr 1984; Willey and McGimsey 1954). The research in Costa Rica links the presence of pottery with sedentism and food production (Fonseca Zamora 1998; Hoopes 1992, 1994; Snarkis 1992:142–143). In other areas such as Peru and Mesoamerica that had been considered the pristine areas where civilization developed in the Americas, pottery appears in both areas 500 to 2,000 years after it was manufactured in Florida, northwestern Colombia, Ecuador, and Brazil.

In Mexico, the early evidence of pottery production comes from the Purrón pottery in the Tehuacán Valley and the Pox and Espiridión complex in Oaxaca dated between 3900 and 3500 B.P. (Flannery and Marcus 1994; Marcus 1983). The apparent initial use of pottery occurred in quite small quantities among mobile hunter-gatherers who also cultivated some plants. Only after 3500 B.P. does pottery become more common in frequency, and it then appears in many regions. This change is associated with the establishment of sedentary villages that depended heavily on agriculture for their subsistence. This early pottery has been interpreted as being an imitation of gourds (tecomate-shaped) and even as being the result of press molding a clay vessel inside a gourd. Some evidence of this manufacturing process is argued for the Tierras Largas phase (Marcus 1983). The same gourd-imitation technique is proposed for the early Barra and Ocos pottery of Soconusco, Chiapas (Clark and Blake 1990). With this proposition we still do not know the function of the pottery or context in which it developed. In the case of Chiapas an explanation of the occurrence of pottery argues that pottery was adopted as part of the political process in the early development of sedentary chiefdom societies. In other words, pottery was adopted as a result of a social strategy in which it played a significant role in sharing of food and risk in public rituals (see also Aldenderfer 1998:305). This also explains the relatively large amount of stylistic decoration observed in the archaeological record (Clark and Blake 1990). In Chiapas, Clark and Gosser (1995:215) also describe a negative correlation between fire-cracked rock use for cooking and tecomates that suggests a gradual process of technological change in cooking techniques.

In Peru, pottery appears in the northern regions only after 4000 B.P. Evidence of early clay baking is known from figurines found in contexts dated around 4500 B.P. at Huaca de los Sacrificios and interpreted from unbaked clay at Huaca de los Idolos in Aspero (Feldman 1985). Early pottery has been found in different sites from the coast to the highlands and in general is simple in form (see Burger 1992:58–60). Aldenderfer (1998:74–75) mentions finding some fiber-tempered pottery in a rockshelter called Cueva San Agustín at an elevation of 4,430 m and dated later than 3460 ± 160 B.P. He also found in the context of an open-air site fiber-tempered pottery similar to that recovered from a rockshelter in the Río Chila drainage that dates to 3660 ± 60 B.P. What is interesting in the case of Peru is that pottery appears long after the development of complex societies. These societies are represented by a complex of monumental architecture at preceramic sites such as La Galgada, the Temple of the Crossed Hands at Kotosh, Huaca Prieta, El Paraíso, and the terraces at Salinas de Chao and Aspero (see Burger 1992; Grieder et al. 1988; Moseley 1992; Shady and Leyva 2003). The economic contexts of the early prepottery populations are still in debate in relation to the rise of such complexity in an "egalitarian" and sedentary society that depended on the overproduction of fish resources rather than agricultural production (see Burger 1992; Moseley 1992).

In synthesis, does the presence of pottery indicate sedentism? On the basis of the available information as presented above, the evidence indicates that in the majority of cases the presence of pottery is linked to mobile hunter-gatherers. In other words, pottery generally does not indicate sedentism. One of the exceptions to this is in Ecuador where early pottery is always associated with sedentary populations (Damp and Vargas 1995; Marcos 1988; Raymond 1998). In all cases, however, pottery does appear to be related to a decrease in mobility (logistic mobility) and the occurrence of special-purpose redundant sites that are utilized to obtain resources that are seasonally abundant. In these terms the relationship between pottery, sedentism, and the origins of food production involves the degree of seasonality of an environment and a change in the type of territoriality that groups utilize to survive in the environment. It is in the context of archaeological comparison that it is possible to argue for a variation of pottery association with mobility and sedentism. Only in a social and economic context can one begin to answer the question of why pottery production developed in mobile or sedentary hunter-gatherer societies or in food-producer societies.

CONCLUSION

Given these theories on the origins of pottery, sedentism, and food production, in terms of mobility and food acquisition, it is hypothesized that, first of all, an increase in sedentism resulting from the use of logistic mobility strategies will occur as a means to cope with changing environments that are becoming more unpredictable in nature. Such environments would include savannas with strong seasonality. Evidence for logistic mobility in the archaeological record is expected. Such evidence can be found in the variability of a site's assemblage (grain size) and in the spatial distribution of features at a site. Considering that the spatial distribution and variability of assemblages reflect the function of a site (base camp, special-purpose camp) and are related to the strategy of mobility, increases in assemblage redundancy are expected more often in special-purpose locations and are least likely in residential camps of logistically mobile groups. Feature use is also expected to be redundant and feature distribution random in special-purpose camps. On the other hand, if the settlement formation process is the result of a permanent year-round occupation lasting for several years, the existence of a spatial pattern of aggregated or clustered features is expected as is more variability in the site assemblage. Second, signs of economic and social intensification are expected in the form of large numbers of artifacts used to process foods (i.e., ground stone technology) (economic intensification) and other artifacts that might indicate group identity or have social significance (i.e., pottery, beads) (social intensification). Economic and social intensification is expected to be correlated with other evidence of the early stages of food production (i.e., botanical remains). Third, the recovery of botanical remains focused on one or a few species is expected. These species should be indicative of seasonally abundant plants that are attractive to human groups and that have reproductive structures, such as seeds, that must be processed to make usable and potentially storable food items.

The fourth hypothesis, as well as the final two hypotheses, suggests what we should expect in the context of the early adoption or initial production of pottery: pottery is culturally selected for when internal social or economic conditions of the household favor the production of pottery as a response to changing conditions from predictable to unpredictable environmental conditions. In a previous article (Oyuela-Caycedo 1995b; cf. Rice 1999) the argument has been made that the explanation for the origins of pottery lies in the fact that these changing conditions require an intensification of social interactions, such as the exchange of gifts (food, drink, and so on) to accommodate an increase in demand for kinship labor, and/or of economic forms of food processing/cooking technologies. In both cases pottery will be selected for favorably. Fifth, the initial use of pottery involves a specialized function that is expected to vary from group to group. In some groups, pottery may have been used to extract oil from nuts; in other groups, it may have had a totally different function such as that of receptacles for the serving of food and drinks. The specific use is not as important as the fact of the specialized function itself. Sixth and finally, although pottery is selected by a group to assist in the process of social or economic intensification, this does not mean that it is competing against or is used instead of other kinds of technologies. It is added to the cultural assemblage because it is used for intensification and is a new form not previously exploited. A later broadening of the uses of pottery could be the result of further internal changes that favor pottery over other technologies of cooking, storing, or other activities.

3   The Strata and Features

Stratigraphy in archaeology is the backbone to any excavation. Stratigraphy is the vertical association of soils, features, and artifacts in specific episodes of time. Soil deposition and activities in time are laid down in layers or strata. In archaeology, the differentiation of strata at a site allows for the differentiation of activities through time. Features in archaeology, on the other hand, are the horizontal associations of soils, artifacts/ecofacts, and other constructions that indicate by association a specific activity. Both the stratigraphy and spatial distribution of features at San Jacinto 1 are presented in this chapter. They are particularly important pieces of evidence that allow for the identification of the geomorphological location of the site and changes in the surrounding landscape through time and of the seasonality of the occupations at the site (see Oyuela-Caycedo 1998 for a previous publication on this topic).

THE STRATIGRAPHY AT THE SITE

Much of the depositional and postdepositional history of San Jacinto 1 seems to have been affected by the same kinds of processes that modify the landscape today. The floodplain where the site is located is very small and runs parallel to the entrenched stream of San Jacinto. The floodplain extends no more than 500 m from the stream channels. The catchment area of the San Jacinto stream is located close to the site in a radius of 2 km to the west (Figure 3.1). Most of the streams that contribute water and form the main stream are seasonal. The only permanent water is one of aquifer origin that supplies the main stream even during the driest months (January–February).

As previously discussed, the zone has two major seasons: rainy and dry. The first rainy period starts in late April–June and is followed by a short dry month around July–August (Veranillo de San Juan). After this, precipitation increases until the end of November, reaching a peak in October. Then the rains stop in early December, leaving January and February as the driest times, with some years having no precipitation at all in these months. This climatic regime drastically changes the green landscape of November into a dry environment of dead grasses from January to March. This bimodal climatic regime also has a strong impact on the availability of fruits and the growth cycle of annuals

The Strata and Features

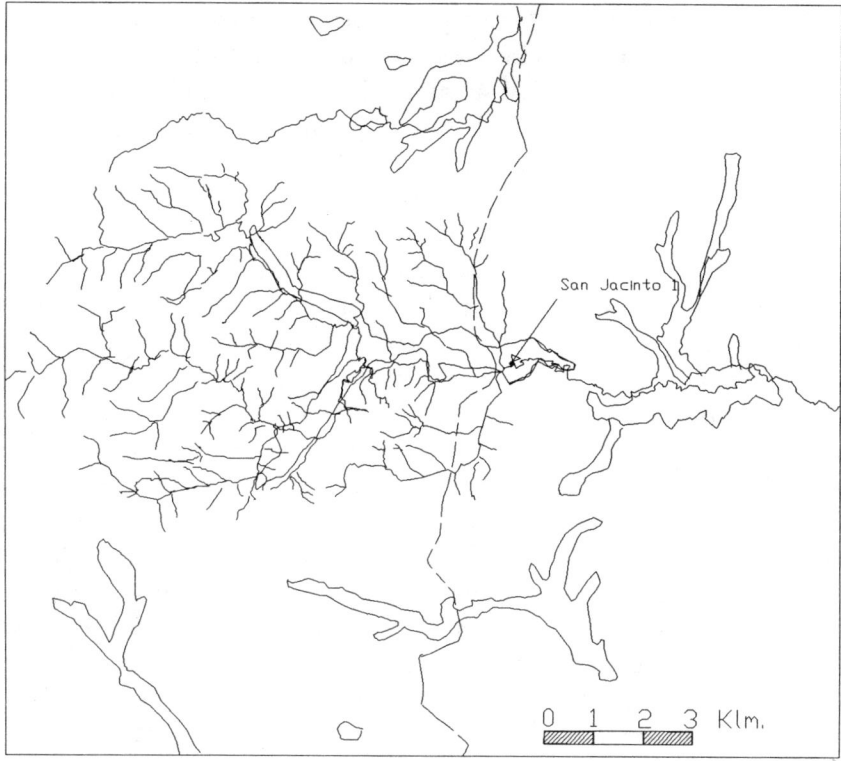

Figure 3.1. Stream catchment and alluvial floodplains.

and perennials (see Bonzani 1998; Walsh 1981) as well as on the cycles of animal availability (for example, mud turtles, iguanas, and fluvial and land snails).

As a consequence of this climatic regime, the alluvial floodplain of the San Jacinto stream is today affected by flooding episodes during the torrential storms. The flooding episodes last for short amounts of time, such as a few hours, and occur when the stream channel cannot cope with the waters of the upper part of the drainage system. During the year the chances of flooding are especially high during the months of April to November. However, most of the year is characterized by a water deficit in the region (see Figure 1.6) that favors the concentration of resources around streams during the dry season. It is this rainy-season flooding regime that has greatly affected the depositional history of the site of San Jacinto 1 and has led to the stratigraphy encountered during the excavations at the site.

Twenty-six layers or strata and facies were defined during excavation and systematic augering of the site and its surroundings (Appendixes 1 and 2).

These strata were numbered from top or surface to bottom. Evidence of anthropic activity is found in nine layers. The most recent corresponds to the present topsoil or humus, called stratum 1. The second period of human activity is registered in stratum 5. The most ancient period of anthropic soils occurred in strata 9, 10, 12, 14, 16, 18, and 20 (Figures 3.2 and 3.3).

The physical and chemical analyses of the soils (Figure 3.4) indicate that the human activity of the early occupation (strata 9, 10, 12, 14, 16, 18, and 20) developed beside and/or close to the channel of a stream.[1] With the help of a computer program that extrapolated data from the augering, it was possible to establish the spatial distribution of stratum 9, confirming an oval form for the settlement and reconstructing a U-shaped dumping area (Figure 3.5). Based on this general spatial interpretation, the size of the activity area in stratum 9 was calculated until the 30-cm contour interval. This space is estimated to be 346 m^2, of which 75 m^2 was excavated. Based on the form of the site, it was also possible to calculate the area lost by the current meander cutoff of the stream. The minimum activity area destroyed was 35 m^2; thus a majority of the site was intact at the time of excavation. By considering the stratigraphy, the paleotopography, and the spatial distribution of sediments and soils, it is concluded that the early human occupation of San Jacinto 1 was located on a point bar of a meandering stream system.

Given the stratigraphic sequence and process of formation, flooding episodes are indicated as the major factor of accretion at the site. The process of soil and sediment formation at San Jacinto 1 seems to be similar to that of other alluvial systems studied around the world (see Ferring 1986; Gladfelter 1985; Guccione et al. 1988; Hassan 1985; Mandel 1992). The excavation also yielded evidence of characteristic features in the development of a point bar. These include lateral accretional (epsilon) cross-bedding related to the migration of the point bar in a meander and the current of the water (see Brooks and Sassaman 1990; Collinson 1986; Reineck and Singh 1975). Based on these results, an interpretation of the pedogenic changes that occurred at San Jacinto 1 are presented in Table 3.1. As noted in Table 3.1 and Figure 3.4, the accretion sequence depended mainly on flooding during the rainy season and the mobility of the stream channel.

Therefore, from the stratigraphy and geoarchaeological perspective alone it can be said that (1) the inhabitants of San Jacinto 1 settled in a point bar environment, (2) flooding was a variable that affected the site during the rainy season, making it too risky to be occupied at those times, and (3) the migration of the channel was a variable that affected the development of living floors and produced cross-bedding stratigraphy. The end of the human reoccupation of the site was very likely the result of a displacement of the stream by a neck cutoff process or avulsion.

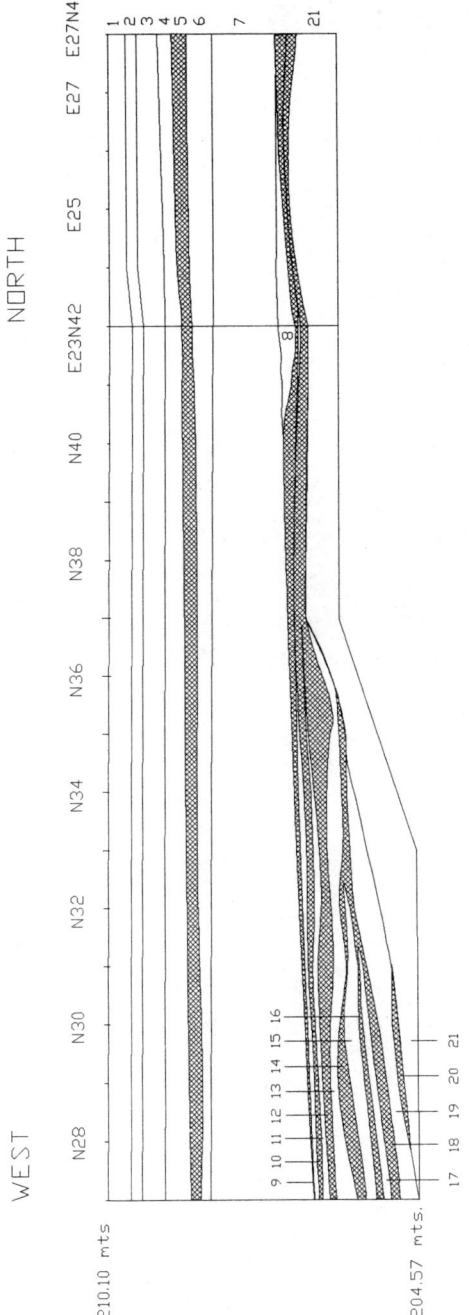

Figure 3.2. Stratigraphic illustration of western and northern walls.

Figure 3.3. Stratigraphy of the site as revealed in profile (corner of E23N27).

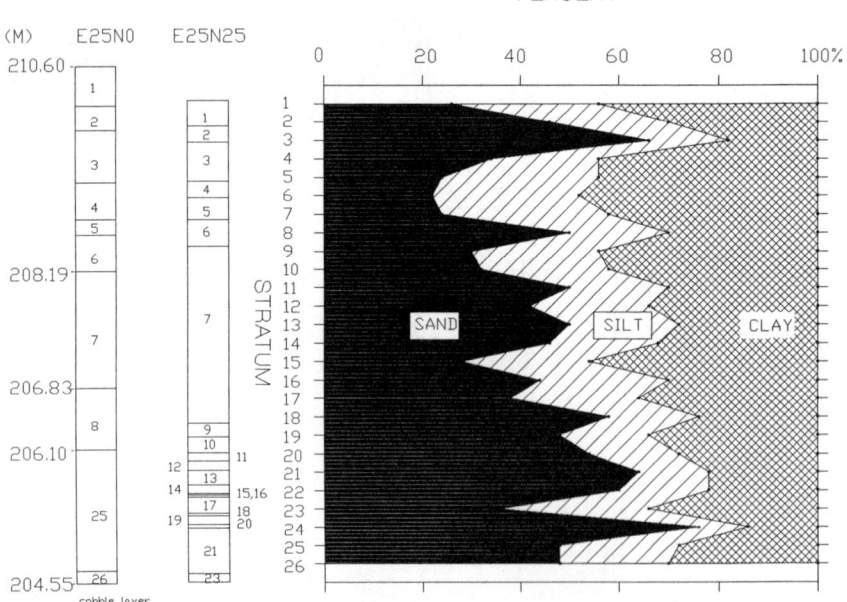

Figure 3.4. Physical characteristics of strata and example of relationship with two augered perforations.

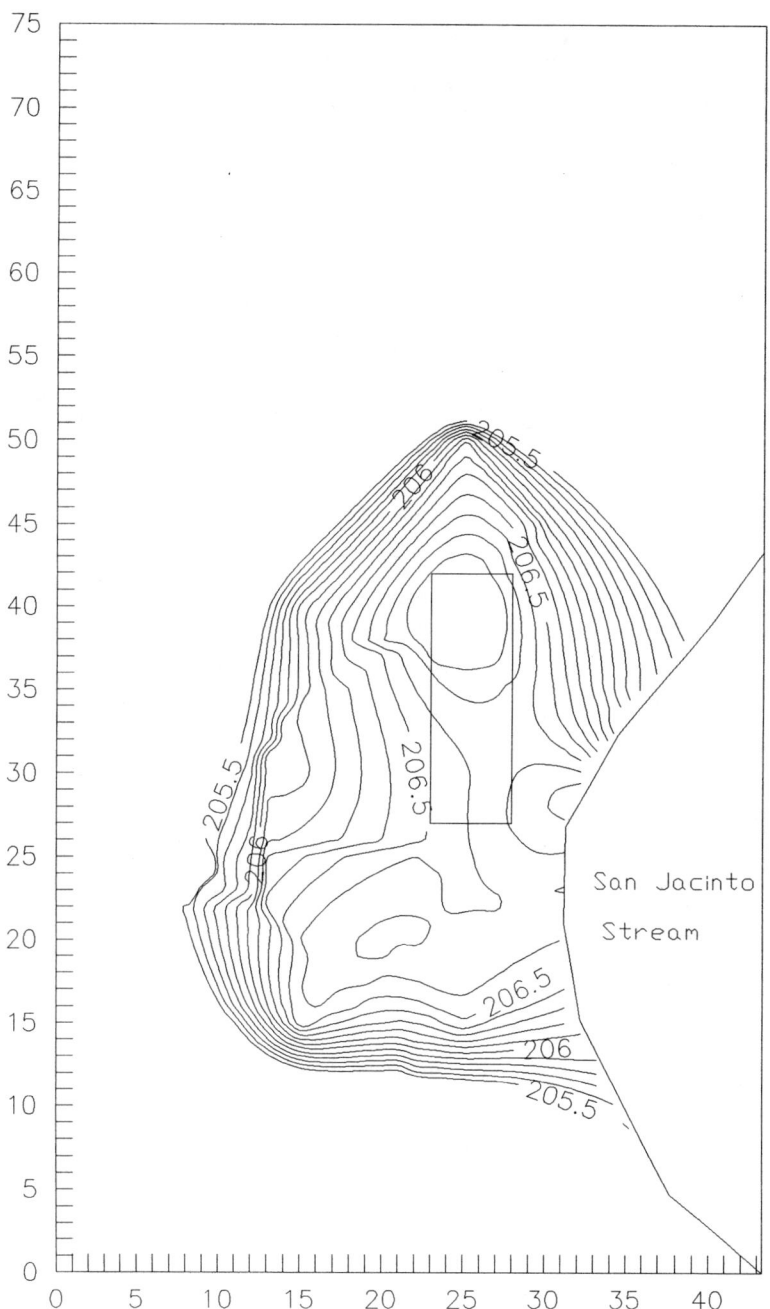

Figure 3.5. Computer illustration of the spatial distribution of the site based on the extrapolation of the stratigraphy obtained during coring; box indicates location of the area chosen for excavation.

Table 3.1. Soil formation sequence of San Jacinto 1

Formation Sequence Units	Stratum	Characteristics
IVd	1, 2	Flood basin, slow rate of sedimentation, development of organic soils
IVc	3	Single flooding event, high rate of sedimentation
IVb	4, 5, 6	Flood basin, low accretion and rate of sedimentation, development of organic soils
IVa	7	Flood basin, medium rate of sedimentation of fine materials (finely laminated)
III	8	Abandoned channel is filled with fine sediments of flood basin; medium rate of sedimentation
IIc	9 to 20	Upper point bar, epsilon, foreset beds of cross stratification; high sedimentation rate
IIb	21, 22, 23	Lower point bar accretion, high sedimentation rate
IIa	24	Lower point bar–scour pool, high sedimentation rate, single flooding event
Ib	25, 26	In-channel deposits, coarse\fine material
Ia	27	Channel floor

In synthesis, the major factor that regulated the occupation and formation process of the site was the rainy season. The high risk of flooding inhibited the occupation of areas like this during those times. Furthermore, during the dry season, because of the deficit of water in the region, these areas became optimal locations for the concentration of subsistence resources.

One can now ask how frequently and for how long the point bar was occupied during the dry season. To answer these questions a new approach and methodology was required that utilized the features recovered from San Jacinto 1.

THE FEATURE TYPES RECOVERED

The excavation uncovered a total of 174 features in the seven lowest anthropogenic strata, which represent a time span of approximately 800 years (6000 to 5200 B.P.) (Figure 3.6). Of these, 112 were defined as earth ovens or fire-pits while the 62 other features included post molds, mollusk concentrations, and other artifact associations. Earth ovens or fire-pits were the most abundant feature type encountered at San Jacinto 1. It seems very likely that the earth ovens were used in the same manner as today by hunter-gatherer populations

The Strata and Features

Figure 3.6. Excavation revealing features recovered at San Jacinto 1.

around the world or by populations that depend heavily on wild food collection or hunting. Today earth ovens are used in baking cakes or bread made from the seeds of wild grasses or from flour from nuts (Johnson 1978:355; LaPena 1978:339; Zigmond 1986:399–403). Fire-pits are also employed in the steaming or roasting of roots and meats (Bartram et al. 1991; Reid 1984a:58–60; Wandsnider 1997; Wedel 1986) and even in the roasting of hearts or heads of agave (*Agave* sp.), sotol (*Dasylirion texanum*), and prickly pear (*Opuntia* sp.) (Dering 1999; Fish et al. 1992). Most of the pits at the site seem to have been used one time and then refilled with the extracted soil.

Earth ovens are characterized by being pits from low to deep depth that contain medium amounts of fire-cracked rock (Figures 3.7 and 3.8). Presence of a carbonized layer of wood below a layer of fire-cracked rocks at the bottom of the pit occurs. Most of the time total thermal alteration of the feature including walls and base is present and marked by a red color. Sixty-eight pits are cooking ovens. Examples of this pit type are feature numbers 38, 53, 55, 57, 61, 63, 67, 85, 117, 118, 133, 143, 151, and 154.

The open fire-pits are characterized by being small- to medium-sized pits with relatively low amounts of fire-cracked rock in the refill (Figure 3.9). Those fire-cracked rocks present do not form a layer. Also present is a layer of carbonized wood at the bottom. These pits seem to correspond to hearths dug

Figure 3.7. Example of excavation of earth oven: Feature 57 (location E24N38, strata 10).

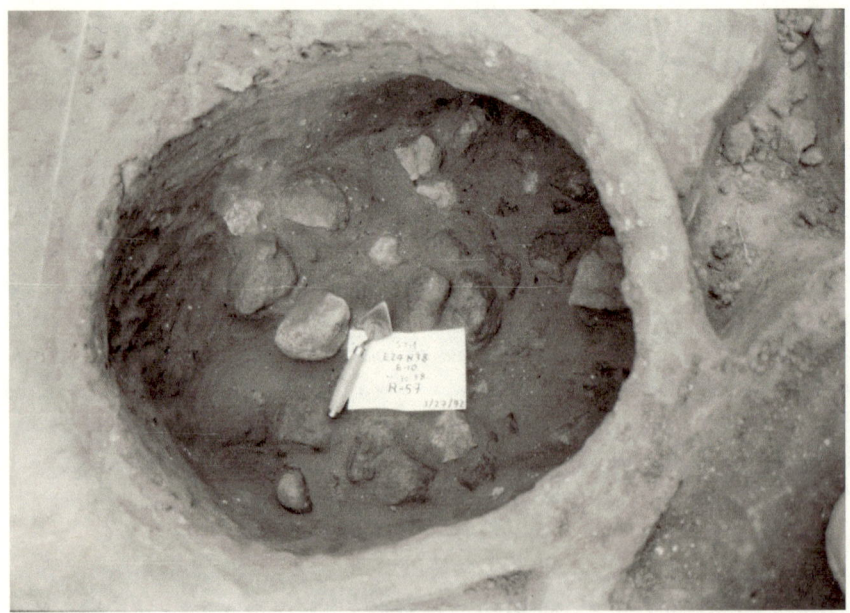

Figure 3.8. Detail of excavation of Feature 57 (location E24N38, strata 10). Note variation in the fire-cracked rocks employed.

The Strata and Features

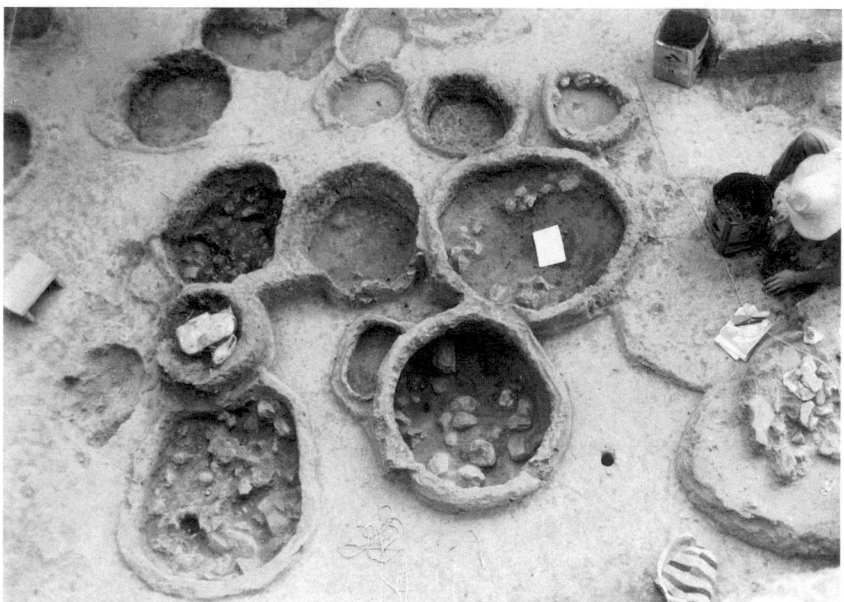

Figure 3.9. Example of variation in feature sizes and volume of fire-cracked rocks. Note that cultural layers have been removed, leaving only the pits exposed.

in the ground for direct and open cooking (Figure 3.9). In some cases the pits are completely refilled with charcoal that had been displaced out of the pit onto the surrounding floor. Forty-four pits are in this category. Examples of this pit type are feature numbers 15, 16, 22, 29, 31, 49, 52, 59, 71, 73, 79, 82, 86, 89, 99, and 101 (Figure 3.10).

The other feature types include post molds and mollusk concentrations. Post molds are less than 10 cm in diameter and indicative of temporary windbreak constructions that could be built in one day and generally lasted no longer than a few days to a few weeks. Mollusk concentrations (Figure 3.11) are often situated with broken pieces of pottery and are made up of from 10 to 20 mollusk shells in small clusters located throughout the strata. Concentrations of beads made of mollusk opercula (see discussion in ch. 5) were also recovered as feature associations.

The following analysis utilizes the earth oven and fire-pit features to determine seasonality of occupations at the site of San Jacinto 1.

FEATURE DENSITY AND DISTRIBUTION AS INDICATORS OF SEASON-SPECIALIZED OCCUPATION

It is argued that variation in the pattern of distribution of features is directly related to the frequency of occupation and indeed even to the strategy of

Figure 3.10. Example of feature sizes and thermally altered walls after the excavation of the anthropic soils.

mobility. Features as a unit of analysis have the advantage of not being distorted by redeposition, which affects artifacts and other remains. The rates of sedimentation and the geomorphological dynamics of the site location affect features. Even in environments of high sedimentation rates, geological events occur at a slower rate than does feature formation by human activity. Therefore, two different occupations of a site in the same season are not recognizable in the archaeological record. Accepting this, the alternative for study of this problem is to look for patterns that show the asynchronic effect of different events that are the product of occupations within and between seasons. The following analysis explores this approach.

The study of patterns of feature distribution as a function of hunter-gatherer seasonal behavior is important since it contributes, first, to defining the kind of mobility pattern that most likely produced the observed synchronic pattern of features. Second, it refines the relationship, if there is one, of mobility strategies and the environmental seasonality of the area. Third, it establishes the frequency of site reoccupation within a season. Finally, it defines the probable seasons of reoccupation.

Binford (1983, 1989) considers the patterns that we should expect in ar-

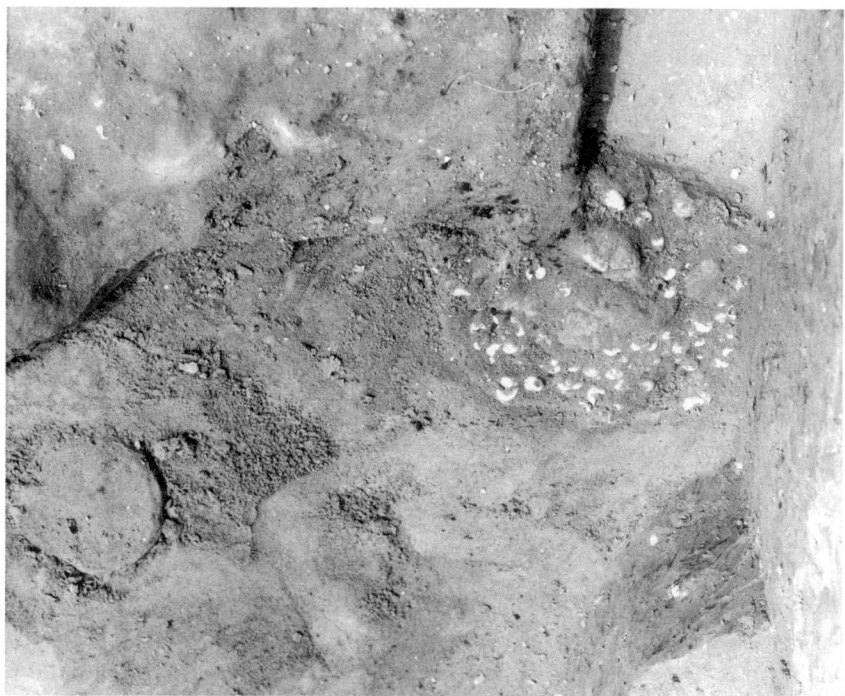

Figure 3.11. Mollusk concentration recovered from San Jacinto 1. Note pottery fragment located in situ with the mollusks.

chaeological assemblages of different kinds of camps. One of the variables he discusses is the degree of assemblage redundancy generated by logistically mobile populations (Binford 1983:357–378, 1989:223–263). In his analyses "assemblage" is used to indicate artifactual remains and may apply to ecofactual remains as well. "Redundancy" indicates the amount or quantity of reoccurrence of an artifact type. The pattern of assemblage redundancy is interpreted according to a "middle range theory" that is very limited in its development. The most useful components of it are based on studies of the logistically mobile Nunamiut, a population that depends to a high degree on hunting (Binford 1978). Before reviewing this pattern, one must consider whether the interpretation of assemblage redundancy creates a problem when the case study has plant resources as its major food supply. This appears not to be a problem. Other studies conducted in relation to foraging hunter-gatherers in Africa and Australia (see Gamble and Boismier 1991; Gould and Yellen 1987; O'Connell 1987) seem to corroborate and refine the interpretation of the reoccupation of sites from assemblage redundancy and feature density.

The variation in the spatial distribution of assemblages reflects the function of a site (e.g., base camp, special-purpose camp) and is related to mobility

Table 3.2. Relationship between mobility strategy, variation between sites, seasonal reoccupation, and assemblage redundancy

Mobility Strategy	Variation between Sites	Seasonal Reoccupation	Degree of Assemblage Redundancy
Residential	Low	None or low for camps	Low or none
Logistic	High	None or low for base camps	Low
		High for special-purpose sites	High
Sedentism	High	Permanent camp	Low or none
		Permanent special-purpose sites	High

strategy (Binford 1983, 1989). Increases in assemblage redundancy are expected more often in special-purpose locations and less often in residential camps of logistically mobile groups. Residential base camps are relatively long occupations in which the full array of daily activities takes place each day until the occupation is abandoned. Special-purpose camps are short-term occupations in which only specific tasks, such as resource acquisition, are performed. Residential base camps are generally occupied for longer periods of time and contain a greater array of activity types than do special-purpose sites. Further, in the ethnoarchaeological cases considered, it is rare for one base camp to be directly on top of another. Instead, different types of occupations tend to occur in the archaeological sequence of a site. Special-purpose sites, however, do tend to occur in the same locations because of the patterning of the required resource. With these considerations in mind, variation of the artifact assemblage is expected to be greater in base camp sites than at special-purpose locations (Binford 1983:328, 330–331). Assemblage redundancy is expected for special-purpose locations. This variation and/or redundancy in assemblages allows for the diagnosis of the strategies of seasonal mobility that most likely generated the archaeological record under study (Binford 1980; O'Connell 1987). The set of relationships proposed is synthesized in Table 3.2.

From this perspective, the development of a concept of feature redundancy seems to be the way to approach the diagnosis of the kinds of occupations at San Jacinto 1. It also permits the anticipation of the kinds of sites that are expected in a region with a variable system of logistic mobility (see Aldenderfer 1998:276–307; Ebert 1992:127–156). Furthermore, this concept allows for the differentiation between features generated by residential mobility and those generated by logistic mobility, at least at the two extremes of the mobility spectrum prior to sedentism.

As indicated, the term *feature* is used to refer to the material manifestation (artifacts, ecofacts, or soils) of a discrete activity. *Redundancy of features* refers to the reoccurrence of that feature type, as defined by its material components and its spatial distribution and context. The concept is important because, as noted in Table 3.2, the degree of assemblage redundancy at permanent camps or special-purpose sites of sedentary populations is expected not to differ from that at the corresponding sites produced by logistically mobile populations. When addressing how to differentiate the assemblage redundancy generated by sedentary populations of hunter-gatherers from that produced by logistically mobile populations, the answer logically appears to exist at the level of spatial patterning and density of features.

Before passing to the analysis of the case of San Jacinto 1, it is important to consider that there are factors that may affect the visibility of the spatial arrangement of features in the archaeological record. It is necessary to acknowledge that the pattern of variations in feature density can also be the result of unknown activities unrelated to the type of occupation. The problem is that ethnoarchaeological studies of the behaviors that can produce alternative effects on feature density and spatial arrangement are still very poorly developed.

In order to analyze the degree of redundancy, each cultural stratum must be studied in its own context. It is in this vertical context that it might be possible to see variation in the strategies of seasonal occupation and mobility. Utilizing Binford's (1983, 1989) argument of assemblage redundancy and the ethnoarchaeological work of O'Connell (1987), the following hypotheses are proposed. First, if the settlement formation process is the result of a permanent year-round occupation lasting for several years, one should expect nonredundant behavior in the base camps, nonredundant feature types, and a spatial pattern of aggregated or clustered features with low density. This pattern would be a consequence of the reuse of features and spatial differentiation of activities that can take place. In the case of special-purpose sites generated from a permanent camp, there should be high redundancy of the archaeological assemblage, but the density of features associated with the function of the site will be low as a consequence of feature maintenance and reuse. Clearer spatial differentiation of activity areas also should exist. Second, if the site is an accumulation of seasonal special-purpose camps, which in general are reoccupied several times during the same season (with resources moved to the base camp), one should expect high redundancy of the activities. As a consequence, redundancy of feature type and a random spatial dis-

Table 3.3. Feature redundancy and mobility

Feature Characteristics	Sedentary Sites	Logistic Base Camps	Special-Purpose Sites
Degree of redundancy	Low	Low	High
Spatial pattern	Clusters or agglomerations	Random	Random
Density	Low	Low	High

tribution of features are expected that are related to the opportunistic behavior of gathering resources when available. There would be little concern for reuse of features, and no clear definition of activity areas would occur. The density of such features should increase in direct relation to the number of times the site is reoccupied within a season as well as to the number of seasons of occupation. Third, in the case of seasonal base camps of a logistically mobile group, one should expect nonredundant behavior, nonredundant feature types, low feature density, and a near-random spatial distribution of features. Furthermore, there should be observable differentiation of activity areas. These expectations are restated in a simplistic and operational form in Table 3.3.

In this study, therefore, it is assumed that, first of all, the density of features has a relation with the length of occupation of a site. The longer the continual occupation of the site, the more likely the continual reuse of facilities or features will be and, as a consequence, the lower the density of features. In an inverse relationship, the shorter and more frequent the reoccupation of the site is during each season, the higher the density of features will be. Second, a base camp will have more variation in feature types as a consequence of more diverse activities. In a special-purpose site the diversity of features is less as a consequence of the occurrence of more specific activities.

To assess lithic assemblage redundancy, Binford (1978:495–497, reinterpreting the work of Vierra 1975) suggests the use of factor analysis. Binford argues that techniques such as factor analysis can help in understanding the degree of redundancy of a site. Using this technique, he suggests that if a site was a seasonal base camp, then significant changes in the activities of the site are expected and variability among the assemblages in each stratum would be explained by different factors. To the contrary, if the continual reuse of the site for the same seasonal special purpose occurred, then the variation of the assemblage by strata would be explained by a single factor.

For San Jacinto 1, a site that seems not to have a long sequence of occupation, factor analysis may be useful. The only problem with this technique is that it does not give us a definition of the degree of feature redundancy. It is for this reason that other techniques such as nearest-neighbor statistics seem more appropriate. Nearest-neighbor statistics can give a measure of the degree of departure from randomness of spatial feature distribution toward clustering or regularity in space. The method measures the spatial relationship between items, using the exact horizontal locations of features, and it has the power to detect patterns of clustering or regularity of any size or scale.

The basic equations of nearest-neighbor statistics have been described elsewhere (Clark and Evans 1954:447; Pielou 1959; for a review see Wilson and Melnick 1990). For the present research the methodology and equations described by Whallon (1974) have been followed, using corrections for the boundary effect proposed by Pinder et al. (1979). In basic outline, the nearest-neighbor statistics can be interpreted as follows. The statistical value of a random distribution is 1. A lower value, down to a minimum of 0, indicates agglomeration or clustering of items. A higher value, up to a maximum of 2.15, indicates more regular spacing. This value has to be interpreted with respect to the significance of the pattern and degree of departure from randomness (see Pinder et al. 1979:fig. 5). As mentioned above, each site type should generate a unique spatial distribution of features. Specifically, special-purpose camps of logistically mobile hunter-gatherers are expected to generate a random distribution of features as a consequence of the multiple reoccupations of the site and repetition of the behavior of the group (within the same season or during the same season year after year).

Features such as cooking pits, storage pits, and any other kind of pit in general are well represented in the archaeological record. In the present case, all the pits found at San Jacinto 1 seem to relate to food-processing activities. Since pits reflect the kind of subsistence activities performed at a site, this makes it easy to differentiate special-purpose sites from base camps. The function of the pits, however, is irrelevant to this part of the research; the aim is merely to establish their spatial arrangement. The data are the locations of all pits encountered in the excavation in their stratigraphic contexts. Only strata 10 and 12 are useful for this analysis because only a small sample of pits was found in the other strata (three in stratum 9 and four in stratum 14). The low number of pits in stratum 9 is interpreted as being the result of a different occupational pattern at the site, and the pits in stratum 14 are the products of other factors; these are considered in more detail at the end of this chapter. The thickness of each of the cultural strata ranges between 6 and 27 cm. The thickness of the cultural strata appears to be the result of repeated visits to the

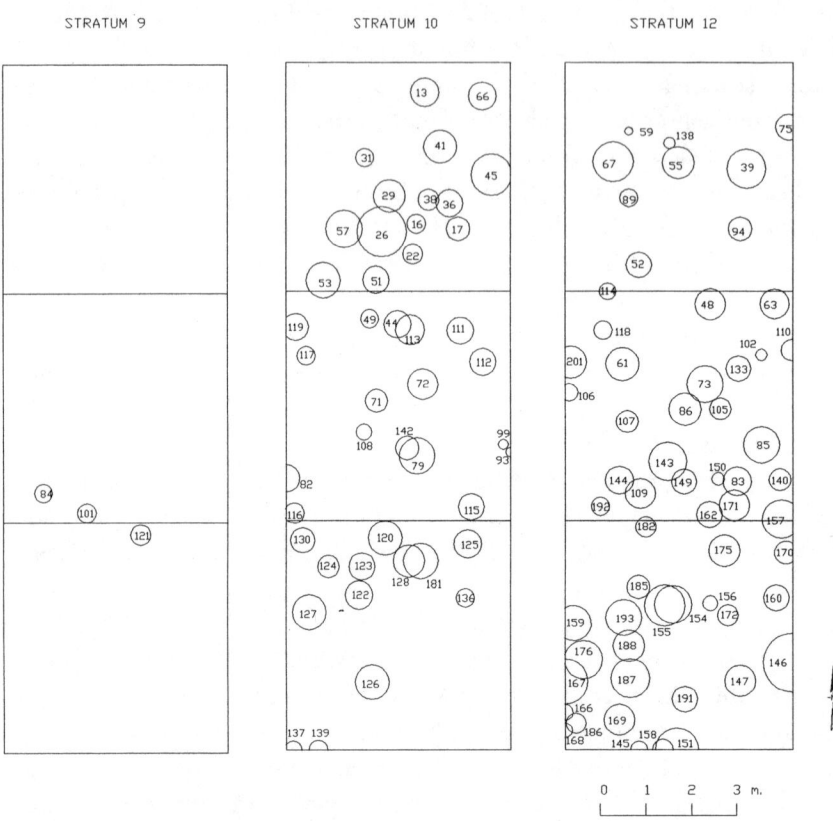

Figure 3.12. Distribution of fire-pits in strata 9, 10, and 12.

same location year after year prior to major flooding episodes that completely covered the site. The results of the nearest-neighbor analysis on the features from strata 10 and 12 are presented above (Figure 3.12).

Forty-five pits were excavated in stratum 10. The density of pits is 0.6 per square meter. The average observed distance from each pit to its nearest neighbor is 0.734 m, with a standard deviation of 0.335. The expected distance from each pit to its neighbor in a random distribution is 0.691, with a standard error of 0.059 m. The ratio of the observed pit distance to the expected average nearest-neighbor distance is 1.063. This ratio indicates that the mean nearest-neighbor distance is only slightly different from that expected in a random distribution. The significance of this slight departure from the expected distance is also very low (df = 44, t = 0.729, $p < 0.5$).

Sixty pits were excavated in stratum 12. The density of pits is 0.8 per square meter. The average observed distance from each pit to its nearest neighbor is 0.711 m, with a standard deviation of 0.289; the expected distance from each pit to its neighbor in a random distribution is 0.592, with a standard error of 0.044 m. The ratio of the observed pit distance to the expected average nearest-neighbor distance is 1.201. This ratio means that the observed nearest-neighbor distance differs from that expected in a random distribution in the direction of more regular spacing. The significance of this departure from the expected distance is high (df = 59, t = 2.705, $p < 0.01$).

The results of the nearest-neighbor analysis suggest that the high density and near random distribution of features is indicative of redundant behavior. This behavior was very likely the result of seasonal reoccupations of the site in which new features were produced with each reoccupation and without regard to previously emplaced ones. In other words, the results follow the expectations of a pattern that is the product of a logistically mobile group that used the site as a seasonal special-purpose camp. Further, it is probable that the site was occupied for a few days at a time, possibly on several occasions during a season.

The tendency toward regular spacing or symmetry in the distribution of features in stratum 12 may be explained as a consequence of the lateral and frontward accretion of the point bar. As the point bar grew to the north, activities and feature emplacement moved northward as well. By the time of the occupations in strata 10 and 9, point bar accretion northward would have been slower as the meander was cut off. It is also important to note that in each occupation there was a strong emphasis against the reuse of pits. This can be understood in terms of the function of the pits (as roasting and/or fire-pits) and explains why the pits were refilled after each occupation.

It is further interesting to note that the mean distance between features is extremely low in comparison to that observed from ethnographic work on base camps in Africa and Australia. For the !Kung and aboriginal desert Australians (groups with residential mobility), for example, the distance between hearths ranges from 4.65 m to 11.52 m and the distance between roasting pits is even higher (O'Connell 1987). The nearest-neighbor analysis conducted for such groups indicates that there is no relationship between distance between hearths and length of occupation or the size of household (Gould and Yellen 1987). As has been described elsewhere, features such as hearths are associated with activities that require less space than pits because individuals sitting around the fire do most of the activities conducted around them. To the contrary, pits require extensive activity areas, as they generally involve activities that are performed standing up. Binford (1988:169) estimates that an area of around 17–24 m^2 of space is required for a pit. This ethnoarchaeological information gives us a clear idea of how a pattern of pits, such as is observed at San Jacinto 1, is very likely associated with a logistically mobile group that performed the same activities at the same site, season after season. No indicators of permanent huts or structures were found in the excavated area of San Jacinto 1, again pointing to the special-purpose nature of the site.

This interpretation seems to be valid for strata 10 and 12, but what happened with strata 9 and 14, where pits were found in lower densities? In the case of stratum 14, the low density of pits is understandable because the stratum is a facie that only becomes differentiated in the secondary refuse area of the stream channel. In the case of stratum 9, the distribution of features as well as the spatial distribution of artifacts suggest a totally different pattern from that described for the other strata. The occupation of the site in this stratum seems to have more of the characteristics of a continual seasonal base camp occupied during the dry season, where activity areas were clearly differentiated. Stratum 9 is the only layer that permits the reconstruction of activity areas and living areas during the season of site occupation. The total living area of stratum 9 probably conforms to the 346 m^2 identified during the augering of the site (see Figure 3.5), with only a small portion of this undergoing excavation (75 m^2). The clustering of features, as well as of activities (see distribution of fire-cracked rocks and pottery in Chapter 4) (Oyuela-Caycedo 1993, 1995b), suggests that the site was occupied as a base camp for a longer period of time, very likely the whole dry season. It is interesting to note that no burials were found in any part of the early stratigraphic sequence. Human remains of an adult were found dispersed on the "living floor" of stratum 9, however.

CONCLUSION

The data collected from the site of San Jacinto 1 illustrate the importance of the use of stratigraphy and feature definition in archaeology. The use of concepts such as assemblage and feature redundancy are also very helpful for the recognition of patterns of camp variability as well as for confirming feature distribution patterns in terms of seasonality of occupation. Nearest-neighbor statistics seem also to be a powerful measure of spatial structure, facilitating the interpretation of the seasonal behavior that explains the distribution of features at San Jacinto 1.

From the analyses of the stratigraphy and features it was determined that the site of San Jacinto 1 was located on a point bar on a stream. The site underwent strong seasonal flooding episodes that made its occupation in the rainy season highly risky. Feature density and distribution indicate that the site was occupied for short periods of time in the dry seasons with new earth oven and fire-pit features being constructed upon each visit.

The results from San Jacinto 1 support the expectancy of Binford's model that the region should have populations that exhibit logistic behavioral strategies marked by strong variation in the archaeological assemblages between different kinds of sites. According to the model, the factor that most likely is constraining the mobility of the group into a defined territory is the environment with its timing of resource availability. This explanation is acceptable, just by considering the redundant seasonal occupation of San Jacinto 1.

4   The Pottery and Lithics

This chapter presents an analysis of the pottery and lithic types recovered from San Jacinto 1. These types of artifacts are usually the cornerstones for any interpretation of an archaeological site. This chapter focuses both on the source of material of the lithics and on the time invested for construction of both the lithic tools and the pottery to better define the mobility range and strategy and type of subsistence activities of the inhabitants of San Jacinto 1. The technologies from the inland site of San Jacinto 1 are then compared with the technologies associated with the river delta site of Monsú and the shell midden of Puerto Hormiga[1]. An analysis of the relationship between pottery and fire-cracked rock in terms of technology is also presented to demonstrate that the most likely function of this early fiber-tempered pottery at San Jacinto 1 was for serving or social purposes as opposed to cooking.

THE POTTERY TYPES RECOVERED

Artifacts recovered included 78,697 grams of pottery found in all cultural strata (Table 4.1). The recovered pottery fragments have a very restricted spatial distribution and appear to have been broken at the site and swept off to the side. The pottery was not found in a context of abandonment on the surface or guarded in caches for later use. This suggests that pottery vessels may have been carried in the move to another base camp. The pottery was also never found in association with the context of the fire-pits, clusters of fire-cracked rocks, or any artifact related with cooking. However, some fragments were found associated with the *Pomacea* snails.

Most of the vessel forms are semiglobular pots and globular vessels (Pratt 1999a, 1999b) similar to the one excavated at the site of Puerto Chacho (Figure 4.1). The ceramic forms include bowls with incurving rims, jars with spouts, and neckless globular jars with deeply incised and excised handles and luglike handles with excised and modeled zoomorphic motifs (Figures 4.2, 4.3, 4.4, and 4.5). Vessels were made by direct modeling and are frequently decorated (Figures 4.6 and 4.7) (Raymond et al. 1994, 1998; for a typology, see Oyuela-Caycedo 1987). The paste is a uniform black color with carbonized fibers that were not totally burned. The plant fibers are grasses (Poaceae)

The Pottery and Lithics

Table 4.1. Pottery fragments recovered by type and stratum

Stratum	Weight in grams						
	WW	WR	WDW	WDR	WL	WS	Total
9	12,215	803	107	90	262	20	13,497
10	30,857	3,143	264	260	313	135	34,972
11	733	45	0	0	0	0	778
12	10,021	579	155	57	35	20	10,867
13	315	9	0	0	0	0	324
14	5,455	184	0	125	135	14	5,913
16	9,349	354	83	60	50	70	9,966
18	1,955	130	40	165	0	20	2,310
20	50	0	0	20	0	0	70
Total	70,950	5,247	649	777	795	279	78,697

WW = Weight of plain fragments; WR = weight of rim fragments; WDW = weight of decorated wall fragments; WDR = weight of decorated rim fragments; WL = weight of lugs; WS = weight of spouts.

chopped into small pieces (Figure 4.8). Most of the time the plant fiber impressions can be observed with the unaided eye on the clay. There is no orientation in the dispersion of the fibers in the clay because of the direct modeling.

The pots were fired at a low temperature in reduced atmospheric conditions, and the surface color is the product of exposing the pots during cooling to the outside air. Two types of surface treatment are evident. The brown type is characterized by the following colors: reddish yellow (7.5YR 6/6), pale brown (10YR 6/3), and very pale brown (10YR 7–8/4). The color is in most cases homogeneous inside and outside of the pot. The red type has colors ranging from light red (2.5YR 6/6–8, 10R 6–8) to reddish yellow (7.5YR 6/6) as a result of the slip. The fragments recovered break easily with the pressure of the fingers. The texture is homogeneous with some asymmetry in the finishing.

THE LITHIC TYPES RECOVERED

Lithic artifacts recovered from San Jacinto 1 include 145 complete and fragmented metates (Figures 4.9, 4.10), 101 manos, 93 mortars, and 20 hammerstones (Castro 1993; Oyuela-Caycedo 1993). Stratigraphic location, source materials, use-wear patterns, and forms are presented in Tables 4.2 through

Figure 4.1. Vessel from Puerto Chacho, dating around 5000 B.P. (21.5 × 38 × 30.5 cm). Located at the Museo Nacional de Colombia, Bogotá (photo by Vic Krantz).

4.9, and a detailed description of these lithic types is given below. The recovery of 145 metates and 101 manos is exceptional for an Archaic/Formative period site, as these ground stone tools are usually associated with the processing of maize to make corn meal for mush or bread (Katz et al. 1974; Lowell 1999:450; Stahl 1989). However, metates and manos are also known to occur at sites where wild grass seeds have been processed (Flannery 1986; Henry 1992:195–196; also see Hillman 1996; Hillman et al. 1989).

Based on the cross-section form of the metates, three forms were differentiated, slab, block, and basin shaped. The stratigraphic distribution of the 101 handstones is similar to that observed for the slab metates. After the slab metates, the most abundant artifact is the mortars. Most of the mortars are very small, corresponding to what are called nutcrackers. The distribution through the strata is very similar to that observed for the metates. Rocks that were picked up for the special purpose of working as hammerstones were not common. Half of the 20 hammerstones recovered were discarded and reused as heating stones (fire-cracked rocks) in the fire-pits. The distribution of hammerstones throughout the stratigraphy was somewhat different from that observed for the metates and other ground stone technology. Hammerstones

Figure 4.2. Zoomorphic lugs from San Jacinto 1 found in the same context and location (E23N31, stratum 16, Level 11–20). In permanent collection at the Museo Nacional de Colombia, Bogotá (photos by Vic Krantz).

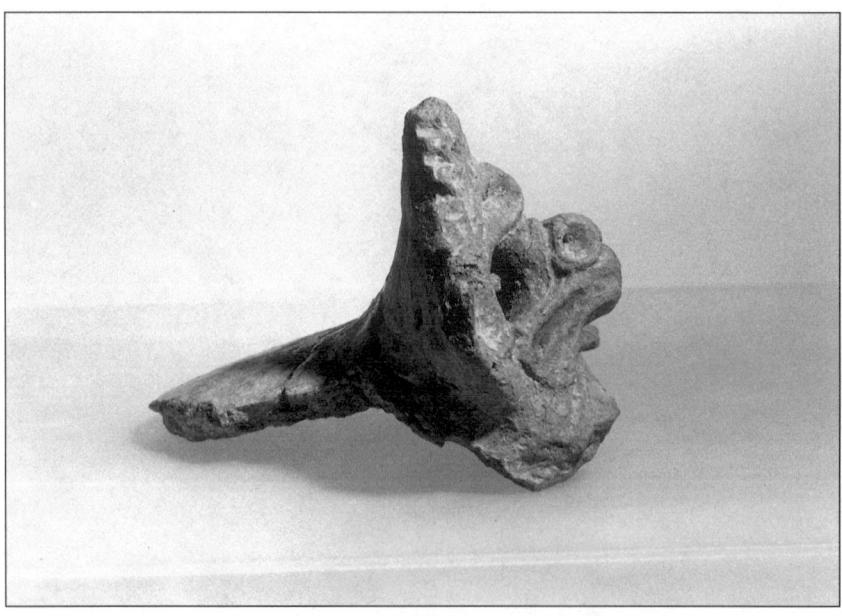

Figure 4.3. Lug from San Jacinto 1 with representation of bird (location E25N40, stratum 9, Level 11–20). Top, view from the top of vessel; bottom, lateral view. In permanent collection at the Museo de Oro, Banco de la Republica (photos by Vic Krantz).

Figure 4.4. Lug from San Jacinto 1 with representation of a bird (location E23N27, stratum 10, Level 0–10). Top, view from the top of vessel; bottom, lateral view. In permanent collection at the Museo de Oro, Banco de la Republica (photos by Vic Krantz).

Figure 4.5. Lug from San Jacinto 1 with unidentified representation (location E24N34, stratum 9, Level 0–10). Top, view from the bottom of the vessel; bottom, lateral view. In permanent collection at the Museo de Oro, Banco de la Republica (photos by Vic Krantz).

Figure 4.6. Typical decoration of top part of vessels (location E23N29, stratum 16, Level 0, Feature 199). In permanent collection at the Museo de Oro, Banco de la Republica (photo by Vic Krantz).

Figure 4.7. Edge decoration of vessel (location E23N30, stratum 16, Level 0, Feature 199). In permanent collection at the Museo de Oro, Banco de la Republica (photo by Vic Krantz).

Figure 4.8. Impressions of grasses (Poaceae) in the fiber-tempered paste. Surface has been removed; detailed view.

Figure 4.9. Block metate found cached in situ in Feature 63 (location E27N36, stratum 12).

Figure 4.10. Basin-shaped metate from Feature 76 (location E25N33, stratum 12, Level 0–10). Part of the permanent exhibition at the Museo Nacional de Colombia, Bogotá (photo by Vic Krantz).

Table 4.2. Cross-section form of slab, block, and basin-shaped metates

Cross-Section Form of the Faces	Slab	Block	Basin Shaped	Total
Flat and concave	6	2	0	8
Flat and convex	1	1	0	2
Flat and flat	96	0	0	96
Convex and convex	1	0	0	1
Concave and concave	1	3	30	34
Concave and flat	0	2	2	4
Total	105	8	32	145

Table 4.3. Total number of complete metates recovered by stratum

Stratum	Slab	Block	Basin Shaped	Total
10	5	0	0	5
12	1	1	1	3
18	1	0	0	1
Total	7	1	1	9

Table 4.4. Total number of fragments of metates recovered by stratum

Stratum	Slab	Block	Basin Shaped	Total
9	7	1	3	11
10	47	2	19	68
12	34	4	9	47
14	3	0	0	3
16	6	0	0	6
18	1	0	0	1
Total	98	7	31	136

Table 4.5. Direction of use-wear (DW) and type of metates

DW	Slab	Block	Basin-Shaped	Total
Lineal	11	2	0	13
Circular rotation	89	2	19	110
Pecked	0	1	1	2
Lineal and rotation	0	1	6	7
Rotation and pecked	1	1	4	6
Lineal and pecked	0	1	1	2
Unclear	3	2	1	6
Total	104	10	32	146

Table 4.6. Raw material types selected for metates

Rock Type	Slab	Block	Basin-Shaped	Total
Sandstone	90	2	7	99
Granite	0	1	1	2
Travertine	4	0	0	4
Limestone	11	3	4	18
Basalt andesite	0	2	17	19
Unclear	0	0	3	3
Total	105	8	32	145

were relatively more abundant in stratum 9 in relation to the distribution of the other artifact types.

In addition, the excavation at San Jacinto 1 yielded 2.18 tons of fire-cracked rocks (Tables 4.10 through 4.12). Fire-cracked rocks are the most abundant remains recovered at the site and represent the most common technology used in cooking. Fire-cracked rocks are typically described in Archaic sites of collectors (see Binford et al. 1970; House and Smith 1975; Latas 1992; Lovick

Table 4.7. Stratigraphic distribution of handstones (manos), mortars, and hammerstones

Stratum	Handstones (Manos)	Mortars	Hammerstones	Total
9	13	7	6	26
10	49	46	8	103
12	22	29	4	55
14	5	3	2	10
16	7	4	0	11
18	4	1	0	5
20	0	1	0	1
Unclear or missing	1	2	0	3
Total	101	93	20	214

Table 4.8. Raw material types selected for handstones (manos)

Rock Type	Total
Sandstone	14
Crystalline limestone	8
Limestone	10
Travertine	5
Basalt andesite	53
Rhyolite	2
Undefined	9
Total	101

Table 4.9. Use-wear patterns on mortars

Use-Wear Pattern	Total
Rotation and pecking	44
Pecked marks	15
Hard battering marks	30
Missing data	4
Total	93

1983; Wedel 1986). Fire-cracked rocks are found at San Jacinto 1 in three contexts: as random patterns on living floors, forming clusters of piles of rocks, and in the stone fill of fire-pits (Tables 4.11 and 4.12). Fire-cracked rocks were used in rock-boiling cooking as well as in fire-pit or steam cooking (see Binford et al. 1970; Frison 1983, 1991; Reid 1989). The astonishing number of fire-cracked rocks recovered from San Jacinto 1 indicates that they would have been used only a few times and discarded and that they came from rock types near the site.

Table 4.10. Raw material type of fire-cracked rocks by number and total weight in stratum 9

Raw Material Type	No.	Weight (g)
Sedimentary rocks		
Sandstone of fine-grain	1,467	58,023
Limestone	866	38,069
Crystal limestone	577	24,331
Travertine	344	27,645
Fossil "lumaquela"	1	20
Igneous rocks		
Rhyolite	79	6,118
Granite	6	840
Basalt andesite	269	25,282
Unclassified rocks	28	20
Total	3,637	1,800,348

Table 4.11. Stratigraphic distribution of fire-cracked rocks by sedimentary raw material type and weight

Stratum	R1	R2	R3	R5	R7	Total (g)
9	58,023	38,069	20	24,331	27,645	148,088
10	541,385	195,927	8,410	87,839	43,071	876,632
11	4,125	1,325	0	150	40	5,640
12	461,000	139,105	8,780	51,800	24,200	684,885
13	1,325	630	0	295	40	2,290
14	25,110	13,597	300	9,000	8,475	56,482
16	47,470	21,230	0	11,270	8,050	88,020
18	18,205	6,485	0	1,550	5,735	31,975
20	230	400	0	100	20	750
Total	1,156,873	416,768	17,510	186,335	117,276	1,894,762

R1 = Fine-grained sandstone; R2 = limestone; R3 = fossil "lumaquela"; R5 = crystalline limestone; R7 = travertine.

SOURCES OF ROCKS FOR LITHIC ARTIFACTS AS AN INDICATOR OF RANGE OF MOBILITY

One aspect that seems to be very enlightening in relation to the degree of mobility of a group is the source of the lithic material employed in the manufacture of tools. The point that is important to stress here is that all of the raw materials for the lithic tools recovered at San Jacinto 1 are found in a radius of 10 km from the site. This is expected in a hunter-gatherer society with a

The Pottery and Lithics

Table 4.12. Stratigraphic distribution of fire-cracked rocks by igneous raw material type and weight

Stratum	R4	R4B	R8	RU	Total (g)
9	6,118	840	25,282	20	32,260
10	34,210	7,020	83,225	0	124,455
11	80	520	550	0	1,150
12	30,995	4,301	60,055	40	95,391
13	0	0	1,550	0	1,550
14	2,160	360	4,560	0	7,080
16	1,140	710	14,505	0	16,355
18	1,090	3,000	3,710	0	7,800
20	0	0	0	0	0
Total	75,793	16,751	193,437	60	286,041

R4 = Rhyolite; R4B = granite; R8 = basalt andesite; RU = unidentified.

restricted range of mobility and where the abundant availability of sources in the catchment area of a logistic group favors an opportunistic behavior in the manufacture of tools. The expedient technology that characterizes this society is demonstrated by the exploitation of raw material available in the area. For example, in relation to fire-cracked rock, the most exploited material is that which is most accessible to the site. One should expect that the fire-cracked rocks were collected in the stream, considering that in the floodplain no rocks occur. As a consequence, it is argued that the 2.18 tons of fire-cracked rocks at the site were picked up from the streambed and reflect the materials to which the hunter-gatherers had access for making tools. Using the material from stratum 9 as an example, it is obvious that the selection of fire-cracked rocks included all the raw material classes used in the lithic tools (Tables 4.6, 4.8, 4.10, 4.11, and 4.12; see Oyuela-Caycedo 1993:appendix 3 for the distribution of rock classes in all the strata).

All of the ground stone was made using the same universe of materials as well (Tables 4.6 and 4.8), with preference for igneous rocks in specific artifacts such as hammerstones. The only raw material source that is not found in the streambed beside the site or that was not used as a fire-cracked rock is a silica that was employed in flake cutting tools. The most common material used for such tools comes from chemically sedimentary rocks such as lidita (flint) and limolite silica, both of which are silica (SiO_2), which produces very sharp edges. The raw material for these artifacts, even if they were manufactured in an opportunistic way, was extracted in the mountains upstream from the site, where outcrops are found. All of the decortification processes for the production of cores were done most likely in the same place as the outcrop. This conclusion is based on the absence of primary flakes recovered at the site (this statement is based on field observation). Quarries for the extraction of the lidita and limolite silica are expected to be found, considering that the samples collected in the stream are too meteorized and saturated with veins to be useful. Because site inhabitants sought out high-quality raw materials such as the ones used for the manufacture of cutting edges, extraction of the material most likely occurred at quarries. This implies that we should expect to find a very different kind of site associated with such an activity. Likewise, high concentrations of primary and secondary flakes associated with any quarry sites are expected.

In synthesis, among all the materials recovered, there is not a single artifact that indicates exploitation outside of a radius of 10 km. Taking into account the catchment area and the raw materials, their use is very likely to be understood as a result of the logistic and opportunistic behavior of this population among which expedient technology was the strategy for tool manufacture. An explanation of the concepts of expedient and curated technology follows, with discussion of their usefulness in defining mobility and subsistence strategies.

THE RELATIONSHIP OF EXPEDIENT AND CURATED TECHNOLOGIES TO SUBSISTENCE

In past studies, subsistence strategies have been technically approached in three forms. The first approach is botanical, wherein the unit of analysis is the macrobotanical or microbotanical remains (Bonzani 1995; Miller Rossen 1993; Morcote 1996; Newsom and Molengraaff 1999; Pearsall 1988, 2000; Piperno and Pearsall 1998; Rodríguez 2001). The next approach is chemical, wherein analyses of residues in bones or on artifacts yield information on diet (Katzenberg et al. 2001; Norr 1984; Tykot 2002; Tykot and Staller 2002; Tykot et al. 1996; van der Merwe et al. 1993). The third and oldest approach used by most archaeologists involves the analysis of the technology for subsistence by studying tool design (form→function), use-wear by experimentation and replication, or the spatial pattern and context of tool association. All of these approaches are valuable, but in view of the need for corroborating evidence, as is demanded by research today, the ideal would be to employ all of these approaches to confirm the arguments or hypotheses proposed. This chapter deals with the third of these approaches.

Technological strategies to make tools like lithics and pottery are subject to the direct influence of social and economic variables. These variables are considered to be adaptive responses to the changing environmental conditions (Nelson 1991; Torrence 1989). In this context, certain technological strategies, such as the time invested in the manufacture of tools, depend on the degree

Table 4.13. Basic general rules of technology

Technology	Energy Expended in Production	Maintenance	Replacement	Discard Rate
Curated	High	High	Low	Low
Expedient	Low	Low or none	High	High

of mobility and the available resources to be processed. It has been proposed that technology should be viewed as a strategy in which two forms of organization are recognized: curated and expedient. Curated technologies require a high investment in time and energy for manufacture and have a low replacement and discard rate. Curated technologies are often associated with highly mobile groups who can freely move to a raw material source, collect and manufacture a tool, and then carry the tool with them to new locations. Expedient technologies, on the other hand, require low amounts of time and energy to be expended in tool manufacture and have a high replacement and discard rate. Expedient technologies are more often associated with groups with reduced mobility who cannot move to distant raw material sources but instead utilize whatever material is at hand and discard the tool after its use and upon moving to new locations. At the new location the available raw materials are then utilized as new expedient tools. These general rules are listed in Table 4.13 and have been described in detail elsewhere (Binford 1979, 1989; Ebert 1992:34–38; Keeley 1982; Koldehoff 1987; Parry and Kelly 1987; Odell 1998; Shott 1986; Nelson 1991).

These two forms of organization of technology are a continuum. When they are examined in relation to mobility, it is observed that they are a key component in any understanding of subsistence. For instance, a correlation among expedient flake technology, increased sedentism, and scheduling for subsistence resources has been found (Binford 1980; Kelly 1995; Shott 1986). This increased sedentism is further linked to logistic strategies by hunter-gatherers in North America as well as in Mesoamerica among whom plant collecting supplies the major food sources of the subsistence base (Adair 2003; Gardner 1997; Koldehoff 1987; Kuhn 1989; Parry and Kelly 1987; Nelson 1991; Newsom and Pearsall 2003; Scarry 2003; Simon 2000; Smith and Cowan 2003; Winterhalder and Goland 1997; see Lurie 1989; cf. Ebert 1992:213–222). This dual organization also seems to be a feasible approach to a more global explanation of the variability of strategies selected by humans in coping with their changing environment (see the concepts of planning depth and tactical depth in Binford 1989:465 and of scheduling in Flannery 1986). Therefore, expedient use of raw materials and manufacture of lithics such as ground stone are likely to be associated with a reduction in mobility and processing of plant resources that are only seasonally available and necessitate easily obtained and manufactured tool technologies.

Parry and Kelly (1987) further argue that expedient core technology is not tied to other technological innovations such as ceramic technology or ground stone axes (which can be considered curated technologies) or to the origin of food production (this is compatible with the model presented on the evolution of pottery production; see Oyuela-Caycedo 1995b). However, a strong correlation between expedient core technology and subsistence changes does seem to exist, as evidenced in the increase in ground stone technology and the shift toward maize as the major dietary staple in North and Central America. An even stronger correlation seems to occur in relation to settlement pattern changes, with nucleation in villages and, of course, decreases in mobility being associated with expedient lithic technology. Accepting that changes in the organization of technology may have a correlation with changes in subsistence and mobility, one can also expect to see certain patterns in subsistence strategies related to these technological changes (Binford 1980, 1989, 2001; Kelly 1995; Shott 1986). These would include the following:

1. A stronger emphasis on grinding and pounding of harvested wild seeds would occur before a shift toward food production. Expedient use of ground stone technology would be visible archaeologically. Cooking techniques to process bulky material for later consumption are also expected, considering the availability of a resource in a short time period (fruiting time).

2. Spatial variability in subsistence technology would result from the spatial-temporal variability of patchy resources available for processing.

3. Relatively small territory size would occur, considering that constant monitoring of resource availability is required, even in very predictable environments (i.e., scheduling). This monitoring is very likely done during hunting trips as part of the logistic strategy and would generate a form of spatial-temporal territoriality in which only limited sections are covered or defended when resources are temporally available. This would imply movement to the location of a resource before it reaches maturity. The limited territory of mobility should be reflected in minimal evidence of raw materials from distant areas (which would be a pattern more typical of residential strategies with curated lithic technologies).

4. Reduced base camp movement is expected. Such movement would occur only after seasonal depletion of the bulky food or when a new, more appealing bulky food resource becomes available for collecting or harvesting. Increased time of occupation of the base camp should occur

year after year until the conditions of the surrounding location change or a new, more optimal location is defined.

These last three predictions have been tacitly presented for foraging strategies in patchy environments by Binford (2001), Flannery (1986), Dyson-Hudson and Smith (1987), and Cashdan (1984) and biologically explored in Pianka (1980) and Morse (1980). The concept of spatial-temporal territoriality, which is very useful for understanding the constraints on mobility, is from Holldobler and Wilson (1990).

Are these expectations confirmed in the artifacts recovered from San Jacinto 1? First of all, for the site of San Jacinto 1, the use of the term *expedient* is amplified to include other kinds of artifact types such as fire-cracked rocks, ground stone tools, and the flaked stone technology as well as the fire-pits. Why are all of these diverse kinds of artifacts and features considered to be typical of an expedient technology? The answer is that all correspond to the proposed definition of Parry and Kelly (1987) for expedient core technology. This is generalized for other artifacts as follows: "The tools are made with little expenditure of time or effort, to be used in specific tasks[;] once the task is complete, the tools are discarded just as quickly as they were made." It is true that a fire-cracked rock is not intentionally made (with the exception of fired clay balls used in some places of the world where there is limited access to rocks). However, they are selected according to form and volume, and it is in this sense that they can be considered "made." Each of these kinds of assemblages of tools and the feature types at San Jacinto 1 is examined in this regard, starting with a brief review of the flaked stone technology.

The Flaked Stone Technology

Flaked stone technology is part of the food-processing technology up until a certain point. It is, however, also part of the technology used to make other tools, for example, those made of wood. For this reason, only with a more intensive analysis of the material excavated will it be possible to discriminate between these two different functions by the use of activity area analysis and use-wear patterns. For the moment, we can recognize some general patterns that are more related to mobility than to subsistence.

Primary flaking of the cores was conducted at the source of extraction of materials. Cores at the site were already decortified. The rocks mainly used were limolite silica, lidita, and basalt, the first two being chemically sedimentary rocks found in the stream headwaters less than 5 km from the site (Tables 4.6 and 4.8). The latter rock is an igneous volcanic rock found in some locations at the headwaters also close to Cerro Maco, located about 10 km from San Jacinto. Mobility was, therefore, limited to within 10 km of the site. The

Figure 4.11. Examples of flake technology at San Jacinto 1.

technique of flaking was opportunistic. No evidence of retouch has been found. A flake was discarded as soon as it accomplished its task and after it lost its functional quality, and the technology can be classified as expedient. It is interesting to note that thermal alteration is very frequently present in the lidita and limolite silica cores and flakes (Figure 4.11). This heat-treatment technique enhances the quality of the rock for cutting purposes and very likely was performed close to the place of raw material extraction.

The analysis of expedient technology used in food processing and food cooking is now presented.

Stone Grinding/Pounding Tools

All of the different kinds of artifacts that fall into this category have as a common feature selection based on form. They have no intentional working or reshaping and only reveal use-wear patterns. Tools of this type include grinding-stone plates or slab metates (Castro 1993), block metates, and basin-shaped metates, mortars, handstones, edge-ground cobbles, hammerstones, and nutting stones (Oyuela-Caycedo 1993:appendix 5). All among this lithic assemblage have a large diversity of facets or crushing surfaces, and some of the tools may have had multiple functions, but none indicates an intentional process of manufacture or even maintenance. The artifacts are just rocks selected because they had the appropriate form for a specific task. Once the tool was no longer useful, it sometimes was reused in the refill of the fire-pits or as a fire-cracked rock. As an example, most of the broken metates were reused as fire-cracked rocks in the refill of the fire-pits. One complete block metate was used several times and was saved in a pit that was later reused as a cache (Feature No. 63; see Figure 4.9).

All of these grinding/pounding implements are interpreted as having been used for the processing of plants, especially seed plants such as wild grasses and possibly wild rhizomes collected during the site's special-purpose use (Castro 1993). The occurrence of ground stone technology before the intensified use of domesticated plants has also been observed for the Natufian Period and later in the Levant (Henry 1992:195–196), as well as in Mesoamerica (Flannery 1986). The following is a more detailed analysis of the grinding/pounding stone technology found at San Jacinto 1 by category.

Metates: A total of 145 complete and fragmented metates were recovered at San Jacinto 1 (see Oyuela-Caycedo 1993:appendix 5). All the metates were classified according to shape, which has a close relationship with the use-wear pattern observed. For this work the previous classifications made by Kramer and Thomas (1983) and Flannery (1986) were considered. Based on the cross-section form of the metates (Table 4.2), three forms were differentiated: slab, block, and basin shaped.

A comparison of the cross sections indicates that the most common difference among the metate types is the existence of two flat surfaces for the slab metates. In 61 percent of the fragments both surfaces were used. On the other hand, the use of block and basin-shaped metates was unifacial. The basin-shaped metates have, as the name suggests, a more concave form as the result of the unifacial use (Figure 4.10). Block metates show higher variations in the form of the faces than do the other metate types. This could be the result of the diversity of functions for which they can be used. However, one feature seems to be common to all of the metate types, that is, the inclination of the work face. This inclination would facilitate the collection of the processed food at one end.

Another difference among the metates is their volume. Slab metates are small. Using all the data from fragments and complete metates, a difference in thickness among the three categories can be seen. Slab metates have a mean thickness of 24.72 ± 1.055 mm. Block and basin-shaped metates have a more similar mean thickness (block mean thickness = 60.39 ± 5.373 mm; basin-shaped mean thickness = 66.50 ± 8.294 mm). Another difference is in the weight of the complete slab metates recovered. Two categories of weights exist, one smaller with weights between 300 and 810 g (five artifacts) and the other with higher weights ranging from 1,150 g up to 3,100 g. This difference within the slab metates will be discussed later. In contrast, both the complete block metate and the complete basin-shaped metate weigh around 42,000 g. This variation in weight related to form suggests that the two heaviest were most likely placed on the floor and not moved frequently. However, the main difference between the two seems to be related to the function of their use.

Accepting the existence of three types of metates, a total of nine complete metates were recovered (Table 4.3), the slab metates being the most commonly used form and the block and basin-shaped metates being less frequent. The large amount of fragments of metates (Table 4.4) also indicates similar behavior but with the difference that basin-shaped fragments were more abundant than block metate fragments. The reason for this difference may be simply that a block metate is less likely to break than is a basin-shaped metate. Considering this point, it can be argued that the difference in fragmented metates does not reflect a preference in the use of one over the other. In any case, it can be safely said that the most abundant artifact types at the site are the slab metates, followed by the block and basin-shaped metates.

Having defined what kind of metate is most abundant at the site, it is possible to go into more detail in regard to their function by analyzing first the use-wear pattern in relation to the type of metate. In this regard, a clear pattern is observed (Table 4.5). In the case of slab metates, there is a strong indication of a use-wear pattern made by the rotation of an artifact over the plate. Considering the smooth surface of the slab metates, it is concluded that the most likely way to generate such a shape is not by using a handstone or a hammerstone but, more likely, by rotating the flat surface of one slab over the other (Figure 4.12). This would indicate the use of two different sizes of slabs, one at the bottom as an immobile base and the other of smaller size like a hammerstone as the mobile artifact. This difference creates a problem considering that the two kinds of artifacts performing the same function generate the same kind of use-wear marks, making it possible to differentiate between them only when the artifact is complete.

Block metates reveal marks with no clear pattern indicating a single direction of use-wear. This suggests a more multipurpose use of the blocks in contrast to the more specific use of the slab metates. In contrast, the basin-shaped metates, even with the same diversity of use-wear patterns as the block metates, do reveal a preference for a rotational movement. Considering the depressions created by the rotational movement, it can be said that this was produced by handstones most likely round in form. It is interesting to note that associated with the only complete basin-shaped metate found at the site were two spherical handstones (Feature No. 76; Figure 4.13).

Having considered the direction of use-wear and the potential different

The Pottery and Lithics

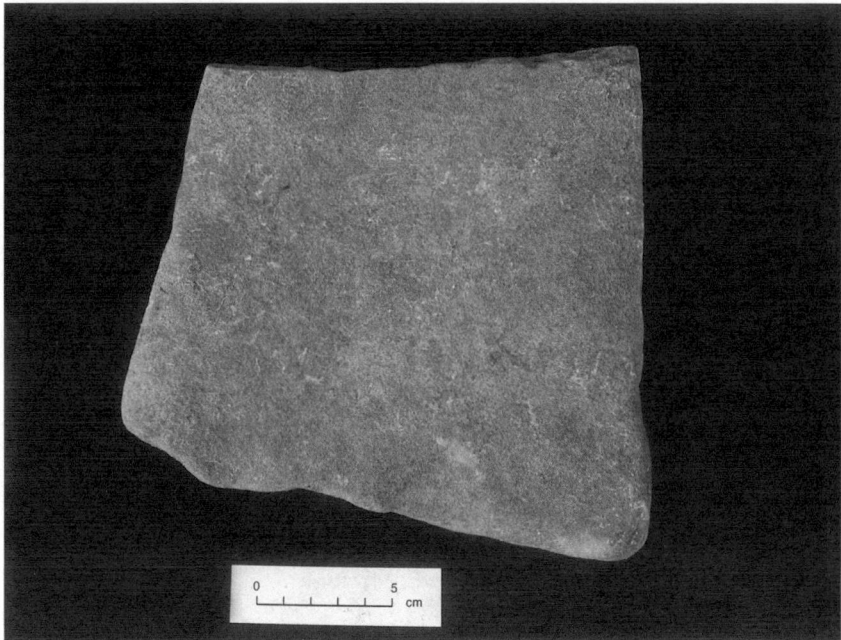

Figure 4.12. Slab metate Pl #1 (location E26N39, stratum 10, Level 35–40, Feature 38).

functions of the three types of metates for the activity of food processing, it is logical to also expect a close relationship among form, use-wear, and preferred rock material type. The preference of one kind of rock over another has to do with increasing the performance according to the food-processing activity required. As was expected in the case of the slab metates, the most preferred raw materials were sedimentary rocks (sandstone, limestone, and travertine) (Table 4.6). In contrast, the basin-shaped metates were made from harder rocks such as basalt andesite, followed in frequency by sandstone. In the case of the block metates, as was expected, there is no significant preference of a specific raw material for the processing activity conducted.

These differences observed in relation to the three kinds of metates lead to the following conclusions:

1. Slab metates were employed in the food-processing activity of grinding by the rotation mainly of two plaques, one that worked as a handstone and the other that functioned as a base. This is an activity that can be performed by placing the larger plaque over stone legs or on the floor. The rotation of the plaques would have the effect of reducing the relatively small grain food particles to powder.

Figure 4.13. Handstones from San Jacinto 1 (left: location E26N23, stratum 12, Level 0–10, Feature 76; right, location E24N41, stratum 10, Level 0–10, Feature 146).

    2. Block metates seem to have been used for multiple activities that required the use of handstones with variable forms, including edge-ground manos.

    3. Basin-shaped metates seem to have been used for food processing not only for reduction of particle size but also mainly for breaking and pounding activities that required the use of heavier handstones (see Stahl 1989).

In synthesis, it can be said that the difference in the metate forms and use-wear patterns may be related to the stage in the processing activity in which they functioned (see Lowell 1999:459–460). The first stage would demand the use of basin-shaped metates and possibly also block metates in some cases. The use of the slab metates was likely for the final stage in a process leading toward the production of flour.

In order to check this interpretation, the handstones are examined for characteristics similar to those of the block and basin-shaped metates.

Handstones: A total of 101 specimens of manos were recovered. The stratigraphic distribution of the handstones is similar to that observed for the slab metates (Table 4.7).

Figure 4.14. Handstones from San Jacinto 1 (left: location E27N36, stratum 12, Level 35–55, Feature 63; right: location E25N30, stratum 12, Level 9–19, Feature 155). Note grinding edge.

The variation in the shapes of the manos is limited. Although 55 broken specimens did not give a clear indication of shape, the most frequent forms identified were spherical (26 percent), rectangular (24 percent), subrectangular (32 percent), discoidal (9 percent), and irregular (8 percent) (Figures 4.13, 4.14, 4.15). Accepting that most of the manos were used in relation to basin-shaped and block metates, it can be argued based on the use-wear pattern that spherical and discoidal manos most likely were used on the basin-shaped metates. The rectangular and subrectangular manos more likely were used on the block metates. Contrary to the observation made previously, this would imply a more abundant use of block metates than basin-shaped metates. This possibility is likely in that it is very difficult to establish the exact number of metates in these categories just based on the metate fragments and in that the basin-shaped metates produce more fragments than block metates.

One aspect that confirms the opportunistic and expedient use of manos is observed in their discard context. Considering the opportunistic use of rocks for various functions, 16 complete handstones were found in the context of fire-pit refill as fire-cracked rocks, and 22 were discarded outside of the pits on the living floor. A similar pattern occurred for the fragments, indicating no preference for the use of fragments for fire-cracked rocks over complete artifacts. In relation to raw material types preferred for use as handstones, there

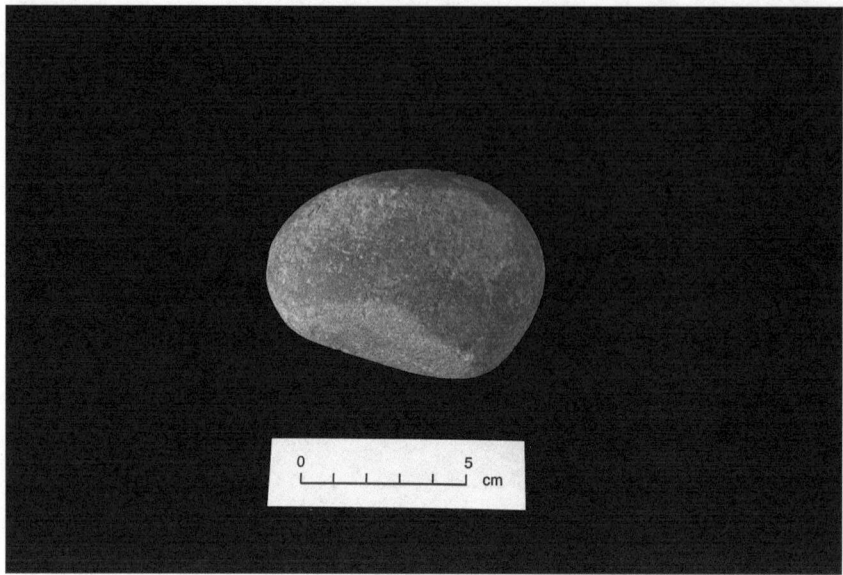

Figure 4.15. Handstone (location E23N32, stratum 12, Level 28–58). Note grinding edge.

is a preference for the use of hard rocks such as basalt (Table 4.8). As has been stated before, none of the artifacts used as manos has any intentional manufacturing process. They were selected because of their natural form and up to a certain degree because of the physical properties of some of the rocks such as basalt.

Mortars: After the slab metates, the most abundant artifact is the mortars. Most of the mortars are very small, corresponding to what Reichel-Dolmatoff (1971:342) calls small anvil stones. The distribution through the strata is very similar to that observed for the metates (see Table 4.7).

The shapes of the mortars are mainly rectangular (52 percent) and oval (24 percent). Practically all of them can be held in one hand (Figures 4.16, 4.17, and 4.18). The bases in general have a flat shape (50 percent), are concave (29 percent), or are angular in form (11 percent). Because of their function, it was expected that there would be a strong preference for the use of harder rocks, but this was not the case. Sedimentary rocks were preferred for use as mortars (77 percent) and in lesser frequencies hard volcanic rocks such as basalt and rhyolite (9 percent) were used. This unexpected pattern is understood when the use-wear marks of the mortars are examined. As is indicated in Table 4.9, the most common form for mortars is the result of pounding and grinding activities made by pecking and rotation.

For what purpose were mortars used at San Jacinto 1? To define a single purpose seems not to be possible. It is very likely that considering the shape

Figure 4.16. Mortar or nutcracker (location E27N30, stratum 12, Level 0–18).

Figure 4.17. Nutcracker (location E24N31, stratum 10, Level 0–10).

Figure 4.18. Mortar (location E24N39, stratum 12, Feature 67).

of a depression that can hold a nut, it is not so illogical to think that these are good artifacts for breaking nuts. However, there are also other mortars with wider working surfaces that can be used for breaking anything. One of the mortars has residue of snail attached to it. This makes difficult the functional interpretation of the mortars, because breaking the snail's shell could also be an alternative way to get meat from the snail. In any case, considering the size of the mortars, they do not suggest an activity involving large-scale processing. Instead, a very individualistic use in the processing of small amounts of foods is suggested, if they were even used for that.

Hammerstones: Rocks that were picked up for the special purpose of working as hammerstones were not common. Even with the presence of 93 mortars, only a small number of hammerstones, a total of 20, was recovered. Half of these were discarded and reused as fire-cracked rocks in the fire-pits. The distribution of hammerstones throughout the stratigraphy was a little different from that observed for the metates and other ground stone technology (see Table 4.7). Hammerstones were relatively more abundant in stratum 9 in relation to the distribution of the other artifact types.

The preference for using any irregular form of rock (14 artifacts) as hammerstones seems to be the rule. Only four have a subrectangular form and two have a discoidal form. In contrast, there was a preference for basalt as the raw material type for hammerstones (14 artifacts). The low number of hammerstones indicates that most likely there was not a real preference for having a

Figure 4.19. Hammerstone (location E24N38, stratum 10, Level 11–20, Feature 57) (photo by Vic Krantz).

specialized artifact. Instead, it seems that what most likely occurred was that each time the inhabitants needed to crack a nut or any other item they used whatever rock was at hand (Figure 4.19). The preference for using subrectangular hammerstones of hard material like basalt may be more related not to food-processing activities but to other activities such as flaked stone production.

In synthesis, after examining the opportunistic selection of rocks for use as ground stone artifacts, it is clear that the artifacts most frequently used and reused at the site were the metates. These artifacts are clearly reflective of an expedient technology of raw material choice and of little effort exerted in the manufacturing process. Indeed, most of the ground stones were only modified during use and discarded, at times being reused as fire-cracked rocks in the features. As has been argued, most of these artifacts suggest that the main activity of use was for the production of mush (wet) or flour (dry), probably from grass seeds or C_3 plants. It is also suggested that the variation in metate form may be related to use in food-processing stages. These stages go from grinding and pounding to release of chaff to a reduction in the size of particles of the food to be consumed by using slab metates at the end of the process of flour production (see Lowell 1999:459–460; Stahl 1989). In these terms the ground stone lithics from San Jacinto 1 confirm the association among expedient lithic technology and an increase in plant collection and processing and a decrease in mobility, based on the sources of the lithic raw materials.

The other type of evidence of the food-processing stages registered at the site is now examined.

The Cooking Technology: Fire-Cracked Rocks and Fire-Pits

Fire-Cracked Rocks: Fire-cracked rocks are the most abundant artifact recovered at the site and the most common technology used in cooking (see Oyuela-Caycedo 1993:appendix 3). Fire-cracked rocks are typically described in Archaic sites of collectors (see Binford et al. 1970; House and Smith 1975; Latas 1992; Lovick 1983; Lowell 1999; Wedel 1986). Fire-cracked rocks are found at San Jacinto 1 in three contexts: (1) in random patterns on living floors, (2) forming clusters of piles, and (3) in the stone fill of fire-pits.

Fire-cracked rocks were used in rock boiling cooking as well as in fire-pit or steam cooking (see Binford et al. 1970; Frison 1983, 1991; Reid 1989). In the excavation at San Jacinto 1, 2.18 tons of fire-cracked rocks of variable shapes and sizes were recovered (Tables 4.10 through 4.12). This astonishing number permitted the assessment that fire-cracked rocks were the most frequent "tool" type used and discarded. This last process seems to have been done after a few uses of the fire-cracked rock. This aspect may be related to the kind of rock used, which became decomposed after a few uses, if it were used for direct cooking (in other words, the continued use of a previously used fire-cracked rock would produce too many particles in the soup or pit). The discard rate of fire-cracked rocks in the pits was also very high. Most of the pits conserved the original rock filling; the inhabitants seem not even to have tried to recover these rocks.

As was mentioned previously, there was no preference for a particular type of rock to be used as fire-cracked rocks; even broken artifacts ended up being useful for such a purpose. In this sense the frequency of one kind of rock type over the other is reflecting just the relative abundance of the rock types near the site.

Fire-Pits: Fire-pits are the most abundant feature type encountered at San Jacinto 1. It seems very likely that fire-pits were used in the same manner as today by hunter-gatherer populations around the world or populations that depend heavily on wild food collection or hunting. Today fire-pits are used in baking cakes or bread made of seed from wild grasses or of flour from nuts (Johnson 1978:355; LaPena 1978:339; Zigmond 1986:399–403). Fire-pits are also employed in steaming or roasting roots and meats (Bartram et al. 1991; Reid 1984a:58–60; Wandsnider 1997; Wedel 1986) and even in the roasting of hearts or heads of agave (Fish et al. 1992).

Most of the pits at the site seem to have been used one time and then refilled with the extracted soil. This is indicated by the fact that in none of the pits was found any indication of wall degradation by rain or of other effects of being exposed for a long time to external conditions. In addition, no refill occurred by postdepositional effects. The rapid degradation of pit walls was observed at the end of the excavation when a heavy rain damaged most of the excavated pits. Fast flooding of the site was not a factor either in the pit refill, as was observed from the soil characterization (see Oyuela-Caycedo 1993:appendix 1). Only in one case was a refill registered that was not the typical sandy clay loam soil that most of the features contained. This was the case for Feature 53, which has a refill of a loamy sandy soil with a large proportion of particle sizes between 0.5 and 0.25 mm (79.64 percent sand, 12.34 percent silt, 8.2 percent clay). This soil characterization contrasts with the other pits' refill, which has more than 24 percent clay and smaller particles of sand. The excavation of Feature 53 did not reveal any particular reason why the refill was different. This soil was restricted to the refill and was not encountered outside of the feature, indicating that it was intentionally placed in the pit. For this reason it is interpreted that the sand was carried to the feature. Another aspect of Feature 53 is that it was the best preserved of all of the excavated features, especially in terms of the red color of the burned clay walls produced by the reduced atmosphere of pit cooking. One concern of the excavation of the pits was to analyze whether the walls of the pits were a kind of plaster different from the soil matrix. A grain size analysis of one of the burned walls (Feature 126) did not show any difference from the soil matrix.

How can the variation observed in the fire-pits help us to determine the range of possible different functions that they may have had? Do all of them have the same function or does the variation in size and content indicate variation in the kind of food that was processed in them? In the field, the existence of strong variation between features was clear, at least in terms of size and content. As indicated in the previous chapter, the pits seem to group more or less into two categories: open fire-pits and earth ovens.

How the earth ovens worked is interpreted as follows, considering ethnographic cases and taking into account the context of the pits. The pits were dug to the desired size. Abundant wood was burned outside the pits and rocks were put directly on the fire to heat them. Only the burnt charcoal was placed at the bottom of the pits (this is interpreted based on the fact that none of these features had ashes) and the heated rocks were placed inside, making a bed over the charcoal. Over the fire-cracked rocks were placed the foods to be cooked, and the pits were refilled with more hot fire-cracked rocks. It seems that in some pits at one point water was added over the rocks to potentially reduce the high temperature of the topmost rocks and produce steam before the pits were sealed. This is evident by the presence of fire-cracked rocks with strong marks of thermal shock due to fast changes of temperature. These marks include thermal spots and cracks and are found only on some fire-cracked rocks in areas where the food seems to have been placed. The last part of the cooking process involved the complete sealing of the pits, possibly with earth obtained from the digging. Once the food was cooked and very likely when the oven was relatively cool, the food was extracted and the removed earth was used to refill the pits.

Why were these earth ovens not reused? The answer seems to be related to one aspect. After the pit had been used once, the walls were completely burned. Because of the high content of clay in the soil matrix these walls were transformed into hard and well-cooked walls (thicknesses up to 10 cm) that would retain heat instead of diffusing it (Oyuela-Caycedo 1993:appendix 6). These preburned walls would increase the temperature to higher levels than desired for cooking or higher than the one achieved in the first use.

Finally, it can be said that these ovens in some way may be viewed as large pots for cooking large quantities of food. The hearths seem to correspond more with daily cooking of meals with the use of direct fire and boiling using fire-cracked rocks. Considering the large numbers of earth ovens (68 cases), it seems obvious to argue that the ovens reflect an intensive and primary reason for the special-purpose use of the site. The use of the fire-pits is interpreted as the final stage of food processing. The food cooking process, as has been stated, starts with grinding and pounding for flour (dry) or mush (wet) production. This would result in an incredible reduction of the bulky material to be cooked. The dry flour or other products of the harvest may have been stored at other locations, as no evidence of storage occurred at San Jacinto 1. This would have produced a potentially large quantity of food prepared in a form that made it feasible to prolong its conservation. The wet mush may have been wrapped in leaves and placed in the earth ovens for steam cooking. These types of processing may have resulted in food products that could be eaten immediately or utilized in a few to several days. On the other hand, the hearths reflect only the subsistence activities of food processing on a daily basis in small quantities and just to satisfy the task group.

The Curated Technology of San Jacinto 1: Pottery

San Jacinto 1 pottery is characterized by the use of plant fibers, most likely grasses, as temper and by firing in reduced conditions (possibly in earth ovens). Fiber-tempered pottery seems to be manufactured mainly by direct shaping and was produced by the household for the household (Raymond et al. 1994, 1998). The fiber temper that is found in the early San Jacinto 1 pottery appears to have come from grasses (Oyuela-Caycedo 1987, 1995b). The ceramic forms include bowls with incurving rims, jars with spouts, and

The Pottery and Lithics

neckless globular jars with deeply incised and excised handles and luglike handles with excised and modeled zoomorphic motifs (Figure 4.3). The San Jacinto 1 pottery is characterized by its great diversity in decorative motifs, as is the early pottery at San Jacinto 2. It might represent an early stage of this technological invention in which experimentation with designs appears to be the rule. Each of the motifs is unique, unlike in later periods such as at San Jacinto 2, Puerto Hormiga, Puerto Chacho, and Monsú, where decoration became repetitive and standardized.

Pottery with no doubt is a curated technology that has a low presence at the site. It is important to note that pottery was not found at the site in a context of abandonment on the surface or guarded in caches for later use (see Oyuela-Caycedo 1993:appendix 2). The pattern of discarded fragments observed seems to be that of those pots that got broken during the use of the site and were swept to the side or became part of the floor matrix. There is not a single debris accumulation on the surface at the time of abandonment that indicates that the inhabitants left behind a complete vessel. This suggests that pottery vessels may have been carried in the move to another base camp, and this corresponds to behaviors associated with curated technology.

Going back to the data, does pottery show any indication of variability in forms that may suggest different purposes? The preliminary analysis of the vessel forms suggests little variability. Most of the vessel forms are semiglobular pots and globular vessels (Pratt 1999a, 1999b). An analysis of the pottery through the cultural strata also does not show any relevant variation in time (Table 4.1). No evidence of direct contact with fire in the form of burned surfaces or of indirect cooking by rock boiling (vessel size is too small) is apparent. Pottery does have a very restricted spatial distribution. Even in the strata with highly redundant reoccupation, the discrete distribution of pottery was clear. In the deepest strata, such as 12, 14, 16, 18, and 20, pottery was found concentrated in the dumping areas.

Pottery, however, was never found associated to the context of the fire-pits or even the clusters of fire-cracked rocks or to any artifacts related with cooking (see below). This lack of association to cooking activities does not mean that pottery was not used for other purposes in food processing such as fermentation. The early function of pottery is interpreted to be tied more to social behavior than to economic process (Oyuela-Caycedo 1993, 1995b; also see Cauvin 2000a, 2000b). It is interesting to note that Reid (1989), in his study of hunter-gatherer pottery, argues that a covariant relationship exists between the exploitation of carbohydrate seeds and the use of starch pots built for boiling. In the case of San Jacinto 1, this relationship is not clear considering the almost null evidence that pots were ever used for cooking. Another aspect of Reid's argument is that cooking pots in comparison with cooking pits will be selected against because cooking pits are a more energy-efficient way to process quantities of bulky plants. This part of his argument seems appropriate for San Jacinto 1 and this may explain the large quantities of fire-pits. As is described in the previous chapter, these fire-pits were produced by the many reoccupations of the site by a small band that seems to have been living mainly from gathering wild plants, here as in other late Archaic sites.

ROCKS VS. CLAY: THE EVOLUTION OF POTTERY TECHNOLOGY

The change from lithic to pottery times has been considered a temporal marker of a major transformation in the evolution of human societies. However, little is known of the meaning of this technological change and less is known of the impact that it had or of why pottery was accepted or invented multiple times. In this section these questions are addressed by analyzing the spatial and functional relationships between fire-cracked rocks and pottery technologies in the case of San Jacinto 1. The results help in the understanding of how and why pottery develops by checking some of the explanatory models of this process of technological change.

The data set used for the present research was the weight of pottery recovered in each square meter excavated. For comparative spatial distributions the same data were obtained for the fire-cracked rocks. Some exploratory analysis was also conducted to define the best approach for recognizing patterns. The technique used for the spatial variation analysis follows that described by Charles Spencer and Kent V. Flannery (1986). For the determination of a correlation value between the two spatial distributions, the standard Pearson's correlation was used (see Whallon 1986).

A comparison of the two basic statistics between pottery and fire-cracked rocks indicates that their distributions are not evenly dispersed (Table 4.14). A multimodal distribution across the excavated area occurs in a pattern that seems to be far from random. Some squares have lower amounts of pottery or fire-cracked rocks or none, while others have large quantities. Pottery seems to have a more clearly defined pattern of concentration or clustering than do fire-cracked rocks.

The Pottery

From stratum 9 were recovered almost 9 kg of pottery. All of the fragments were found to form a clear pattern of distribution in 53.3 percent of the 75 m^2 excavated. Only 42 fragments of pottery rims were recovered associated with the stratum (Table 4.15). The pottery analysis suggests that in the 75 m^2 only a few vessels were present, possibly fewer than 10 concentrated in nine peak

Table 4.14. Basic statistics of pottery and fire-cracked rocks by weight

Material	No. of Squares	Min. Weight (g)/Square	Max. Weight (g)/Square	Mean Weight (g)/Square	Standard Deviation	Coefficient of Variation	Variance/Mean Ratio
Pottery	75	0	980	119.827	194.961	1.627	317.2
Rocks	75	0	9385	2327.173	1733.544	0.745	16.33

Table 4.15. Pottery fragments from stratum 9

Pottery Fragments	Weight (g)	Percentage
Plain sherds	8,205	91.2
Rims	468	5.2
Decorated walls	15	0.2
Decorated rims	60	0.7
Decorated lugs	239	2.7
Total	8,987	100

areas (see Table 4.15 and Figure 4.20). The discrete pattern of pottery distribution forming clear clusters does not indicate a direct relationship with the features or with the distribution of the fire-cracked rocks.

The low frequency of pottery also was observable during the excavation of the lower strata. This pattern contrasts radically with that observed at sites such as Monsú, Puerto Chacho, and Puerto Hormiga, where pottery is highly visible.

The Fire-Cracked Rocks

Contrary to pottery, fire-cracked rocks are the most abundant archaeological material recovered in terms of number and weight, a pattern common in base camps of collectors (Binford et al. 1970; Latas 1992). A total of 174.5 kg (3,511 items) of fire-cracked rocks were recovered in stratum 9 (Table 4.16). The mean weight of the rocks is 49.7 gm.

Fire-cracked rocks were found in three contexts. First, they were dispersed on the stratum in a random distribution (distributions of less than 1,000 g/m^2 seem to behave in this manner). Only two of the square-meter sections had no fire-cracked rocks (see Figure 4.20). Second, they were found forming clusters in piles that had on occasion up to 9 kg of rocks in a pile. These were classified initially as features (most of the peaks observed contained more than 2,000 gm of fire-cracked rocks per square meter; see Figure 4.20). Third, fire-

Figure 4.20. Distribution of pottery (A) and fire-cracked rocks (B) in stratum 9. Pottery concentrations are shown in 100-g levels and fire-cracked rocks in 200-g levels.

cracked rocks were found in the interior of fire pits or earth ovens. In stratum 9 only four fire-pits were identified. These features were mainly associated with strata 10, 12, 14, and 16.

All of the fire-cracked rocks were classified according to rock formation and composition. Sedimentary rocks account for 89.91 percent of the fire-cracked rocks; the rest (10.02 percent) are composed of igneous volcanic rocks (Tables 4.10 through 4.12). A Pearson's correlation between pottery and fire-cracked rocks for all the excavated units confirms an extremely low correlation (0.083), which suggests fire-cracked rocks are not related to pottery in the context of cooking activities (see Table 4.14 and Figure 4.20). The distribution

Table 4.16. Total weight and number of fire-cracked rocks in stratum 9

Rock Type	No.	Weight (g)
Sedimentary rocks		
Sandstone of fine grain	1,427	56,078
Limestone	823	36,699
Crystal limestone	573	23,966
Travertine	336	25,735
Igneous rocks		
Rhyolite	78	6,008
Granite	6	840
Basalt andesite	268	25,212
Total	3,511	174,538

of fire-cracked rocks in or near earth ovens indicates a relation with cooking practices, such as stone steaming or boiling, which may employ other kinds of perishable containers, such as bottle gourds (*Lagenaria* sp.), *totumos* (*Crescentia cujete*), leather bags, and baskets. Finally, it is clear that the main association of fire-cracked rocks is with cooking activities linked to the features (earth ovens), which were the main form of food cooking at San Jacinto 1.

The results of this analysis suggest that there is no relationship between pottery and cooking activities as represented by fire-cracked rocks and features. This interpretation favors the argument that pottery at this site had a function different from that related to cooking. Pottery seems not to compete at this point in its developmental process against fire-cracked rocks. The two do not appear to be directly associated with the same activities as indicated by the Pearson's correlation and the graphics of spatial distribution (see Table 4.14 and Figure 4.20).

It can also be noted that the distribution of pottery is limited to 53.3 percent of the excavated squares. Fire-cracked rocks, on the other hand, occur in all but two squares (97.3 percent). Brown (1986:605) notes for Early Woodland archaeology a similar phenomenon for pottery of low sitewide density and concentration in highly localized areas. The results here suggest an initial restricted role for pottery in its process of incorporation by the inhabitants of San Jacinto 1, as also seems to be the case for the Early Woodland period of North America.

Likewise, the difference between the quantities of pottery and fire-cracked rocks is substantial and points to an initial secondary and limited role for pottery as compared with fire-cracked rocks. A later reversal in the visibility of pottery vs. fire-cracked rocks at sites such as Monsú and Puerto Hormiga occurred as pottery was more fully incorporated into the inhabitants' activities and it competed with and took over roles previously fulfilled by other material culture such as fire-cracked rocks.

CONCLUSION

The evidence from San Jacinto 1 indicates that the basic unit of technological production, maintenance, and consumption was very individual. For none of the recovered technologies, either expedient or curated (pottery), were part-time specialists required. Interregional exchange is absent, and no exotic materials are present. The raw materials used for the lithics are all present within 10 km of the site and none of the lithics indicate time-consuming construction techniques. This type of expedient technology is what is expected for groups who have reduced mobility and do not travel long distances to obtain raw materials (Binford 1989:252–255; Kelly 1995).

The pottery technology, on the other hand, was curated, and some time and effort were necessary for its construction. The ceramic forms include bowls with incurving rims, jars with spouts, and neckless globular jars with deeply incised and excised handles and luglike handles with excised and modeled zoomorphic motifs. The pottery vessels were most likely carried from one site to another. The lack of association of the pottery to the cooking technologies of fire-cracked rocks and earth oven features indicates that the reason for the invention and use of pottery at this site was not for cooking purposes. Instead, the pottery most likely served a role in social interactions, such as for the fermentation of drinks and serving.

The analysis of the technology of food processing and cooking suggests that the major staple of the diet came mainly from harvesting and processing seeds of C_3 plants and a possible low use of rhizomes. This interpretation is based on the technology of grinding/pounding reflected in the large numbers of metates and handstones recovered and the cooking technology indicated by intensive use of fire-pits as roasting, steaming, or cooking ovens. Indeed, the recovery of 145 metates and 101 manos is exceptional for an Archaic/Formative period site, as these ground stone tools are usually associated with the processing of maize to make corn meal for mush or bread (Katz et al. 1974; Lowell 1999:450; Stahl 1989). However, metates and manos are also known to occur at sites where wild grass seeds have been processed (Flannery 1986; Henry 1992:195–196; also see Hillman 1996; Hillman et al. 1989). Further information in this regard concerning the carbonized botanical remains and the low presence of faunal remains is presented in the next chapter. All of this evidence suggests a heavy dependence on plant processing very typical of sites that have been traditionally classified as Archaic.

The subsistence technology most similar to that at San Jacinto 1 is found in the Great Basin and the American Bottom for the middle and late Archaic (Emerson and McElrath 1983:224–225, 232–233; Fortier 1983:248–251, 256–259; Phillips and Gladfelter 1983); in Oaxaca (Flannery 1986; Lorenzo 1958); and in other places of the world such as the Levant (Bar-Yosef and Belfer-Cohen 1991, 1992; Belfer-Cohen and Bar-Yosef 2000; Kuijt and Goring-Morris 2002; Molist n.d.). In these areas populations depended heavily on wild grass collection at one point in their trajectories. Good ethnographic evidence that describes similar patterns in the associated technology is found among plant-collecting bands in western North America (Castetter and Bell 1951; Hunter 1992; Smith 2001:30) including California and the Great Basin; in the present and in dream times in Australia (Binford 1989:223–263; Cane 1989; Harney 1951; Jones and Meehan 1989; Tindale 1977); and in other groups of Oceania (Barrau and Peeters 1972). In Africa, studies on groups in the Sahara and sub-Sahara also yield good information on wild grass harvesting (Harlan 1989) and on camp structure, as indicated by the Kua San hunter-gatherer camps (Bartram et al. 1991). These cases from around the world seem to be extremely similar and useful for comparison to the lithic technology that was found at San Jacinto 1.

Based on the findings, it can therefore be argued that the site represents a special-purpose camp where cooking activities were performed during the dry season. This implies that San Jacinto 1 represents just one site type among the multiple types that this band could have generated. Considering the diversity of seasonal microenvironments, one should expect to identify other kinds of camps or stations in the area with very different and distinctive variations in the subsistence technology.

5 The Ecofactual Remains

The ecofactual remains recovered from archaeological sites can reveal a wealth of information about the lifeways of the inhabitants and the environments and ecosystems in which they lived. Ecofactual remains include faunal remains and botanical remains (DeFrance et al. 1996; Hastorf 1999b). They yield information on the environment at the times of the site's occupations, on the diet of the inhabitants, on other natural resources utilized for various purposes, and on the seasonality of the site's occupations. By tying all of this information together, it is also possible to help identify the social and economic strategies that peoples utilized to adapt to their environment.

The ecofactual information from San Jacinto 1 to date focuses on the mollusks and macrobotanical remains recovered. A focus on the mollusk remains was necessary since they made up 95 percent of the faunal remains recovered. The amount of bone recovered from birds and mammals at San Jacinto 1 is so small that its use in arguing for the seasonality of the site appeared to be minimal (Grayson and Thomas 1983:434; Oyuela-Caycedo 1993). The analysis of the botanical remains focused on the macroscopic identification of carbonized seeds and fruits with the use of scanning electron microscopy (SEM) photography to aid in future identifications of fragmented remains. The identification of carbonized wood recovered from the site is ongoing. Microscopic botanical analyses conducted at the site in the form of palynological studies yielded no results (Bonzani 1995; L. Herrera, personal communication, 1992). Phytolithic analysis to date has only been conducted on one sample from Feature 63, an earth oven that yielded grass and arrowroot (*Maranta arundinacea*) phytoliths (D. Piperno, personal communication, 1995). The results of these analyses and a discussion in terms of the seasonality of the occupants' movements, the ecological setting of the site, the use of resources, and social/economic interactions follows.

ENVIRONMENT, ECOLOGICAL SETTING AND MOBILITY, AND SEASONALITY

Environmental Context

The faunal and macrobotanical remains recovered from a site indicate what types of animals and plants had to be present during the site's occupation. Further, by determining the ecological requirements of these animals and plants, one can define the types of environments that had to be present at a site for these taxa to occur. In the case of San Jacinto 1, the recovery of plant remains like *Malvastrum* (Malvaceae) and land snails, which are found in dry xerophytic communities or thorn woodlands under arid conditions, is indicative of a past environment that was more arid than today. These tree snails, *Drymaeus* sp. and *Orthalicus* spp., live predominately in environments with less than 500 mm per year of precipitation. For these snails to be utilized during the occupations at San Jacinto 1, the environment must therefore have been similarly dry. Such environments in the tropics are defined as savanna woodland or as tree and/or shrub savanna (Sarmiento 1983:246–247, table 10.1). These savanna types fall into the subhumid to semiarid savanna types outlined by Harris (1980). The subhumid type falls in terms of precipitation received just below that of the present-day environment (1,000 mm per year), with the current dry season being approximately 5 months long. With less precipitation, the dry season would have been from 5 to 7.5 months in duration. If the area was much drier than present with less than 500 mm per year of precipitation, then a tree and/or shrub savanna type occurred, and the dry season would have been from 7.5 to 10 months long.

Currently, the vegetation directly over the site is dominated by members of the families of Poaceae (13 percent) and of Malvaceae, particularly *Malachra rudis* (26.4 percent) (Bonzani 1995). Members of this genus are scattered shrubs found in the hot lowlands of the Americas (Castañeda 1965:226). Similar botanical specimens recovered both archaeologically and in the modern-day collections conducted in the area in 1991 and 1992 include *Eupatorium* (Asteraceae), *Cyperus* (Cyperaceae), *Sida* (Malvaceae), and members of the Poaceae, Leguminosae, and Sapotaceae. These similarities indicate a general continuity in the plants that would have been available to the inhabitants utilizing the site some 5,000 to 6,000 years ago.

The ecofactual information recovered from San Jacinto 1 corroborates the climatic interpretations based on pollen column analyses and shell midden formation (Oyuela-Caycedo 1996; Van der Hammen 1974, 1983, 1984; Van der Hammen et al. 1991). Combining the evidence from the pollen analyses with the association of the land snail species and xerophytic vegetation, it is now possible to argue that around the time of occupation of San Jacinto 1 (ca. 6000 to 5200 B.P.) the environment was more arid than today. Precipitation would have been less than or equal to 500 mm per year (current precipitation, 1,000 mm per year), resulting in a more prolonged dry season than currently occurs (5 months) (Harris 1980; Walsh 1981).

Ecological Setting and Mobility

The ecological setting of the site of San Jacinto 1 during its occupations was near some body of water, most likely a stream, as is its present location. As originally defined by Oyuela-Caycedo (1993) using soil analysis studies, this type of ecological setting is confirmed by the recovery of plants known to grow in flooded or semiaquatic environments. In particular, the members of the family Cyperaceae and *Polygonum* indicate such a location. Members of the Cyperaceae grow in swampy or seasonally flooded conditions (Gentry 1993:120–122), as do the semiaquatic species of *Polygonum* (Gentry 1993:693–698). The modern-day collection of *Cyperus odoratus* from the area of the site near the stream confirms such a distribution.

Other plants recovered archaeologically that are known to be semiaquatic or weedy plants that adapt to disturbed seasonally flooded conditions include *Portulaca* sp. and *Sida* sp. *Sida rhombifolia* was collected from the present-day floodplain of the stream passing by San Jacinto 1. *Portulaca meracioides* was collected as a weed growing in a patio of a house in the town of San Jacinto. Both *Portulaca* and *Polygonum* have known growth habitats along floodplains and are commonly used as foods by Archaic/early Formative groups throughout the world (Bonzani 1984; Renfrew 1973; Smith 1992; Yarnell 1986).

Thus, as defined by Oyuela-Caycedo (1993) and confirmed by the recovery of macrobotanical remains, the site was located on a seasonally flooded area such as a point bar along a stream or river meander. The site was probably abandoned because of changes in these conditions as might occur by a stream meander cutoff. Such a context would provide the setting for plant genera that require disturbed areas for growth (Poaceae, *Portulaca, Polygonum*) and those that need wetter or swampy conditions to survive (members of the Cyperaceae).

Stream meanders and cutoffs are known to produce oxbow lakes or areas where swampy conditions might occur even in areas with drier climates. It is perhaps just such an environmental setting that made the site of San Jacinto 1 so attractive to humans that they returned to the same location for hundreds of years. Given that the general climatic conditions from 5,000 to 7,000 years ago in this region of South America were potentially much drier than today, an area with permanent water would have been particularly attractive to any groups living in the region. When resources were available in the area, numerous groups would have been drawn to them and the location would have been very desirable to groups who needed resources growing in such areas or rich soils for planting. The site was clearly a focal point for groups who visited on a yearly basis to plant, collect, or obtain resources (also see Smith 2003:164). The available resources were probably used for food and beverages and to obtain important fibers for matting, baskets, or pottery making. Task groups or groups of larger families would have visited the spot and may have come into contact with members of other groups. To avoid conflict or to attract additional labor, social activities probably occurred, as is evidenced by the pottery forms and uses. However, during the rainy season and at other points

The Ecofactual Remains

in the dry season when resource abundance fell off at this location, the visiting groups would have had to move elsewhere to avoid the floods and to collect other resources. San Jacinto 2 seems to be one such site that has the characteristics of a base camp, being located on the top of a modified hill with possible evidence of a pithouse structure (Oyuela-Caycedo 1987).

There is, as well, evidence that the inhabitants of San Jacinto 1 also utilized other resources located in different ecological zones near the site, such as in tropical cloud forests. This evidence is in the form of the bead opercula and shells recovered from the mollusk genus of *Neocyclotus* as well as in the recovery of phytoliths of arrowroot. Both the mollusks and members of the Marantaceae are found in wet environments, typically with palms and cloud forest. The closest such environment to San Jacinto today is the Cerro Maco, which is located about 10 km from the site. No other ecofactual or lithic materials recovered are located at a distance farther away than this. In general, the recovery of these remains and the lack of more exotic materials indicate a restricted mobility for the hunter-gatherer groups utilizing San Jacinto 1. Task groups from a centralized base camp could have collected the snails and opercula of *Neocyclotus* and the roots and leaves of the Marantaceae for activities that occurred at San Jacinto 1 after the local rains ended. These activities included the use of the opercula to make beads and potentially the cooking of roots or the use of leaves to wrap prepared foods, probably from seeds of C_3 plants, for cooking in the earth ovens. Once this spatial territoriality was established that utilized diverse ecological zones, it was only a matter of waiting and watching for the changing yearly cycles to know when to return to San Jacinto 1. This form of spatial-temporal territoriality, once established, would have been the key to the successful adaptations of the groups living in such a savanna environment.

Seasonality

As well as defining the changing environment and ecological setting of the site, information on the seasonality of the site's occupations can also be obtained from the faunal and botanical remains recovered from San Jacinto 1. If one ties the identified macrobotanical remains to the present-day seasonality of plants in the Savannas of Bolívar, the data should give an idea of the type of site and time of use by its inhabitants at 5900 to 5200 B.P. To obtain the data on the modern-day seasonality of plants in the region, surveys on the seasonality of 50 plant taxa used for food or other purposes were collected from six informants from the town of San Jacinto. Informants who accompanied the authors in the field during the collection of specimens were also asked about plant seasonality. The flowering, fruiting, planting time, and harvest time of plants were also noted during collection (Bonzani 1995, 1999).

From the data collected, a number of observations can be made based on the seasonality of modern-day plant use at San Jacinto. First of all, the cultivation of plants in the region where seasonality is based on a bimodal distribution of rainfall requires at least two different schedules of planting based on physiographic area. For the purpose of simplicity, these areas are terraces and floodplains. On floodplains, planting occurs after the floodwaters recede in late October to November, as with the type of maize known locally as *maíz de sereno* (maize of the mists). This name may be in reference to morning mists that lie along the rivers and streams and help to water the plants. These floodplain soils are productive and the harvest (*la cosecha*) can occur three to five months later in January through March.

In fields on terraces, crops must be planted before the rainy seasons and collected after the rainy seasons are over. This schedule of cultivation occurs both over the major rainy period of September, October, and November and over the shorter rainy period of May–June. From the data on terrace fields (Bonzani 1995:tables 3.16–3.22), planting tends to occur in September and in March, April, and May. Harvesting occurs from October to January. When planting occurs in September, the harvest (*la cosecha*) is ready in January, as with maize when the cobs have formed and the grass has dried out. When planting occurs in March through May, harvests can be ready in June to August, as with pepper, squash, or a second crop of maize, or in October, as with the tubers sweet potato and manioc and with beans (*Phaseolus lunatus*). Achiote, bottle gourd, and cotton are also planted in April–May and harvested in the dry season in December–January. Tobacco harvests are longer and can run from August through December but with a concentration in December. Some cultivated plants like passion fruit and papaya have become available all year round.

The second observation is that fruiting of different families of trees tends to be seasonal. However, the majority of the genera and species of trees fruit in May during the shorter rainy season, which occurs after the major dry period in the area. These trees include members of the families of Anacardiaceae, Annonaceae, Guttiferae, Polygonaceae, and *Persea americana* of the Lauraceae. Other families are noted to have their major fruiting period during the months of the major rainy season in October and into November. These families, however, may also fruit in May, though informant information and collections of fruits in the field by Bonzani show a clear concentration of fruiting times in October and November. These plants include members of the family Myrtaceae and *Ocotea* of the Lauraceae. Other families that have a more extended period of fruiting are the Mimosaceae, with *Inga densiflora* fruiting from October to February and *Prosopis juliflora* fruiting from August to November. Of note, fruits from *Inga densiflora* may not have been available in this region (at 210 m asl) in Archaic and Formative times since the tree is found in Colombia from 800–1700 m asl (Bartholomäus et al. 1990). The availability of fruits from trees of other families appears to fall more into the beginning or early part of the major dry season in the region that begins in December and runs until March or April. These families include the Sapotaceae, the Sterculiaceae, and *Phyllanthus acidus* of the Euphorbiaceae, which fruit in December through February, and the *Cassia grandis* of the Caesalpiniaceae, which fruits from December to March. Although native to Colombia or northern South America, three fruiting trees were unknown to local informants or, if known, the season of fruiting or flowering was not known. These include *Chlorophora tinctoria* of the Moraceae, *Chysobalanus icaco* of the Rosaceae, and *Genipa americana* of the Rubiaceae.

Thus, the major fruiting period of trees occurs in the short rainy season around May. Fruiting in the major rainy period around October is found in the Lauraceae, Myrtaceae, and Mimosaceae. Dry-season fruiting occurs in the Sapotaceae, Sterculiaceae, Euphorbiaceae, and Caesalpiniaceae.

The third noticeable observation from these data is that the availability of palm fruits is not as highly seasonal as that of some of the other plant families. Fruiting of palms in seasonal environments of the Amazon runs from the dry season in December through the wet season around May. The data from the palms indicate that they may not be as useful to define site seasonality as would be other fruit tree families, though more information on seasonality of palms in the region of San Jacinto is clearly needed.

In addition, the seasonality of the use of tubers in this region of Colombia may be hard to determine as tubers can be left in the ground for a number of months and collected as needed. In general, tuberous plants (*Manihot esculenta, Ipomoea* spp., *Dioscorea* spp.) are planted vegetatively in April and collected during the major wet period in September to October. Collection in the wet season may be a matter of taste preference, as was indicated by informants for manioc (Doorman 1982); tubers of these same genera are also noted to be collected in January.

The fourth observation deals with the availability of grasses. Grasses are an important resource for humans, as indicated by the archaeological and ethnographic record (Cane 1989; Castro 1993; Harlan 1989, 1992a; Jones and Meehan 1989; Oyuela-Caycedo 1993:209–213, 1995b; Tindale 1977; Wetterstrom 1993). In the Savannas of Bolívar the occurrence of grasses is highly seasonal, with seed and other reproductive structures available at the end of the rainy season (end of November) and beginning of the dry season (December). If maize is planted on the terraces, then the collection of cobs and kernels would occur after the rainy season when the plant is reaching maturity in December to January. By the middle of December the other grasses and plants in the region are drying up and dying. For maize planted along the floodplains, maturity is also expected to occur in three to five months with early maturity probably due to soil productivity. Collection of the plant would still be expected to occur in the dry season.

When the data on plant seasonality are compared to the botanical remains identified to date at San Jacinto 1, the site can be tied to a time of occupation at the beginning of the dry season from November to March. The dry season is the season when the plant remains recovered from the site would have had flowers and seeds and fruits. This season of occupation can be confirmed by the recovery of seeds from the families Malvaceae and Sapotaceae, both of which fruit in November to January–February in the San Jacinto region. Members of the Malvaceae in the region, including *Malachra rudis* and *Gossypium,* flower at the end of October into November and have fruits in November and December. For instance, the immature fruits of a wild, near-arborescent shrub of *Gossypium* found near the site were noted to be just opening on November 15, while the fruits of the cultivated form of cotton are collected in December (Bonzani 1995:tables 3.21 and 3.22). The other identified seed types of the genus *Portulaca* and the families Leguminosae and Cyperaceae are also indicative of a period of availability at the beginning of the dry season. Modern-day samples of seeds of *Portulaca meracioides* were collected in December as were bulbs and reproductive structures of *Cyperus odoratus* from the town of San Jacinto and from near the archaeological site, respectively (Bonzani 1995:table 3.21). Most of the herbaceous plants in the region die back by the middle to end of December.

No macrobotanical remains from the site have been identified to date that indicate occupation before the rainy season in August or September. These data point to the fact that it is very unlikely that any resources utilized at the site were being planted or cultivated before the rainy season at San Jacinto 1. Instead, plant seasonality points much more strongly to the likelihood of intensive collection and processing of seeds in November or December after the rains and floodwaters in the area receded. Likewise, no botanical remains recovered to date indicate a seasonality of April–May, when the majority of trees fruit in the region.

Thus the data from the botanical remains of San Jacinto 1 confirm the observation that the site was occupied during the dry season, probably in December and possibly into January when the area was not in danger of flooding. The collection of the mollusks at the site was also most likely done when the stream was low in the dry season. The site occupations could have occurred numerous times during one dry season or over the years. Before subsequent occupations, flooding occurred, as evidenced by each cultural layer being separated from the next by sterile fluvial depositions. After the rains and floods at the beginning of each yearly dry season, the groups in the region would have descended upon the site to collect the seasonally abundant resources that grew well in this semiaquatic ecological setting. These resources were probably only abundant for a short period at the beginning of the dry season before they either died off, as did the grasses, or their fruiting period ended. The seasonality of resource use in this case outweighs the importance of whether the resource was cultivated. In this scenario, the site of San Jacinto 1 would have been a seasonal oasis where members of various groups gathered to possibly plant and later collect and process seed resources. Such special-purpose sites would have been only one type of site and location that these groups would have occupied. The necessity of utilizing other resources and locations at different times of year would have limited the usefulness of the site for permanent or even semipermanent occupation. The resources found at San Jacinto 1 also would have been only a small part of the yearly diet that the inhabitants of the region would have had to utilize to adapt to an environment that was potentially much drier than today. In this sense, these resources were probably initially much more important for social reasons of adaptation than for longer term, year-round economic group survival.

THE BOTANICAL REMAINS RECOVERED AND USES

One way to recover macrobotanical remains is to use flotation on soils that are collected in the field, wherein the lighter carbonized materials float to the top of the water and are collected (Struever 1968; Wagner 1982; Watson 1974). This method was carried out at San Jacinto 1 to obtain the macrobotanical remains from the site (Bonzani 1995). Material for flotation was recovered both from floors and from all types of features encountered. In total, 67 random samples of the features and floors and 10 nonrandom samples of ^{14}C-dated features were analyzed for their macrobotanical content.[1] The 77 samples analyzed consisted of 274.79 kg of soils, which yielded 1,017.9 g of carbonized material (the light fraction), 719.1 g of which was analyzed (Bonzani 1995:appendix 2). Less than 2 g of seeds or fruit material was recovered from the 77 samples and all of the material appeared to be degraded or was recovered in a fragmented state. The majority of the carbonized material was wood, which has yet to be analyzed. Identifications initially conducted in 1994 and 1995 were based on reference collections and photographs presented in the following references: Pearsall (1980), Isely (1947:328–329), Harrington (1977), Pohl (1968), Berggren (1969), and Montgomery (1977).

To obtain comparative information on what the environmental context of the site of San Jacinto 1 was 6,000 years ago, an ethnobotanical study was also conducted among modern-day inhabitants at San Jacinto and neighboring communities (Bonzani 1995, 1998, 1999). This study collected information on modern-day uses of plants as well as on the plants' habit, habitat, and seasonality. It was then possible to compare the identified macrobotanical remains to modern-day reference material and ascertain a good idea of the environment, the site's ecological setting, and the seasonality of use of the site and its resources within its inhabitants' mobility strategies some 5,000 to 6,000 years ago (presented above).

Macrobotanical remains recovered from strata 5 (dated to 2100–1700 B.P.) include one seed identified as *Chenopodium* sp. (Chenopodiaceae) (Table 5.1) (F. King, personal communication, 1995; Montgomery 1977:70). The genus consists of approximately 185 weedy annuals, perennial herbs, and, rarely, shrubs. Most of the species are found in temperate regions of both hemispheres. One species (*C. ambrosioides*) is noted as an effective vermifuge (Schultes and Raffauf 1990:127). Several species, especially *C. quinoa* (known as quinua) from South America, have starch-rich seeds and are cultivated today from Colombia along the Andes through Peru and Bolivia to Chile and Argentina at elevations above 1800 m. A potential wild ancestor of quinua, *C. hircinum*, grows along the eastern margins of the Andes Mountains in Bolivia and Argentina into the more lowland areas of Argentina, Uruguay, and Paraguay (Smith 1995:170–173).

Archaeologically in South America, *C. quinoa* has been recovered from the Quebrada de Las Pircas sites in Peru dated to 6200–5500 B.C. (Pearsall 2003:237–241; Rossen et al. 1996). It has also been recovered at Ayacucho Caves of highland Peru dated to 5800–4400 B.C. (MacNeish et al. 1980), and from the Panauluaca Cave in the Junin basin of Peru dated to 3050 and 2050 B.C. The specimens from the Junin basin have thinner testa than wild examples and may represent domesticated forms (Smith 1995:171–173). *Chenopodium* spp. has also been recovered from various sites in Peru, Chile, and Argentina dating from 2500 B.C. to A.D. 1450 (Hernández et al. 1999–2000). Based on this information, a proposed area of origin of domestication for *C. quinoa* is the Peruvian Andes in what has been termed the Andean High-Elevation Complex (Pearsall 1992). No archaeological plant remains of the genus have been reported for Ecuador or Venezuela (Pearsall 2003). In Colombia at the site of Monsú, 13 seeds identified to the family Chenopodiaceae were recovered and associated with the Barlovento Period dated to ca. 1290–1280 B.C. (Reichel-Dolmatoff 1985:171). A single seed of *Chenopodium* was also recovered from the El Venado site located in the Department of Boyacá near Bogotá, Colombia (A. Boada, personal communication, 2002).

The recovery of one seed of this type from stratum 5 dated to ca. 2100 to 1700 B.P. can only be used to indicate that the plant was available in the lowland region of Colombia at this time. This recovery is the first indication of

Table 5.1. Stratigraphic distribution of carbonized botanical remains

Stratum/Level	5	9	9	10	10	12	12	14	14	16	18	20	Total
Feature	3	Floor	8, 10	Floor	11, 16, 31, 34, 45, 53, 57, 78, 116, 125, 190	Floor	55, 63, 162, 171, 201, 211	Floor	193, 195	Floor	Floor	Floor	
Provenience*													
Weight of soils floated per strata (g)	10,890	15,850	5,670	86,330	34,960	67,910	19,520	10,360	4,720	11,360	10,000	2,440	280,010
Weight of light fraction per strata (g)	75.4	6.9	2.1	272.2	215.1	175.4	98	50.3	44.3	50	29.9	2.5	1,022.1
Asteraceae *Eupatorium* sp.				1									1
Chenopodiaceae *Chenopodium* sp.	1												1
Cyperaceae				1		1							2
cf. *Cyperus* sp.											1		1
cf. *Eleocharis* sp.				2				1					3
Leguminosae**				1	2				1			1	5

Continued on the next page

Table 5.1. Continued

Stratum/Level	Provenience*												
	5	9	9	10	10	12	12	14	14	16	18	20	Total
Malvaceae *Malvastrum* sp.		2	1	23	31	25	8	7	4	2	1		104
cf. *Sida* sp.				2				1	1		1		5
cf. Poaceae		1		9	15	2	2	3			1		33
Polygonaceae *Polygonum* sp.											1		1
Portulacaceae *Portulaca* sp.		1		10		9	1				1		22
Sapotaceae					1								1
Total	1	4	1	49	49	37	11	12	6	2	6	1	179
Starchy parenchyma		6	6	24	29	49	23	60	6	71	24	43	335

*For specific coordinates, levels, and features see Bonzani 1995:appendixes 2 and 3.
**The Leguminosae can be divided into three separate subfamilies: Mimosaceae, Caesalpiniaceae, and Fabaceae.

The Ecofactual Remains

the genus's distribution into the lowland regions of northern South America for this time period beyond its documented use by the Chibcha of the Andean highlands near present-day Bogotá (Wilson 1990). Whether the plant was growing wild or was cultivated, whether seeds were being carried into the area from other regions, or even whether the plant was being used at all cannot be determined at this time.

The macrobotanical remains recovered from strata 9 through 20 (dated to 5940 to 5190 years B.P.) include carbonized seeds of *Malvastrum* sp. (n = 104) (Malvaceae), *Portulaca* sp. (n = 22) (Portulacaceae), cf. *Sida* sp. (n = 5) (Malvaceae), *Eupatorium* sp. (n = 1) (Asteraceae), *Polygonum* sp. (n = 1) (Polygonaceae), cf. *Cyperus* sp. (n = 1) (Cyperaceae), cf. *Eleocharis* sp. (n = 3) (Cyperaceae), Cyperaceae (n = 2), and Leguminosae (n = 5, seeds and fruits) and carbonized culms, leaves, or other monocot plant parts identified tentatively as being from the grass family (cf. Poaceae, n = 33) (Table 5.1). Of note, although recovered by hand and not from the floated material, two fragments probably of one seed identified as belonging to the family Sapotaceae (H. Cuadros V., personal communication, 1992) were also recovered from a posthole in stratum 10. Other botanical remains that were initially thought to be small seeds of grasses (Bonzani 1995:152–154, 1997) have undergone further analysis and have been identified as spores of fungi (L. Newsom, personal communication, 2002). Some of the fungi were probably a wood-rotting type (i.e., *Polyporous* spp.) that would have come from dead branches collected from the ground and used for firewood. Genetic analyses on this material were attempted at the University of Missouri but the extraction of DNA from the carbonized samples failed (E. Buckler, personal communication, 1996).

Other starchy carbonized parenchyma fragments (n = 335) were also recovered from the site (Table 5.1) (Bonzani 1995), and carbon isotope analyses of three of these fragments from stratum 20 ($^{13}C/^{12}C$ ratio of −26.1, −25.3, and −23.6) revealed that they are from C3 plants (see Table 1.1) (Cerling 1999; Sage et al. 1999). One of these fragments had gross morphological characteristics similar to a maize cupule (the basic unit of an ear or cob from which two grains are born; Blake and Cutler 2001:95) but yielded a carbon isotope ratio of −23.6, verifying that it was not from maize (*Zea mays*) (Figure 5.1).[2] Another seed fragment from stratum 10 also yielded similar morphological characteristics to those found on maize kernels but probably also represents a fragmented seed from a C3 plant (Figure 5.2).[3] The rest of the fragments are currently undergoing analysis for identification. The parenchyma fragments were recovered from both floor and feature contexts and from all cultural strata excavated (strata 9 through 20).

An SEM study was also conducted on two samples of carbonized parenchyma recovered from stratum 10 at San Jacinto 1 and on carbonized samples

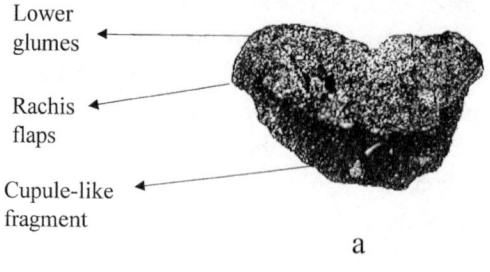

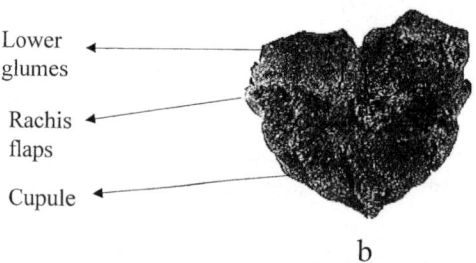

Figure 5.1. a, Fragment from San Jacinto 1, stratum 20 (location E23N27, stratum 20, Level 0–7). Dimensions are 9.9 × 6.4 × 3–3.4 mm (exterior width × fragment length × fragment thickness). b, Maize cupule fragment from the historic period Highbee Tavern site in Fayette County, Kentucky (15Fa222, Unit 10, N993 E1020, Feature 14, 25–56 cmbs). Dimensions of cupule are 9.5 × 7.4 × 4.5 mm.

of modern maize and teosinte. The identification of macrobotanical remains is based on comparison and similarities to modern examples of a known plant taxon in gross morphological characteristics and in the microstructural features of the seed surfaces as revealed in SEM photography (Barthlott 1984). In the case of maize, the mature kernel comprises a number of organs and tissues (Neuffer et al. 1997). These include the pericarp or outer wall. The aleurone or secondary layer follows this primary layer. Within the pericarp and the aleurone is the endosperm. The endosperm generally makes up the majority of the mass of the kernel and is the starchy food source for the enclosed embryo. These three layers reveal important microstructural features such that unidentified parenchyma fragments can be compared with modern reference materials of maize kernels.

Other structures of the maize kernel that can assist in identification are the scutellum and the abscission layer. The scutellum is the recessed area at the base of the kernel in which the embryo sits. It is a band of tissue positioned between the endosperm and the embryo. In carbonized fragments of maize

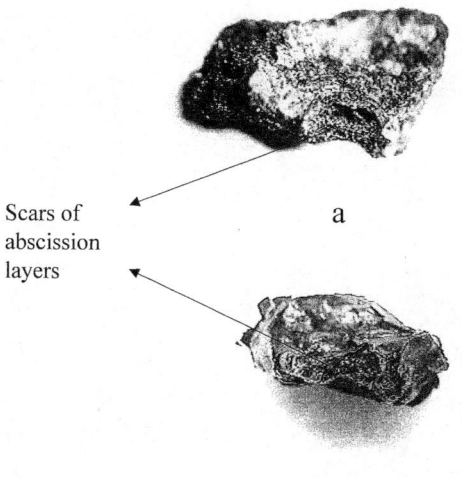

Figure 5.2. a, Seed fragment from stratum 10 (location E24N39, stratum 10, Level 11–20, Feature 31). Dimensions are 3.3 × 2.4 × 2.0 mm (width × depth × thickness). Note the possible scar of the abscission layer at the base of the fragment. Remnants of the pericarp are still visible on the specimen. b, Modern carbonized maize kernel with the scar of the abscission layer in evidence for comparison.

kernels the scutellum is often evident as a depression in the seed resulting from the loss and deterioration of the embryo and surrounding tissues. The abscission layer is the location on the maize kernel where the rachilla or flower stalk is attached. Upon carbonization the flower stalk is frequently lost, leaving the abscission layer as a prominent scar at the base of the kernel.

Utilizing SEM photography to reveal these structures, it was possible to compare modern carbonized kernels of maize (*Zea mays* L.) and modern carbonized kernels of northern teosinte (*Zea mays* ssp. *mexicana* x *Zea mays* ssp. *mays*) with the macrobotanical parenchyma fragments recovered from San Jacinto 1. Prior to SEM analysis, fresh or "green" cobs and kernels of maize were collected and carbonized for comparative purposes (Pearsall 2000:128–132). Dried kernels of teosinte were carbonized from stored reference material. All of the macrobotanical remains from San Jacinto 1 were recovered in a carbonized state.

Analyses of the parenchyma fragments from San Jacinto 1 utilizing SEM photography revealed structural similarities with both maize and teosinte but were inconclusive in allowing for the positive identification of the analyzed specimens from San Jacinto 1 (Figures 5.3, 5.4, 5.5, and 5.6). Samples of maize,

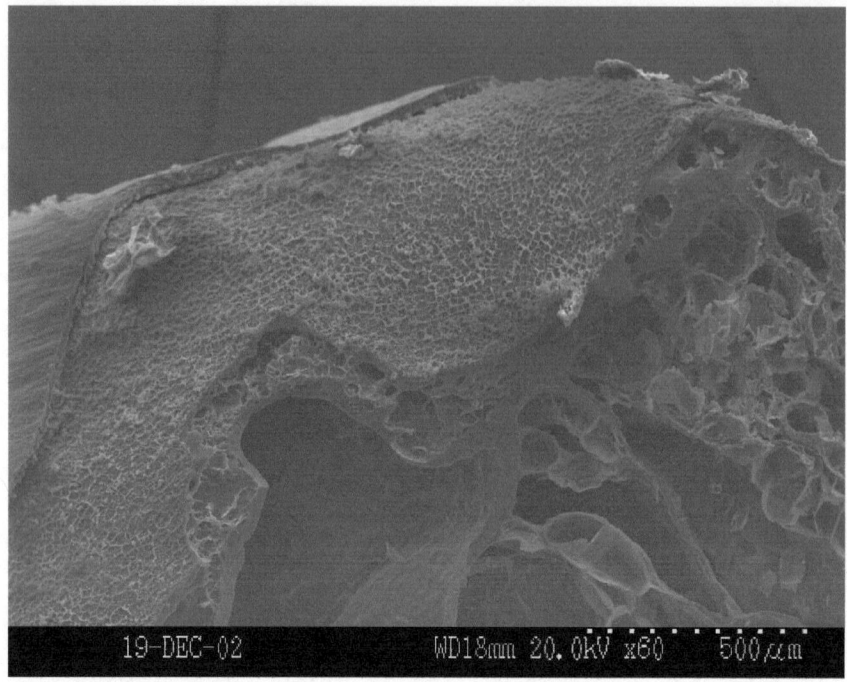

Figure 5.3. SEM photograph showing secondary layer or aleurone of modern carbonized maize kernel (*Zea mays*) (500 μm) (reference number 5MAIZKWALLD06). Diamond or tetragonal shapes evident in outline (top left).

teosinte, and the San Jacinto 1 material all reveal evidence of the three structural layers indicated as being the pericarp, aleurone, and endosperm. The pericarp is difficult to see in all of the examples and is present in the San Jacinto material as an ashy layer resulting from extensive burning and deterioration. However, the secondary layers or aleurones of all three specimens have a very similar primary sculpture or shape of the cells. In particular, diamond or tetragonal shapes are evident on the secondary layers in the samples of modern maize and teosinte and in the fragments from stratum 10 from San Jacinto 1. The endosperm is the most clearly prominent structure in all three specimens. Evident in the endosperm or tertiary layers is a pattern of cellular disintegration caused by heat expansion. The formations visible are probably due to shrinkage deformations of collapsing cells (Barthlott 1984). Both small- and large-scale collapse of cells and development of vesicles are evident and are expected to occur during carbonization particularly in structures with high water content (Hather 2000, 1993). Although enticing in their implications, these results have not led to any clear-cut possibilities for the identification of these fragments recovered from San Jacinto 1. A positive identification

The Ecofactual Remains 123

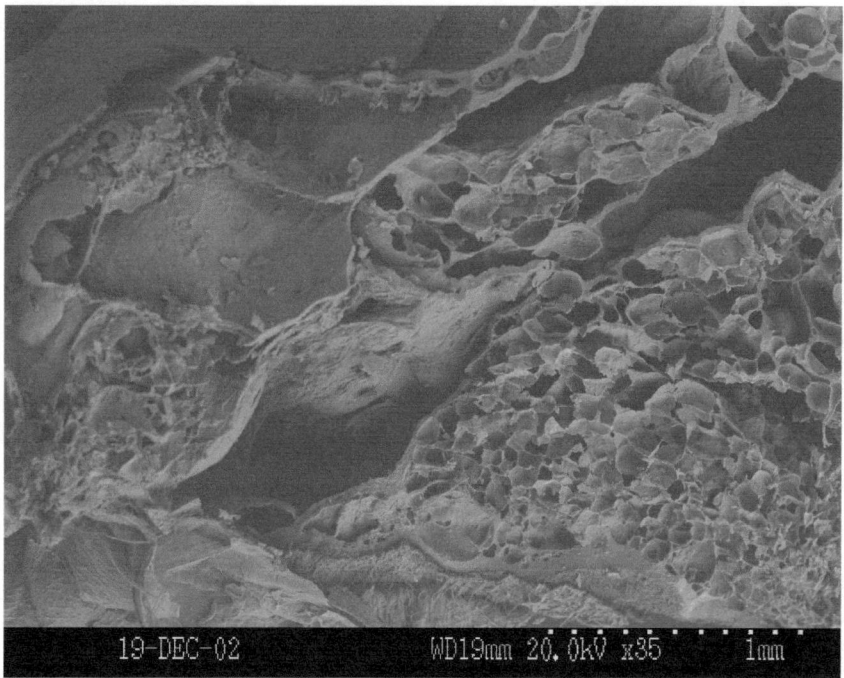

Figure 5.4. SEM photograph showing secondary layer or aleurone of modern carbonized northern teosinte kernel (*Zea mays* ssp. *mexicana* x *Zea mays* ssp. *mays*) (1 mm) (reference number 7bte035bback01). Diamond or tetragonal shapes evident in outline (top left).

must, therefore, await further study at various levels and with various forms of analysis.

However, the macrobotanical remains that were recovered and identified at the site do supply a wealth of information as to the diet and other uses of plants by the inhabitants and the environment and seasonality of the site's occupations. Not including the parenchyma fragments that still need to be identified, the most numerous plant remains recovered at the site to date are from the family Malvaceae. These include *Malvastrum* and seeds tentatively identified as *Sida*. Gentry (1993:591) notes that the genus *Malvastrum* is made up of 12 species of herbs found in dry inter-Andean valleys. Perez-Arbelaez (1978:476–477) notes that members of the genus are found in the lowlands as well as in colder climates in Colombia. The plants are rich in mucilage and the stalks enclose strong, useful fibers. In Tocaima, the leaves are used as brooms for sweeping (Perez-Arbelaez 1978:476–477). In the Department of Bolívar one member of the genus *Malvastrum americanum* is identified as a shrub and is noted to be found in areas disturbed by natural and human

Figure 5.5. SEM photograph showing secondary layer or aleurone of archaeological carbonized parenchyma fragment from San Jacinto 1 (1 mm) (location E27N41, stratum 10, Level 11–16, Feature 34) (reference number COSJ1761MM). Diamond or tetragonal shapes evident in outline (most obvious on left).

factors such as railroad tracks (Castañeda 1965:232–233). Seeds of the genus *Malvastrum* have also been recovered archaeologically at Pachamachay Cave, a hunting base camp in Peru. Its use there is unknown (Pearsall 1980).

Although *Malvastrum* was not recovered in collections of modern plants near the archaeological site, other members of the Malvaceae were. These included *Malachra rudis,* a bush that occupied ca. 26 percent of the area directly over the archaeological site and that was noted to have medicinal uses by local informants (Bonzani 1995, 1999). Cotton (*Gossypium* sp.) was also noted to be growing wild ca. 200 m from the archaeological site in tree and shrub growth near the stream of San Jacinto. Other members of the Malvaceae collected near the archaeological site included *Bastardia viscolor.* Another specimen of the Malvaceae, that of *Pavonia,* was collected ca. 7 km from San Jacinto 1 growing on the outskirts of a cultivated maize field.

The genus *Sida* occurs mostly as weeds in moist lowland areas in Colombia (Gentry 1993:584). The genus consists of 200 species, mostly herbs and shrubs, native to warm areas of the world, especially in the Americas (Schultes and Raffauf 1990:289). The general use of the species of this genus is to clarify

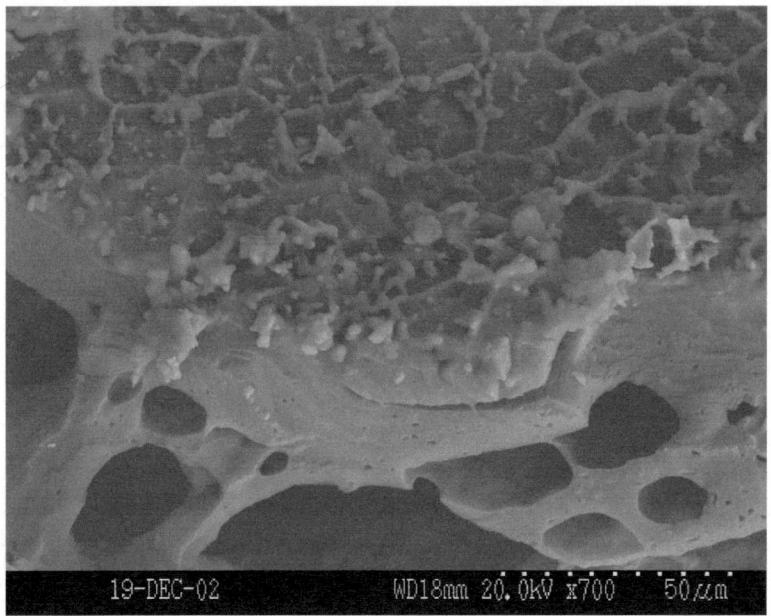

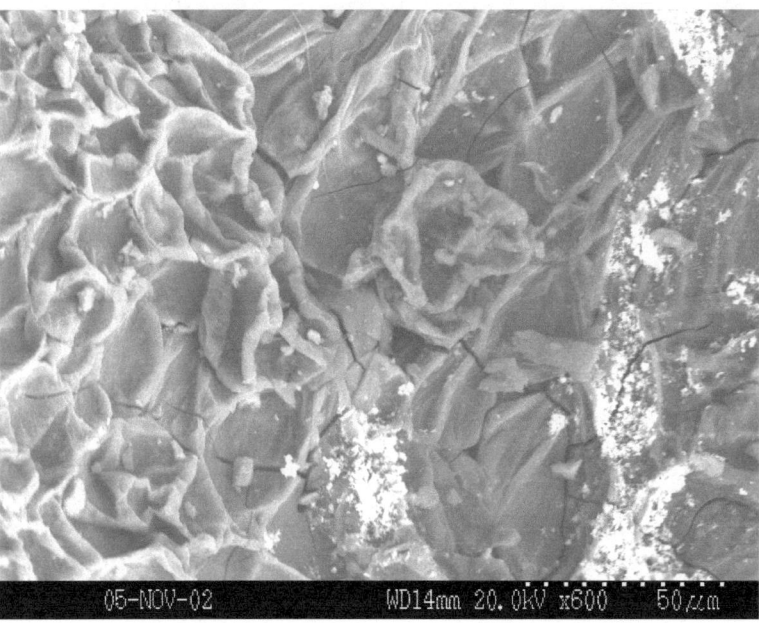

Figure 5.6. Close-up SEM photographs showing secondary layer or aleurone. Top, Modern carbonized northern teosinte kernel (*Zea mays* ssp. *mexicana* x *Zea mays* ssp. *mays*) (50 μm) (reference number 7bteoback04). Bottom, Archaeological carbonized parenchyma fragment from San Jacinto 1 (location E27N41, stratum 10, Level 11–16, Feature 34) (50 μm) (reference number COSJ179.PCI). Diamond or tetragonal shapes are evident in both specimens. Diamond or tetragonal shapes may be a characteristic of the family Poaceae or of the genus *Zea,* as these shapes also appear to occur in maize (see Figure 5.3).

honey to make *panela,* blocks of a mixture of sugar cane and honey, eaten alone or broken up and used like refined sugar (García Barriga 1992:II:184). Two specimens of *Sida rhombifolia* L. were collected at the end of October growing near the archaeological site of San Jacinto 1. Flowers were not yet open by the middle of October. Informants indicated that the plant is used medicinally and is applied to bites (Bonzani 1999). The species is noted to be very common in disturbed areas of hot climates. In popular medicine the species is used in Valle and in Cauca as an emollient. The aerial part of the plant is used in decoction and in baths to wash wounds and it is a good anti-irritant and anti-inflammatory agent (García Barriga 1992:II:184).

Use of the fibers from the stems of *Malvastrum* to make brooms for sweeping and perhaps its use to make cordage to bind up food wrapped in leaves for cooking in the earth ovens are possible reasons for the recovery of this plant from San Jacinto 1. The seeds were recovered from both floors (60 percent of the seeds recovered) and features (40 percent of the seeds recovered), with Feature 34 (stratum 10) having the highest number of these remains (n = 16) (Table 5.1). The recovery of *Sida* from strata 18, 14, and 10 potentially is most likely indicative of the naturally occurring vegetation in the area of San Jacinto 1 during the full range of its occupations from ca. 6000–5200 B.P. Medicinal uses of the genus may have occurred as well.

The carbonized culms, leaves, and other monocot plant parts identified tentatively as being from the grass family (cf. Poaceae) were the next most frequent type of macrobotanical remains recovered from San Jacinto 1. Of note, phytoliths of grasses were also identified from one sample sent for analysis that was collected from under a block metate found cached in situ in Feature 63 (D. Piperno, personal communication, 1995). The specific genus of the grass was undeterminable. Phytoliths of arrowroot (*Maranta arundinacea*) (Marantaceae) were also recovered from this sample. Arrowroot is a tropical forest understory herb that requires 1500–2000 mm per year of rainfall (Gentry 1993:148; Purseglove 1972) and may have had to be collected and brought to the site in a manner similar to the mollusks *Neocyclotus*. These mollusks are found in very humid environments with large amounts of palms and typical of the cloud forest located about 10 km from San Jacinto. The tubers of arrowroot are eaten and the leaves of other genera of the Marantaceae such as *Calathea* and *Heliconia* are used to wrap food for cooking. The leaves of maize are also used for the purpose of wrapping a mush of maize (*choclo*) in both dry and wet forms (Patiño 1990:171–172). The stems and leaves of members of the Marantaceae are also used for fibers to make baskets, hats, and other materials that require durable fibers (Patiño 1967:59–60). Phytoliths of arrowroot have also been recovered from early contexts in archaeological sites such as Cueva de los Vampiros (8600 B.P.) in the lowland tropics of Panama and Ecuador (Piperno and Pearsall 1998). The recovery of both grass and arrowroot phytoliths from Feature 63 (an earth oven) may indicate consumption of both grasses and arrowroot by the inhabitants at San Jacinto 1. It may also point to the use of the leaves of these plants for wrapping prepared foods or for their use as a source of fibers for basket making, pottery making, or other purposes.

Grasses grow in a variety of settings (Plazas et al. 1993; Sarmiento 1983, 1984) including areas naturally disturbed by flooding (Parsons 1980:268; Solbrig 1993), as is presently the case at San Jacinto. This habitat description readily agrees with geomorphological evidence of the location of San Jacinto 1 on a stream point bar that underwent seasonal flooding. Various specimens of grasses were collected in 1991 and 1992 growing wild near the archaeological site of San Jacinto 1 and the stream that cuts through the site (Table 5.2) (Bonzani 1995, 1998). Forty-three percent of these have their origins in Africa, indicating the substantial replacement of native grass species by foreign, introduced ones (Parsons 1980). In this region, the grasses are beginning to be pollinated at the end of October into November, with seed structures not yet developed. A cultivated specimen of *Zea mays* was also collected at the end of November from a field ca. 800 m to 1 km from the site and in association with manioc (*Manihot* sp.) and beans (*Phaseolus* spp. and *Vigna unguiculata*). Cobs were not yet ready for collection. Based on observation and informant interviews, the major planting of maize on terraces in the region occurs in September at the beginning of the rainy season and the fruit is harvested in January when the fruit and climate are both dry. A second minor planting occurs in April with collection during the shorter dry season in August (Bonzani 1998; Tovar n.d.:321).

The most important grass brought under domestication in the Americas is maize (*Zea mays*). The wild ancestor of maize is now almost completely accepted to be teosinte (Beadle 1972, 1980; Buckler et al. 1998; Doebley 1990; Gaut and Clegg 1993; Matsuoka et al. 2002; Wang et al. 1999), although debate in this regard continues (Eubanks 1995; also see Johannessen and Hastorf 1994). Six subspecies were initially considered to be potential ancestors of maize. Two of these (*Zea mays* ssp. *mexicana* and *Zea mays* ssp. *parviglumis*) are annuals and are the closest in morphology and other characteristics to domesticated maize. Genetic research has now indicated that the subspecies *parviglumis* is indistinguishable from maize, being closer to it than to other teosinte samples, and is most likely the ancestor of maize. The distribution of this subspecies is at elevations from 400 to 1200 m along the upper slopes of the central Balsas River in southwestern Mexico (Doebley 1990; Smith 1995).

The earliest macrobotanical evidence of maize in the form of desiccated cobs now comes from the highland site of Guilá Naquitz in the Valley of

Table 5.2. Grasses collected near the site in 1991–1992

Scientific Name	Spanish Common Name	Ref. No.*	Origin
Axonopus sp.	Pajita azul	RB 203	Americas
Cenchrus sp.	Cadillo	RB 249	Pan-tropical
Dichanthium aristatum	Unknown, possibly cochito or hanglito	RB 156	Africa
Dichanthium pertusa	Yerba zorrio	RB 175, 199	Africa
Digitaria insularis	Yerba de zorra, Yerba zorro	RB 157, 189	Tropical America
Hyparrhenia rufa	Faragua	RB 161	Africa
Lasiacis sorghoidea	Bambu, granadilla	RB 162, 217	Unknown
Panicum maximum	Guinea, mirable	RB 155, 158	Africa
Paspalum plicatum var. *villosisimum*	Yerba de zorra	RB 188	Tropical America
Paspalum virgatum	Pajon	RB 210	Tropical America
Sorghum halapense	Pasto gigante, sorgo, yerba vero	RB 139, 208	Africa
Sorghum sudanense	Sorgo migo	RB 251	Africa
Sporobolus indicus	Yerba estrella	RB 187	Pan-tropical
Zea mays	Maíz	RB 218	Tropical America

*Designates reference turned in to the herbaria at JBGP and COL in Colombia.

Oaxaca, Mexico. Cobs from this site have yielded direct AMS dates of 5420 and 5410 B.P. (Benz 2001; Piperno and Flannery 2001; also see Flannery 1986; Iltis 2000; Long et al. 1989; MacNeish 1967; Smalley and Blake 2003; Smith 1997). Other early remains of maize come from the Tehuacán Valley, also in the highlands about 250 km from the Balsas River (MacNeish et al. 1972). In this valley more than 24,000 specimens of cobs, kernels, and smaller husks, leaves, tassel fragments, and so on were recovered. The earliest specimens are from the San Marcos Cave and Coxcatlán Cave initially dated to 5050 to 3550 B.C. (7000 to 5500 B.P.) (Smith 1995). The earliest dates on the maize from Tehuacán, however, are now discarded since direct AMS radiocarbon dates on the 12 primitive cobs from San Marcos and Coxcatlán yielded dates ranging from 2750 B.C. to A.D. 400 (4700 to 1600 B.P.). The four oldest from San Marcos dated from 2750 to 2650 B.C. (4700 to 4600 B.P.) (Long et al. 1989; Smith 1995). Other evidence from cobs recovered from numerous sites in Mesoamerica yields evidence of past use of maize. In the Valley of Oaxaca (Guilá Naquitz) pollen of *Zea mays* ssp. *mexicana* also occurs at 7400–6700 B.C.; at the site of San Andrés on the Gulf Coast of Mexico maize pollen dates to 7100 years ago; at Tamaulipas the species occurs at ca. 2500 B.C.; and in the Basin of Mexico pollen from the species occurs at ca. 5200–200 B.C. (McClung de Tapia 1992; Piperno 2001).

In the interior of Colombia some evidence for plant use and early agriculture has come from a pollen core taken during the Calima project in southwestern Colombia. This study has revealed maize pollen in the region dated to 7000 B.P. (Pearsall and Piperno 1990). Evidence for pollen from maize and manioc dated to 4380 and 4695 B.P. also comes from archaeological sites in Araracuara in the Colombian Amazon (Herrera et al. 1992). Indications of plant processing at El Pital (ca. 6500 B.P.) (Salgado 1987) and of a shift from manioc to maize utilization at the Momil sites (ca. 2150 B.P.) (Reichel-Dolmatoff and Dussan 1956) have also been discussed. The evidence for plant use at Momil is in the form of ceramic *budares* and lithic grater chips for manioc and metates and manos for maize.

Macrobotanical and microbotanical remains of maize have been recovered from other sites in South and Central America and the Caribbean (see Newsom and Deagan 1994; Newsom and Pearsall 2003; Pearsall 2003; Piperno and Pearsall 1998 for a review of these sites). Based on phytolithic evidence from the preceramic sites of the Las Vegas tradition (Stothert 1985, 1988), maize cultivation appears to begin in Ecuador by about 8000–7000 B.P. The environmental context for this tradition is one of a long dry season with a short wet one that resulted in relatively open grasslands with forest cover along rivers (Stothert 1985:630). Phytolithic evidence also indicates maize production at the early ceramic site of Real Alto by the beginning of its occupation

(5150 B.P.) (Pearsall and Piperno 1990). Macrobotanical remains, pollen, and phytoliths of maize as well as pollen from the common bean, papa (*Solanum tuberosum*), quinua (*Chenopodium quinoa*), chocho (*Lupinus mutabilis*), and oca (*Oxalis tuberosa*) were recovered from the Formative village of Cotocollao dating to ca. 3450 B.P. in the highland environment of Ecuador (Villalba 1988:329–344). Macrobotanical remains of maize in the form of cobs, leaves, and kernels were also recovered from the site of Los Gavilanes in Peru (Bonavia 1982; Bonavia and Grobman 1989). Other sites in Peru with maize in preceramic contexts have been reported, though skepticism continues to exist in regard to accepting this information (Bonavia and Grobman 1999; McK. Bird 1984). Maize also occurred in Panama by about 7000 B.P., as evidenced by pollen and phytolithic remains at Cueva de Los Ladrones (Cooke and Ranere 1992a; Piperno et al. 1985). Norr (1984), however, believes that the incorporation of maize into subsistence strategies was only very gradual in Panama. The remains of other grasses have also been recovered archaeologically in South America, including at Chilca Caves on the Peruvian coast dated to between 4200 and 2500 B.C. (Engel 1970, 1973) and at Pachamachay Cave in the highlands of Peru (Pearsall 1980).

Although no definitive evidence of the use of maize at San Jacinto 1 has been recovered to date, there are clear indications from the ground stone technology recovered that grinding of seeds (probably of C_3 plants) was occurring at the site. The seeds were most likely ground using the metates and manos and made into a humid mush or *masa*. The initial humid state of the carbonized fragments recovered from San Jacinto 1 is indicated by the fracturing and expansion of the endosperm that resulted in the numerous vesicles observable in the remains (see Figures 5.2, 5.5, and 5.6). These vesicles occur when plant tissues are in a fresh state and water content is high (Hather 1993, 2000). Charring of dried plant tissue results in few vesicles and good preservation, which was not the case with the remains recovered from San Jacinto 1.

The *masa* could then have been consumed as a fermented beverage with the use of the pottery vessels for serving or fermenting the drink (Oyuela-Caycedo 1995b; Pratt 1999a, 1999b). It could also have been cooked in the earth ovens most likely in the form of a *bollo limpio,* or *masa* wrapped in leaves and steamed in the earth ovens. This practice is common in San Jacinto today, although the *bollo limpio* is boiled and not steamed and is made of maize (Montes and Montes 1975). These food products can be conserved for seven to eight days and it is unlikely that the occupations at San Jacinto 1 lasted for much longer than this.

Seeds of *verdolaga* or purslane (*Portulaca* sp.) of the family Portulacaceae were the next most common macrobotanical remains identified from the site to date. The family consists of about 20 genera and 500 species of annual or

The Ecofactual Remains

perennial herbs and shrubs. The family is distributed worldwide with a focus in western North America and southern South America. The weed *Portulaca oleracea* is at times used as a potherb and in salads. The family is also important for some ornamentals (Jones and Luchsinger 1986:329–331). Archaeologically, in Colombia at the site of Monsú located on the Canal del Dique, an old branch of the Magdalena River on the Caribbean coast, four seeds identified to the family Portulacaceae (Caryophyllaceae) were recovered for the Macaví Period in contexts dating to between 1800 and 1600 B.C. (Reichel-Dolmatoff 1985:171). Members of the genus *Portulaca* have also been recovered at numerous archaeological sites in North America and Europe (Bonzani 1984; Canal and Rovira 1999; Smith 1992:113; Yarnell 1986).

The recovery of 22 seeds of *Portulaca* from stratum 18 through 9 at San Jacinto 1 and its known use as a food allow for the interpretation that this genus may have been used as a food at the site throughout its periods of occupation from ca. 6000 to 5200 B.P. Further, the plant's recovery in all instances but one (one seed was from a posthole) was from floor contexts and the midden and not from the fire-pit or earth oven features. These data indicate that the genus may have been part of meals that were prepared and eaten on the spot and that it was not part of the food being cooked in the fire-pits. Since purslane is a weed, these seeds may also have been part of the background vegetation.

Other identified plant remains from San Jacinto 1 occurred in lesser quantities. These include *Eupatorium* sp. (Asteraceae), *Polygonum* sp. (Polygonaceae), cf. *Cyperus* sp. (Cyperaceae), cf. *Eleocharis* sp. (Cyperaceae), and other members of the families Cyperaceae, Leguminosae, and Sapotaceae. These identifications confirm the presence of these genera and families at San Jacinto 1 from 5,000 to 7,000 years ago and they yield important evidence as to the site's environmental location and seasonality of occupations.

Eupatorium comprises 600 known species (see Gentry 1993:343–348). The literature indicates that all of the species of *Eupatorium* are tonics, sudorifics, febrifugals, and ordinarily emmenagogues; others are also aromatics and diaphoretics and the roots have anticephalalgic properties (García Barriga 1992: III:345–346; Perez-Arbelaez 1978:296). One specimen of *Eupatorium* was collected with flowers in mid-November from near the archaeological site in an area not cultivated for about 10 years.

The genus *Polygonum* comprises 300 species including temperate and Old World taxa. These species are weedy or semiaquatic and usually succulent herbs (García Barriga 1992:I:284; Gentry 1993:693–698; Spjut 1994). Archaeologically, members of the genus *Polygonum* have been recovered in early contexts (5050 B.C.) from sites in North America, causing it to be grouped with "early successional floodplain plant species" and adaptations geared toward their collection (Smith 1992:102). Knotweed (*Polygonum erectum*) is considered part of the Eastern Agricultural Complex of plants initially domesticated in eastern North America (Smith 1992; Yarnell 1986). Several species of *Polygonum* have edible seeds and have also been recovered archaeologically in Europe (Bonzani 1984; Canal and Rovira 1999; Martínez 1999; Renfrew 1973).

The Cyperaceae are grasslike herbs with linear leaves and usually triangular stems. Sedges are especially common in swampy settings. The genus *Cyperus* comprises 600 species including those from the Old World. It is the most common genus of sedges found in the neotropics, tending like the other members of the family to be found in swampy areas (Gentry 1993:120). It is also found in disturbed flooded areas (Wijmstra 1967).

Several members of the genus have medicinal and ritual uses. For instance, in the Amazonian regions of Colombia, Ecuador, Peru, Bolivia, and westernmost Brazil, members of the genus *Cyperus* are cultivated by the Sharanahuas to be used in ritual shaman activities. In this case the rhizomes are pulverized and the powder is placed in a decoction made with the hallucinogenic vines of *ayahuasca* (*Banisteriopsis caapi*) and drunk. In Colombia, Kofán women boil the roots and drink the tea to correct menstrual problems. It is also considered a regulator of menstruation by the Sionas and Secoyas, located in Ecuador and Colombia, and is considered a strong contraceptive by the Tukanos in Brazil (Schultes and Raffauf 1990:157–158). Two species of the genus were collected from October through December in 1991 near the archaeological site of San Jacinto 1 in an area not cultivated for about 10 years. These include *Cyperus odoratus* L. and *Cyperus rotundus* L. A rhizome of *C. odoratus* was collected at the beginning of December and seeds of *C. rotundus* were collected in mid-November. No information was available in the literature concerning the uses of *C. odoratus* (Castañeda 1965; García Barriga 1992; Perez-Arbelaez 1978; Schultes and Raffauf 1990). The tuberous rhizomes of *C. rotundus* are used in popular medicine in Colombia, dried, as powder or in decoction. The dry tubers with yogurt are used to cure ulcers of the uterus opening (*cuello*). Use of the tuber is also said to cure diarrhea from whatever cause and to cure hemorrhaging in any part or organ of the body. It is also indicated to cure problems of arterial pressure, can eliminate intestinal parasites, and can help with stomach gases (García Barriga 1992:III:503–505).

Bulbs of *Cyperus* and/or *Scirpus* were eaten during the Peruvian preceramic and on the coast and in the Andean cordilleras of Ecuador between 5200 and 2500 B.P. (as cited in Cooke 1992b:45). The tubers of wild nut-grass (*Cyperus rotundus*) were eaten extensively at Wadi Kubbaniya in Egypt during the late Paleolithic (19,00 to 17,000 B.P.) with *Cyperus* species use continuing into the Epipaleolithic at various Qarunian sites (9050 to 7980 B.P.) (Hillman 1989; Wetterstrom 1993). *Cyperus* sp. remains have also been recovered in

Mesoamerica in the Basin of Mexico at the Loma Torremonte site dated to ca. 650–300 B.C. and at Terremote dated to 400–200 B.C. (McClung de Tapia 1992).

The genus *Eleocharis* comprises 150 species including those from the Old World. The genus is leafless with round hollow stems and it occurs in swampy or marshy conditions (Gentry 1993:120–122). Some members of the genus (*E. geniculata* [L.] R. et S.) have stems sufficiently flexible and long to be used to make woven mats or wickerwork-type objects. The genus is also used medicinally as a tonic in Venezuela (Perez-Arbelaez 1978:281). A potential use of the plant in matting or bedding for short-term stays at San Jacinto 1 or in basketry is a possibility based on current ethnographic uses of the genus (Perez-Arbelaez 1978:281).

The Leguminosae are a heterogeneous group of leguminous plants traditionally identified as one family with three subfamily divisions. The family is one of the largest and consists of 600 genera with approximately 13,000 species. The division into three separate subfamilies is based on differences in floral structure (see Jones and Luchsinger 1986:356–361). Mimosaceae (Mimosoideae) are mainly tropical and subtropical trees and shrubs. Caesalpiniaceae (Caesalpinoideae) are mainly tropical and subtropical trees and shrubs, and Fabaceae (Papilionoideae) are mainly temperate, tropical, and subtropical herbs, though trees and shrubs do occur. Numerous members of the Caesalpinoideae are medicinal or yield dyes, timber, and ornamentals. For instance, many species of *Senna* are cultivated for their leaves, which yield senna, a base for a laxative (García Barriga 1992:I:434–468; Jones and Luchsinger 1986:358–359). The Fabaceae are an important source of high-protein food and oil and provide forage food, ornamentals, dye, and other uses (Jones and Luchsinger 1986:360–361). The Mimosaceae are of little economic importance except for some timber and ornamentals and as the source of gum arabic or gum acacia (*Acacia senegal* or *A. arabica*) (García Barriga 1992:I:407–408). However, mesquite (*Prosopis*) is an important weedy tree of the arid southwestern United States and Mesoamerica and remains of the use of the fruit as a food have been found archaeologically (Jones and Luchsinger 1986:358; McClung de Tapia 1992; MacNeish 1967; Minnis 1992).

The Sapotaceae family consists of 35 to 40 genera and some 700 species of shrubs and trees. The members are distributed throughout the tropics of both hemispheres. Many species have latex, as for instance *chicle* (*Achras zapota*), and some have edible fruits. Two such species that probably had their origins in Central or South America include *caimito* (*Chrysophyllum cainito* L.) and sapodilla or *níspero* (*Manilkara zapota* [L.] P. von Royen. Syn: *Achras zapota* L.). Caimito is also indicated to have originated along the dry zones of the Magdalena River in Colombia (Bartholomäus et al. 1990:29; Brücher

1989:246; Food and Agriculture Organization of the United Nations 1986:181; García Barriga 1992:II:366–368; Perez-Arbelaez 1978:685–686; Schultes and Raffauf 1990:410; Spjut 1994). Members of this family fruit in December through February in the San Jacinto area (Bonzani 1998, 1995:table 3.17), though immature fruits of *níspero* were seen as early as October. Remains from this family are also noted to occur in preceramic sites in Panama and Colombia and in the early ceramic site of Loma Alta in Ecuador and could have been used as food (Cooke 1992b:48; Pearsall 2003:223; Piperno and Pearsall 1998:205, 217, 249, 252, 293).

Based on the known ethnographic uses of the plants recovered and identified to date from San Jacinto 1, a number of possible uses and activities can be interpreted from these remains. First of all, it appears to be very likely that both grasses and tubers possibly of arrowroot (*Maranta arundinacea*) and of sedges (*Cyperus* spp.) were utilized for food at the site and were cooked in the earth oven features. The recovery of large numbers of metates and manos also indicates the processing of seeds. The leaves of grasses or of members of the Marantaceae may also have been used to wrap the mush or processed foods that were to be cooked in the earth ovens. The leaves or culms of grasses are noted to have been utilized in the fiber of the pottery at San Jacinto 1 (Raymond et al. 1998).

The herb purslane (*Portulaca* sp.) and fruits of the Sapotaceae were probably also eaten at the site on an occasional basis. Other recovered botanical remains (*Malvastrum* sp., cf. *Eleocharis* sp., members of the Marantaceae) are used for fibers in making baskets, mats, brooms, or other tools and these uses and associated activities (collecting, sleeping, cleaning) may also have occurred at the site 5,000 to 6,000 years ago. Other medicinal and ritual uses of many of the identified plants (*Cyperus* spp., *Eupatorium* sp., cf. *Sida* sp., cf. *Eleocharis* sp.) are also known ethnographically.

In general, the botanical remains indicate that the site was in a dry or savanna-like setting with grasses and members of the mallow family (Malvaceae) predominating. They also indicate that the site was close to water or in a semiaquatic location. This information would agree with soil analyses that yield evidence that the site was located on a seasonally flooded point bar. This environmental context would account for the occurrence of taxa that require wet or swampy conditions and disturbed habitats even if the overall precipitation pattern was drier than today.

THE MOLLUSK REMAINS RECOVERED, USES, AND CLIMATIC CHANGES

The most abundant faunal remains at the site in terms of number, volume, and weight of specimens are represented by mollusks. A total of 24,505 individuals were classified in the field according to type of form. Later, a sample from each of these types was classified by Juan Parodiz (Carnegie Museum of Natural History, Invertebrate Section, Pittsburgh, Pennsylvania) (Table 5.3; totals for the two species of *Pomacea* are combined).

The snails recovered correspond to two classes. The first and most abundant are operculated land snails of the class Prosobranchia within the families Ampullariidae and Thiaridae. These land snails have an operculum that can be used to seal the opening of the shell. The second type corresponds to the true land snails of the class Pulmonates. Four species were identified in the first class and three species were identified in the second (Table 5.3). Freshwater bivalves were also recovered in lesser quantity. Two species were identified corresponding to the family Mycetopodidae and three species correspond to the family of Hyriidae (Table 5.3).

Land snails (Pulmonates) are considered to be ecologically sensitive to vegetation, humidity, and temperature. Among the three species encountered in the excavation there is good information for two as regards their ecology. These two are the tree snails of the species *Drymaeus* sp., possibly *virgulatus* (Férussac) and *Orthalicus maracaibensis* (Pfeiffer, 1856), reported also as *Orthalicus undatus* (Bruguiére). The ecological information that exists for these genera is from the Sierra Nevada de Santa Marta (Breure 1984) and from the Cordillera de la Costa National Park "Henry Pittier" in Venezuela. The data from both areas confirm that all the species of these two genera are found in association with dry xerophytic communities or thorn woodlands under arid conditions. This environment has precipitation below 500 mm per year. In this environment in northern Colombia the most common family of trees is the Mimosaceae. The recovery of these land snails is indicative of a past environment more arid than today that corroborates the climatic interpretation based on pollen column analyses and shell midden formation.

Other ecological data, very important for the analysis of human mobility, are in regard to the genus *Neocyclotus* (also a land snail of the class Prosobranchia). This genus is found in very humid environments with large amounts of palms, typical of cloud forest. This environment is also known as subandean forest; it has high levels of permanent atmospheric humidity and can support growth of epiphytic Bromeliaceae. The implications of finding this genus that is adapted to a totally different altitudinal environmental niche than the two pulmonate species are addressed below.

Certain trends are also recognizable in relation to changes observed in the stratigraphy between the occurrences of *Pomacea* and *Neocyclotus* (both of the class Prosobranchia). One is noted when the relationship between the two genera in the stratigraphy is examined. The second is noted in relation to the frequency of opercula found in the strata. In the first relationship a correlation is observed between the two genera through the cultural strata (Pearson's cor-

Table 5.3. Stratigraphic distribution of mollusks

	Stratum									
	9	10	11	12	13	14	16	18	20	Total
Bivalvia--Freshwater										
Family Mycetopodidae										
Anodontites hyrioides (Ortmann)	0	1	0	1	0	1	3	0	0	6
Family Hyriidae										
Diplodon sp.	275	646	5	78	0	2	1	0	0	1,007
Ecuadorea hylaeus (d'Orbigny)	1	0	0	0	0	0	0	0	0	1
Prisodon alatus (Sowerby)	0	0	0	0	0	0	1	0	0	1
Gastropoda, Prosobranchia--Operculated Land or Freshwater										
Family Ampullariidae										
Pomacea cornucopia (Reeve) and *Pomacea elegans* (d'Orbigny)	1,940	7,044	133	2,319	98	773	1,733	266	2	14,308
Neocyclotus cfr. *dysoni* (Pfeiffer)	402	2,185	34	1,885	99	1,270	2,649	614	6	9,144
Family Thiaridae										
Doryssa sp. affinis *D. atra* (Richards)	0	0	0	0	0	1	2	0	0	3

	Pulmonates, Bulimulidae (True Land Snails)									
Drymaeus sp. possibly *virgulatus* (Férussac), genus of tree snails. *Sultana kelleti* (Reeve)	0	5	0	0	0	0	0	0	0	5
Orthalicus maracaibensis (Pfeiffer, 1856), reported also as *Orthalicus undatus* (Bruguiére), genus of tree snails	14	6	0	4	0	1	0	0	0	25
Pulmonates, not identified	3	0	0	1	0	0	0	0	0	4
Prosobranchia, marine, Conidae. *Conus* sp. probably from debris of nearby geological deposit	0	0	0	0	1	0	0	0	0	1
Total	2,635	9,887	172	4,289	197	2,048	4,389	880	8	24,505

Table 5.4. Percentage of *Pomacea cornucopia* and *Pomacea elegans* (PC) in relation to *Neocyclotus* cfr. *dysoni* (ND) by stratum

Stratum	n*	% PC	% ND
9	2,342	82.8352	17.1648
10	9,229	76.3246	23.6754
12	4,204	55.1618	44.8382
14	2,043	37.8365	62.1635
16	4,382	39.5482	60.4518
18	880	30.2273	69.7727
20	8	25	75

*Number of individuals.

relation of 0.651), wherein the percentage of *Neocyclotus* decreases in relation to *Pomacea* (Table 5.4). This change is due to unclear factors and numerous interpretations can be put forth, one being that a reduction in the mobility of the group occurred (fewer trips during the dry season to collect the species of *Neocyclotus* for beads; see below). The other interpretation is that a gradual climatic change led to a drier climate and more arid landscape, affecting the distribution of *Neocyclotus*. The second interpretation seems to corroborate the paleoclimatic evidence of increasing dryness and reduction of humid forest.

One of the problems encountered when dealing with mollusks is recognizing whether their integration into the archaeological record is the result of natural or of human activity. Mollusks were encountered in two contexts. First, freshwater snails formed clear spatial clusters, suggesting one single episode of deposition on a cultural floor (see Figure 3.11). Second, bivalves, freshwater snails, and land snails were found dispersed and redeposited in cultural strata and in the refill of some features. In the exploratory analysis of the spatial distribution of the two genera (*Pomacea* and *Neocyclotus*), a multimodal distribution was expected to occur in stratum 9. The two genera were expected to form clusters and to be localized in the same spots as a result of being collected in a mixed form. This type of collection was assumed to have occurred as a result of their ecological and morphological similarities, both being found close to or in freshwater environments and being members of the same family. At that point in the research the difference in econiche that occurs between members of the *Pomacea* and *Neocyclotus* was not known.

The results of the spatial analysis were different from that which was initially expected. First, there is practically no correlation in the spatial distribution of the two genera (Pearson's correlation of 0.084) in stratum 9, which indicates that different task groups very likely collected them for different

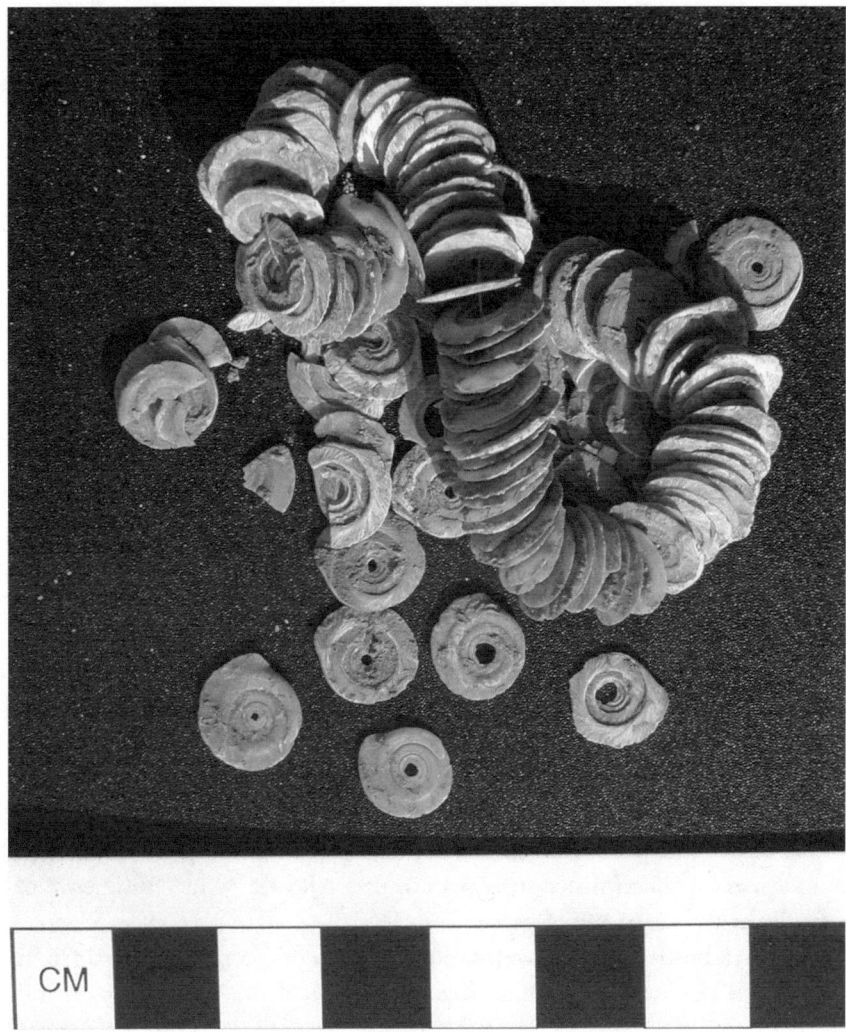

Figure 5.7. Beads made from the opercula of *Neocyclotus* (surface collection from San Jacinto 2; beads identical to those found at San Jacinto 1).

purposes. It is now known that the *Neocyclotus* were collected in an econiche distant from the site and were exploited for making beads (Figure 5.7). Second, a multimodal distribution of the two genera in stratum 9 is observed statistically using the coefficient of variation (Table 5.5). Comparing these variations indicates that the two genera do not overlap and that they are concentrated in separate clusters on the floor, with *Neocyclotus* being more spatially concentrated than *Pomacea*. The most interesting difference in the distribution of *Pomacea cornucopia* (Reeve) and *Pomacea elegans* (d'Orbigny) in

Table 5.5. Basic statistics of the freshwater snails *Pomacea* and *Neocyclotus* by number of individuals

	n*	Min.	Max.	Mean	Standard Deviation	Coefficient of Variation	Variance Mean Ratio
Pomacea	75	0	109	25.867	22.685	0.877	19.88
Neocyclotus	75	0	76	5.36	9.68	1.806	17.48

*Number of excavated square units from stratum 9.

relation to the *Neocyclotus* is the separate distribution of the two genera on the cultural floor (Figure 5.8).

What is the reason for the spatial differentiation between these two genera? The available evidence favors the interpretation that *Neocyclotus* was exploited mainly for extracting the opercula to make beads whereas the *Pomacea* were exploited for food. This differentiation in selection would generate the pattern observed. Furthermore, there is also ecological evidence that supports the argument that the two genera are found in very different ecological niches. *Pomacea* spp. would have been collected in the San Jacinto stream beside the site, probably by children, during the dry season when the snails were easier to find. On the other hand, *Neocyclotus* sp. would have been gathered in the humid forest of the Serranía very likely by a task group of male hunters who traveled there and returned the same day. Another part of the group is expected to have stayed at the site dedicated to plant collecting and processing of foods. As a consequence, this pattern can reflect a gender difference of activities as well as of use of space.

The first beads were recovered during fieldwork conducted in 1986 at San Jacinto 1 as well as at the nearby archaeological site, San Jacinto 2. Initially, it was not recognized from what part of the shell the beads were made. There were no previous reports of the use or discovery of opercula in archaeological contexts in Colombia or in the neotropics until those recovered from San Jacinto 1 were identified as calcified opercula from the genus *Neocyclotus*. The operculum is the plate that closes the snail's aperture when it retracts into the shell. It is located on the dorsal surface of the posterior part of the foot and is used to protect the snail from predators as well as to maintain its interior humidity during the dry season. The structure of the operculum is complex and is formed by calcareous layers. The operculum is considered to be part of the shell (Hunt 1976) and, as a consequence, may be a very good marker of seasonal growth and a means to measure the season when the specimen was killed. These same determinations can be done with the shell. The recovered opercula were perforated in the middle. Considering their form and

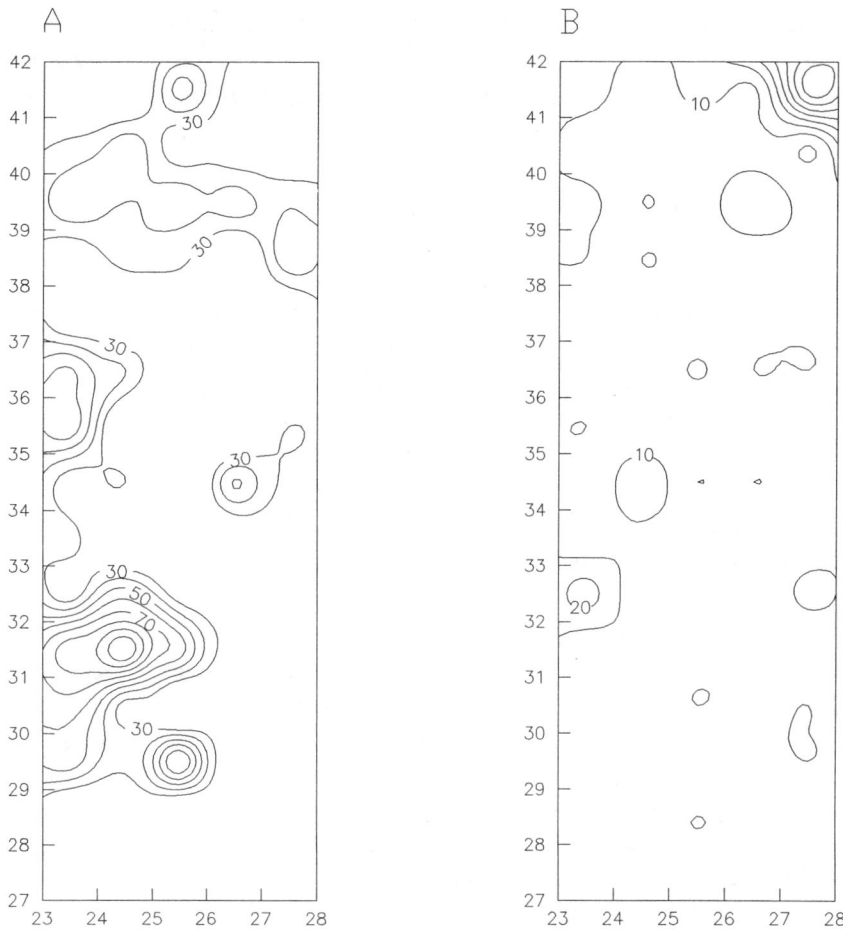

Figure 5.8. Distribution of *Pomacea* spp. (A) and *Neocyclotus* cfr. *dysoni* (B) in stratum 9.

the concentrations in which they were found, they seem to have been used as beads (there are a few cases in which some beads were made using the shell itself in imitation of the form and size of the operculum). All the snails used for this purpose correspond to adults between four and six years old, assuming that the dark marks of the shell and operculum correspond to halted growth periods during yearly dry seasons and considering the homogeneous size of the opercula as well as of the shells. The similar size of the shells and of the opercula and the age of the snails confirm the selective behavior involved in the collecting process of the specimens.

The occurrence and high ubiquity of specimens of *Pomacea* spp. in numerous strata at San Jacinto 1 also indicate a strategy of food use that focused on the seasonal availability of foods. Based on the likely collection of *Pomacea* during the dry season, the site appears to have been utilized during this season on a yearly basis. Few other mollusks or faunal remains were recovered that would point to the occupation of the site at other times of the year.

CONCLUSION

In conclusion, various types of information can be gathered from an analysis of the faunal and botanical remains from San Jacinto 1. First of all, data from the genera of snails recovered at the site and palynological studies from the region (Van der Hammen 1974, 1983; Van der Hammen et al. 1991) point to a drier environment than today's, potentially with precipitation around 500 mm per year. The recovery of grasses, abundant wood, and the seeds of *Malvastrum* also indicates an environment that had all of these resources available for use and one that would have been relatively dry given the present-day habitat of *Malvastrum* and the other remains identified (Gentry 1993:591). Given this information, the environment during the occupations of San Jacinto 1 can probably be defined as savanna woodland to tree and/or shrub savanna (Sarmiento 1983:246–247, table 10.1). These definitions correspond to Harris's (1980) subhumid to semiarid savanna types. The dry season would most likely have been from 5 to 7.5 months in duration, though a longer duration of the dry season cannot be ruled out at this time.

The macrobotanical remains also clearly indicate that the site was located along the stream to which its present location corresponds. These remains include the Cyperaceae and members of the genera *Polygonum, Portulaca,* and tentatively *Sida,* all of which are found in disturbed, semiaquatic econiches along bodies of water (Gentry 1993). This semiaquatic setting would have provided an ideal location for the collection of seasonally abundant resources, most likely after the floodwaters and rains in the region subsided. The current major rainy season in this region runs from September or October to November, with October receiving the highest amount of precipitation (see Figure 1.6).

The seasonality of the site's occupations has also been established to be at the beginning of the dry season when the botanical remains recovered would have had fruits and seeds that were incorporated into the archaeological context. On the north coast of Colombia this period would correspond to December to January and possibly the end of November, depending on the length of the dry and rainy seasons. Grasses, for instance, begin pollination in October and November in this area, develop inflorescence in November and December, and have died off by January. Members of the Sapotaceae and Caesalpiniaceae (subfamily of the Leguminosae) also fruit at this time of year in this region (end of October through March). No botanical remains that correspond to other times of the year were recovered from the site to date.

Data on plant use at the site are indicative of the intensification in the use of C3 plants and possibly grasses and roots such as arrowroot (*Maranta arundinacea*). However, further evidence indicating their storage at an associated base camp would add support to this argument. No evidence of storage has been found to exist at the site to date. No plant remains were recovered from the site that would indicate a period corresponding to planting or collection before the rainy season in September–October. Instead, the seasonality of the recovered botanical remains is better explained by collecting along the floodplain of the stream of San Jacinto after the rainy season in November to December. The resources from C3 plants were probably collected in a fresh or green state and then ground using the abundant number of ground stones recovered from the site. In addition to these foods, other resources such as roots were probably cooked in the earth ovens as well, and herbs like purslane and fruits such as those from the Sapotaceae family were most likely eaten at the site. Other plants recovered from the site may have been used for their strong fibers to make matting, baskets, or brooms or potentially for ritual or medicinal uses.

As indicated by the recovery of the mollusks of *Neocyclotus* and the collection of other localized mollusk species, the territoriality of the groups occupying San Jacinto 1 would have been restricted. However, different ecological settings were utilized, which points to the likelihood that a centralized base camp was occupied at various times of the year from which task groups would have left to visit these other ecological settings to collect resources.

6   San Jacinto 1 in Perspective

The site of San Jacinto 1 has proven to be a fascinating one, well worth the effort of excavating through a deep stratigraphy of alluvial soils. The site has yielded a rich context of material including the earliest fiber-tempered pottery recovered in the New World. From San Jacinto 1, we can begin to get an understanding of ways of life that are usually invisible and undiscovered due to the natural processes of erosion and deposition. Here an early setting for the beginnings of intensive food processing and seasonally specialized activities on active floodplains has been revealed for the first time in the tropics.

The site gives us a glimpse into how people lived in a tropical savanna environment some 5,200 to 6,000 years ago. Here one sees a setting of small groups of people who moved on a seasonal basis within a limited territorial range. All of the raw materials and artifacts recovered from the site could have been obtained within a radius of 10 km. Within this range these peoples would have lived and hunted and collected the resources they needed to survive and reproduce biologically and socially.

The environment at the time of the site's occupations would have been drier than it is today, with between 500 and 1,000 mm of precipitation per year. Palynological evidence from surrounding areas and the environmental conditions necessary for the growth of some of the mollusk genera recovered from San Jacinto 1 (*Drymaeus* sp. and *Orthalicus maracaibensis*) verify this drier period. With such dry conditions, seasonality would have been more pronounced and resources would have been more clustered both in space and time.

Given this setting, the occupants of San Jacinto 1 used the site as a special-purpose camp to collect and process starchy seeds and other resources that were clustered along the stream of San Jacinto in space and that were available for only a short period during the year. This period was most likely at the end of the rainy season and beginning of the dry season in November, December, January, and possibly through March in this part of South America. The site would have been uninhabitable during the rainy season because of the strong and frequent flooding that is in evidence in the soil profile and stratigraphy of the site. The inhabitants would have had to reside elsewhere during the times of year with strong rains. It is therefore likely that the inhabitants at

San Jacinto 1 in Perspective

San Jacinto 1 had a very narrow opportunity both in space and time to collect the resources needed during this season of the yearly cycle.

The animal and botanical resources utilized at San Jacinto 1 include mollusks and plant genera used for various types of purposes. The identification of phytoliths of grasses from one feature points to a conclusion that grasses were utilized at the site. The recovery of metates and manos in various strata verifies the intensive collection, grinding, and processing of seed resources probably from C_3 plants. The seeds were most likely ground to form a mush or flour that could be wrapped in the leaves of the grass or members of the Marantaceae and steamed or cooked in the earth oven features also found at the site. The resources could also have been used to make a fermented drink that was potentially served in the pottery recovered from the site. Other foods such as tubers (arrowroot, *Maranta arundinacea*) were probably also cooked in the earth oven features. Whether these resources were wild or domesticated is not particularly important when addressing the form of adaptations of these groups (Harris 1996a). This is true because the resources processed at San Jacinto 1 would have only been utilized for a short period of time during the year. They would have only made up a small fraction of the food base that these peoples would have had to utilize throughout the rest of the year at other sites, which have not been excavated to date (i.e., San Jacinto 2) (see also Dillehay and Rossen 2002; Gil 2003; Rossen and Dillehay 2000:135–136).

So why go through so much trouble to get these resources, grind them, steam or cook them, and even probably make pottery with which to serve a fermented beverage made from them when it seems to be too much work for such low nutritional qualities (Gremillion 2004)? Part of the answer was stated above in that given the environmental setting these resources would have been highly localized in space and time. A group would have had to know when and where a particular resource would be available and they would have had to adjust their mobility strategies accordingly. These peoples would have needed to adapt to the changing landscape and seasonality of the savanna.

In this environmental setting the ceramics at San Jacinto 1 may have played a role in relation to the resources being processed. Their form and composition all point to the likelihood of use for serving, perhaps of fermented beverages (Oyuela-Caycedo 1993, 1995b; Pratt 1999a, 1999b; also see Iltis 2000; Smalley and Blake 2003 for a discussion of the early use of teosinte and maize). They also may have held mollusks for storage or serving purposes. The large earth oven cooking features as well would have been utilized in food-preparation activities and they may also have served as kilns for pottery manufacture. They would have been utilized to cook potentially large amounts of food such as tubers or *bollos,* which today are made of a wet mush of maize wrapped in leaves and steamed or fried, sometimes also combined with meats and other vegetables (see Jaenicke-Després et al. 2003 for evidence of the domestication of maize prior to its use for making tortillas). Such activities can be seen as a means of social intensification or the beginnings of ritualized behavior (Aldenderfer 1998:303–305; Cauvin 2000a, 2000b; Hastorf 1999a, 1994), which allow different groups to co-interact and avoid conflict. These activities, related to a spatial-temporal territoriality, initially probably restricted, could then have developed into extended social networks and alliances (MacDonald and Hewlett 1999). Social and ritualistic behaviors may have been occurring as a means to alleviate conflict or competition in areas where the territories of adjacent groups overlapped, and the development of new technologies, such as pottery, could have played an important role in this process.

As the population continued to grow, important plant resources would have been utilized further even to the point of relocating the resource in space to gardens or terraced fields or other areas that could be better controlled by one group. The resources also could have been moved in time by planting seeds and using more active management techniques and by controlling the reproductive cycle of the resources, leading to further economic intensification of activities including storage, cultivation, and agriculture. Domestication of the plants' genetic structures in this scenario could have occurred very early in this process, yet the social/cultural adaptations of hunter-gatherer groups would not have been greatly affected or changed.

We now turn to a more in-depth discussion on the origins of sedentism, food production, and pottery in the New World, linking the evidence from San Jacinto 1 to some of the theoretical models presented in Chapter 2.

THE PROBLEM OF THE ORIGIN OF SEDENTISM

We know from palynological evidence from the region and from the mollusks recovered at the site that the environment during the occupations of San Jacinto 1 was drier than it is today. The current dry season runs from four to five months and it is expected that the dry season would have been even more extensive at that time. Reduction of mobility at San Jacinto 1 seems to be just one optimal strategy to cope with a territory in which resource availability fluctuated in time (seasons) and space (changing landscape). This strategy would have been the use of logistic mobility whereby the territorial range of a group is reduced so that resource distribution can be monitored in time and space. The establishment of base camps and special-purpose sites for resource extraction is found in this type of mobility. The evidence of logistic mobility and restricted territoriality at San Jacinto 1 includes the course-grained reso-

San Jacinto 1 in Perspective

lution of activities occurring at the site, the redundancy of features, the seasonal flooding episodes between occupations, and the use of a very localized catchment area.

Of the theoretical models discussed on mobility (i.e., Woodburn 1982; Testart 1982), Binford's (1980) model best takes into account the variation in human strategies of mobility found today as well as in the archaeological record. The results from San Jacinto 1 in terms of mobility and variability of exploited econiches can be summarized on the basis of this model of foragers and collectors. Three important methodological aspects help to link the archaeological record of San Jacinto 1 to the type of mobility that was practiced at the site. These are (1) the grain size of the site, (2) the relationship between assemblage redundancy and logistic mobility in contraposition to residential mobility, and (3) the stratigraphic evidence that reveals the effects of unstable environments in relation to the strategy of mobility. These three aspects are all related to the definition of San Jacinto 1 as a special-purpose site in a system of logistic mobility during the majority of its occupation.

The first methodological aspect, the grain size of the archaeological record, is understood as the resolution of events that take place at a site: the higher the resolution in recognizing an event, the finer the grain of the archaeological assemblage at a site. Binford (1980, 1983, 2001) argues that the factor that regulates the assemblage grain size at a site is mobility. The higher the mobility (residential) is at a site, the higher the resolution of recognizing an event and the finer grained the archaeological assemblage would be. Interassemblage variability would also be great.[1]

In the case of open sites, such as San Jacinto 1, what makes an archaeological record fine or coarse grained in terms of activity areas is related to the kind of activities performed and the degree of mobility. It is clear at San Jacinto 1 that even if one finds an incredible number of features, they do not permit the differentiation of activity areas as a consequence of the short and frequent reoccupation of the site during each dry season. A course grain size in the archaeological record is evident and indicates that the site was not used as a base camp for the majority of its occupation. Instead, the course-grained nature of the archaeological assemblage (low resolution of individual events) indicates that repeated short-term use of the site for similar activities over time occurred. Even in highly depositional environments such as those caused by flooding, it is impossible to differentiate each occupation. The only stratum at San Jacinto 1 that allows the differentiation of activity areas using the features is stratum 9. This can be done because a shift in the use of the site from a special-purpose camp to a possible base camp is indicated. In this case the differentiation of activities can be developed.

The second aspect, the relationship between assemblage redundancy and logistic mobility in contraposition to residential mobility, is based on the feature analysis of San Jacinto 1. The abundance of fire-pits at the site indicates a high degree of redundancy of cooking activities. This redundancy is a consequence of a seasonal mobility strategy exploiting predictable resources that require processing by the use of an expedient ground stone technology, as well as intensive cooking in a kind of cooking oven. According to Binford (1983), it is not likely that redundancy of assemblages occurs in base camps (logistic or residential). This is the result of the fact that base camps have to be flexible in their location in relation to the optimal location of different resources that can be exploited by means of task groups. In other words, in a logistic strategy the possibility that a base camp would have settled on top of another seems to be rare (Binford 1983, 1989; see Gamble and Boismier 1991; Gould and Yellen 1987; Smith 2003:164–166). To the contrary, special-purpose sites, especially those that are mapped onto predictable resources, are more likely to be placed at the same locations until the resource is depleted. This is what creates a high degree of redundancy, which is rarely recognized in the archaeological record because of the lack of research on these kinds of sites. San Jacinto 1 corroborates this relationship between assemblage redundancy and special-purpose sites. The only variation that departs from the argued redundancy is in the last occupation (stratum 9), in which the site changes to a more permanent-looking base camp.

Third, unstable or stable landscapes as determined by the stratigraphy of a site are other factors that affect the strategy of mobility (see Kelly 1995). Alluvial floodplains are seasonally unstable environments; they are risky places to live. This high risk to a population in a seasonally bimodal environment seems to define the location of sites. The data from San Jacinto 1 indicate that the occupation of the site occurred because of the changing conditions from a stable environment without risk of flooding during the dry season to a very risky environment in which flooding occurred during the rainy season. In this type of ecological setting, camps are unlikely to occur in floodplains during the rainy season. However, after the rainy season resources can be collected and/or planted without the high risk of being destroyed by flooding. This pattern leads to the expectation that during the dry season camps would preferably be located close to stream channels, point bars, or other areas that are rich in resource concentrations during those times and that also offer prime locations for planting. In contrast, during the wet season it is expected that the occupation of more stable landscapes such as old terraces, hilltops, and ridges should occur. There is ethnohistorical evidence for this pattern in the grasslands of the Llanos of Venezuela and Colombia (Morey 1975) and archaeological evidence for this variation in the location of sites during the dry season as well as the degree of mobility is observed in the case of San Jacinto 1.

This pattern for the tropics implies a variation in the preservation of sites according to the bimodality of camp locations. Short-term camps and special-purpose sites would be underrepresented in the landscape as a consequence of the taphonomic effects of the environment. This creates a serious problem in the localization of sites such as San Jacinto 1 and the misrepresentation of them in the archaeological record. Furthermore, this variation in preservation creates a problem in understanding the dynamics of any group for which the strategy of mobility is tied to the seasonal variation of resources. As is generally true, there is also a beneficial side to this problem of preservation. This is in relation to the location and preservation of early permanent villages. The early evidence of permanent settlements would be highly visible in any region as a consequence of preferential locations for stable environments such as higher terraces and tops of hills. This aspect would facilitate in a regional study the recognition of when early permanent villages developed. This should be considered in future research toward the understanding of the origin of sedentism.

In synthesis, we see groups that moved on a seasonal basis and focused on specific locations at specific times of the year when resources were available. Although the groups were not sedentary, we also know that they moved within a restricted range or territory. This fact has been verified by the lack of exotic materials recovered from the site. All of the lithic raw materials are located within a few kilometers of San Jacinto 1 and the most exotic ecofacts recovered were beads made from the opercula of snails that typically live in cloud forest. Ecotones of cloud forest in the San Jacinto region are found at Cerro Maco, located about 10 km from the site. The inhabitants at San Jacinto 1, therefore, utilized a logistic mobility strategy to practice a form of restricted spatial-temporal territoriality whereby they would be able to be at a particular location when the right time of year necessitated it (also see Aldenderfer 1998).

It is clear from the evidence available from San Jacinto 1 that the main factor that regulates the degree of sedentism is resource fluctuation in time and space. To cope with such fluctuations groups develop different mobility strategies that allow them to utilize the available resources. In the case of San Jacinto 1, located in a highly seasonal savanna environment, a logistic mobility strategy was utilized to obtain (or plant and collect) resources during the appropriate time of year. To do this a spatial-temporal territoriality was required, which necessitated that the territorial range of the groups be restricted. The groups had to be at prime locations at certain times of the year, but they did not have to stay there all year. In the case of the floodplain environment at San Jacinto 1, they would not have been able to in any case.

THE ORIGIN OF FOOD PRODUCTION

Linking the origins of food production to changes in sedentism is an easier task if one thinks of it in terms of changing territorial patterns and resource distribution. Decreases and increases in sedentism occur because people have to change their mobility patterns to cope with changing environments. When resources are distributed relatively equally in space and time, territorial ranges can be large and mobility high. When resources are clustered in space and time, territorial ranges must be reduced and focused on when the resources are available. Mobility decreases and sedentism increases. When wild resource abundance is relatively predictable yet highly seasonal and the resource is important to human groups, these groups must adjust their mobility strategies and territoriality to the timing and location of the resource. The natural patterning and attractiveness of the resource, however, will lead to conflict and competition over the use of the resource by different groups who live in the area. Territorial ranges will overlap at these intersections of important resources. As there are social means of avoiding conflict and establishing ownership (see below), there are also economic means of avoiding conflict. One of these means, whereby a resource is removed from its habitat and planted in other similar locations, can lead ultimately to food production.

As has been previously stressed (Ford 1985; Harris 1996a, 1996b; Hart 1999; Rindos 1984; Smith 2001; Terrell et al. 2003; Zohary 1989; Zohary and Hopf 1988; Zvelebil and Rowley-Conwy 1986), there are many gradations of plant manipulation and domestication of the landscape that occur before full-scale food production takes place. These gradations of plant and landscape control range from promoting the growth of wild resources, weeding, and tending wild resources to the transplantation and cultivation of wild and early domesticated resources to year-round cultivation and agriculture of fully domesticated plants and large-scale change of the landscape. Clearly, in the case of the origins of food production, we are discussing a stage of plant manipulation that occurs prior to agriculture and a high degree of domestication or labor-intensive control of the landscape. To define the domesticated landscape and terms like *agriculture* and *food production,* the status of the particular plants being utilized (i.e., wild, semidomesticated = able to self-reproduce vs. domesticated = unable to self-reproduce) and the recipient (mode) of and amount of labor-intensive behavior must be addressed (Harris 1996a:446).

In the case of San Jacinto 1 the possible stages that are in evidence for the control of the landscape include plant manipulation in the form of intensive harvesting and processing. This "control" of the landscape is highly seasonal and it is a strategy that utilizes the natural setting (floodplain) and seasons of rain and flooding to the inhabitants' advantage. Little actual change to the landscape is in evidence and indeed the mode of control appears to be directed explicitly toward the plant resource being utilized. If we think of the domestication process as the domestication and control of the landscape, then the evidence from San Jacinto 1 indicates that the early stages of this process do not involve significant changes in the landscape per se. They involve the use of spatial and temporal variability to allow for the manipulation of particular plants. In this case the domestication of the landscape or a high degree of environmental manipulation (Ingold 1996:21; Terrell et al. 2003:329–334) could occur after the actual domestication (genetic changes) of an important plant species. This pattern may help explain why one often is confronted with evidence of a domesticated plant before any other changes to the landscape that are visible archaeologically occur (Smith 2001:13).

The archaeological evidence from San Jacinto 1 in regard to the early stages of food production includes the technology of food processing and the relationship between it and the factors that regulate the reduction of mobility in the region: bimodal seasonality (dry and rainy periods) and predictability of resources. The organization of technology has been argued to correlate with the subsistence and mobility strategies utilized by the occupants of the site. The patterns of tool production, maintenance, discard and replacement rate, and changes in technology are expressed in two forms of organization in hunter-gatherer societies: curated and expedient technologies. It has been argued that expedient technology is highly related to increased dependency on plant collecting and processing as well as scheduling and logistic mobility (Binford 1980; Kelly 1995; Koldehoff 1987; Kuhn 1989; Nelson 1991; Shott 1986). The evidence from San Jacinto 1 seems to correlate with such a relationship. The considerable presence of a ground stone technology, including metates, mortars, and nutcrackers, with unintentional manufacture beyond opportunistic selection, indicates an expedient technology functioning to maintain a strong dependency on starchy seed plants. It is the abundance of this expedient ground stone technology as compared to flaked tools that indicates a general regional change in the resources processed, potentially from the predominant use of animals to a high dependency on plant foods.

Interestingly, no tools that indicate direct changes to the landscape were recovered from San Jacinto 1. Such tools would include axes for the felling of trees or other kinds of tools for digging or hoeing. This lack of evidence indicates that direct control or changing of the landscape had not yet occurred during the numerous reoccupations and uses of the site. Instead, the natural setting of the floodplain, which would have been free of trees, nutrient rich, and watered, offered a prime location for plant collection, manipulation, and potentially cultivation. Labor-intensive activities were directed toward the plants themselves in the form of collection and processing and not toward changing or controlling the landscape for planting purposes at this time. In this case the early stages of food production are indicated by intensification in the labor to collect (harvest) and process the resources (i.e., seeds) regardless of whether or not these seeds were actually planted. The increased food supplies and need for additional labor may then have led to a population increase in the area. However, as indicated at San Jacinto 1, it is only after the initial intensification in the collection and processing of seeds (or a focus on the reproductive stage of a plant's life cycle) that labor-intensive activities geared toward planting (or a focus on the beginning of the plant's life cycle) occur.

The intensity of the grinding and pounding activities, plus the cooking technology of intensive use of earth ovens, suggests the use of a resource that was abundantly available for a short period. The botanical remains recovered are also highly seasonal in nature, occurring predominately at the beginning of the dry season. This time constraint demanded the processing of a food resource at the location in a relatively short period. This scenario is reinforced by the heavy reliance on cooking technologies that involved fire-cracked rocks as well as earth ovens as the main cooking form (Dering 1999; Lowell 1999). This process is similar to that seen in the Levant (Bar-Yosef and Belfer-Cohen 1992; Henry 1992; Kuijt and Goring-Morris 2002) and in the Great Basin, California, and the American Bottom for the middle and late Archaic (Emerson and McElrath 1983:224–225, 232–233; Fortier 1983:248–251, 256–259; Phillips and Gladfelter 1983). These populations depended heavily on wild seeds (acorn, grasses, and other seeds). Substantial ethnographic evidence describes similar patterns of plant collecting and complex processing techniques. These techniques range from intensive grinding, pounding, and leaching to cooking bread in earth ovens similar to those encountered at San Jacinto 1 (Basgall 1987; Binford et al. 1970; Frison 1983; House and Smith 1975; Latas 1992; Lovick 1983; Wedel 1986).

As indicated by the results of the analysis of the material recovered from San Jacinto 1, the following can be stated:

1. Grinding and pounding of harvested seeds occurred before a shift to full-scale food production, involving the year-round use of a food staple, significant changes to or domestication of the landscape, and storage.

2. Utilized resources were available on a seasonal basis, most likely at the beginning of the dry season from December through March based on the identified mollusk and botanical remains. Cooking techniques to process bulky materials for possible consumption up to a few days or weeks later are evident and related to the short time during which the exploited seed resource was available.

3. Utilized resources were spatially localized along the floodplain or beaches of the meandering stream, today known as the "*quebrada de San Jacinto.*" Spatial variability in subsistence technology and ecofactual remains is likely to occur between sites that would correlate with the spatial-temporal variability of patchy resources available for processing.

4. Relatively small territories to monitor the availability of such resources (i.e., scheduling of when to plant and when to collect) are reflected in the low evidence of raw materials from distant areas. Overlapping of territorial ranges would be expected at areas such as San Jacinto 1 where resources were localized in space and time.

5. Reduced base camp movements seem to correlate with seasonality.

How does this evidence from San Jacinto 1 fit into different models for the origins of food production in the tropics? One universal model sees population density as the main factor for the origins of food production (Binford 1968). Binford's model is considered because its mode of change acts in the same way as in other models (Boserup 1965; Bronson 1977; Cohen 1977). Due to the limitations of the record it is not possible to test specifically whether population pressure was present in the area of San Jacinto, but some general comments can be made. Another explanation is also discussed that considers the multifactor relationship of resource distribution, seasonality, and scheduling with the origins of food production (Flannery 1986).

Population pressure is an important factor in Binford's (1968) model (see Cowgill 1975; Owen 1988). He explains where the process of the origin of agriculture is most likely to have taken place, that is, in edge or marginal areas. The argument in summary goes like this: populations of foragers settled down first in the riverine and coastal regions. Then with increasing population density people were pushed to marginal zones, creating an imbalance of resources to populations in these locations. This would force the intensification in food production in environments of low rainfall and diverse plant communities. There is a relationship between degree of complexity and population density as well as between population density and agricultural intensity (Turner et al. 1977). Unfortunately, this relationship does not mean much when one is dealing with long-term processes that start with hunter-gatherer bands of collectors who were restricted in their mobility strategy by the environment and not by their neighbors. However, that neighboring groups could have overlapping territories in areas that were particularly attractive for one reason or another may have led to attempts to control the resources that were in demand. Such control may have included changing the natural occurrence of a resource in time and space to one that could be manipulated and fully utilized by only one group in its particular territory.

Such a scenario can be envisioned for maize (or any other important plant resource) whereby prior to domestication many groups would have been attracted to it during its season of availability (i.e., for sugar and so forth) (Iltis 2000; Smalley and Blake 2003). These locations would be areas where territories of different groups overlapped due to a desire for the resource itself, as well as because of environmental constraints and/or population pressure. Social intensification and means of conflict resolution may have then occurred to allow for the plant's use by different groups. However, through time, continued conflict or movements of dispersion away from these areas would have necessitated other means to control and maintain the use of a plant by a group. One way to do this would have been to become more sedentary and to continually occupy the area where the plant was growing naturally (Rosenberg 1998). Another way would have required moving the resource to other locations in space and potentially later in time. This type of control could be exercised by keeping and planting the seeds of the plant within the territory of one group or at new locations when the group moved. These actions may have required no more than throwing or planting the seed onto a floodplain (e.g., for wild grasses, see Castetter and Bell 1951; Hunter 1992:69–70; Smith 2001:30), and little change to the actual landscape would have occurred. It would also have become possible to plant the seeds at different times of the year that may have been more favorable for the plant's growth in a new location or for the needs (scheduling) of the group. This scenario would therefore have led to the cultivation and domestication of a particular plant resulting from its demand by groups based on their type of territoriality.

Paying attention to the notion of seasonality, Flannery (1986) describes a model that seems feasible for analyzing the trajectories toward food production. According to this model, populations develop diverse strategies of resource procurement that change according to seasonal and annual variations. In order to deal with the timing and variation of resources, populations develop different alternatives, one of these being scheduling of resources. For instance, Guilá Naquitz was a rockshelter occupied by a small group of a foraging population that fissioned into small bands as a seasonal strategy during the dry season and fusioned into a large macroband camp (Geo Shih) during the rainy season. A broad-spectrum use of plants is indicated and the earliest evidence of desiccated corncobs has now been confirmed for the site (5420 and 5410 ^{14}C years B.P.) (Piperno and Flannery 2001).

The problem in comparing the data from San Jacinto 1 with the case of Guilá Naquitz is that San Jacinto 1 is a special-purpose camp utilized repeatedly over hundreds of years while Guilá Naquitz was a temporary shelter not specifically occupied each year to collect a seasonal resource. Another problem is the incomplete picture of exactly what resources were exploited on a year-round basis by the groups that occupied the Serranía of San Jacinto. From the ecofactual analyses of San Jacinto 1, it is possible that starchy plant resources, arrowroot, herbs and fruits, and mollusks were occasionally eaten and were processed by grinding and probably cooked in the earth ovens. It is also clear that these activities occurred at some point in the dry season. This information, however, is only a small part of the yearly cycle of resource exploitation that would have occurred in the region. However, as at Guilá Naquitz, the scheduling of resource acquisition does appear to have been part of a general pattern of territorial utilization of the landscape. By combining the concepts of territoriality with seasonality and scheduling, the information from these sites begins to paint a three-dimensional picture of the strategies that led to plant domestication and food production.

Indeed, the concept of a spatial-temporal territoriality is very important because it helps explain why people become more sedentary (from fluid to more restricted territoriality) and why it might be necessary to continue a process of domestication (planting) in new locations. When looking at spatial territoriality one focuses on landmarks in the landscape to delineate territory (indicating where to go and where not to go). Sometimes these boundaries are passed with ease as with mobile hunter-gatherers. At other times the boundaries become more fixed or the group travels less and territory is more restricted as with collector hunter-gatherers. In more complex societies these boundaries can become permanent and even marked in various ways (Bonzani 1992; Cashdan 1983; Dyson-Hudson and Smith 1978; Peterson 1972; Rowley-Conwy 2001; Wilson 1971:195; Wittenberger 1981).

When one introduces the concept of seasonality and scheduling into territoriality, a temporal dimension is added, which means that landmarks may also be temporarily available in the landscape. These markers would be seasonally available resources such as plants, migrating animals and people, water, and fertile soils (floodplains, lake banks after flooding, and so on). A temporal map is necessary to know when to be in a certain location at a certain time. As Rosenberg (1998) explains, once a group knows a particular resource is going to be in a particular area at about the same time each year, the group has the option of not going too far away from this area and general mobility decreases and sedentism increases. In these areas of seasonal resource abundance, it is expected that other human groups will also extend their territories to encompass the resource.

For various reasons a group may not be able to stay in an old territory or the same region. These reasons may include conflict or competition between different groups interested in the same resource. They may also include intra-group conflict or competition, and internal elements of one group may separate and leave for new locations. In this scenario it would be possible to maintain contact with an important resource, particularly in the case of plants and animals, by bringing it with the group. For a plant it would most likely be recognized that if placed in an environmental setting similar to that from which it came, the plant should grow and it might be possible to still utilize this resource. This process could lead to incipient cultivation and domestication and evidence of such is expected in environments and ecological settings that are similar to those in which the plant's wild progenitor grows. Such environments would not have required extensive or intensive changes to the landscape and may not be easily visible in the archaeological record. Clearly, explanations for the early cultivation and domestication of plants benefit by incorporating the concepts found in spatial-temporal territoriality.

Following this line of thought, one can expect that food production would be just an extension of the preagricultural pattern of activities in time and space that had begun to be performed. Seed plants may have been intensively exploited for a long time and still may not necessarily have generated any cultivars or even a domesticated form (Harris 1996a:446). This pattern occurs for perennial trees such as *algarrobo* (*Prosopis juliflora*) and numerous species of palms found in the area (Bonzani 1995, 1998). On the other hand, if labor-intensive activities are directed toward a particular plant species, the domestication of a plant (genetic changes) might actually occur prior to evidence of human-induced changes to or domestication of the landscape (Smith 2001; Terrell et al. 2003). The potential view of year-round resource specialization does not make sense when the availability of food plants that can be exploited in the area is considered and when populations of mobile collectors have to plan in depth to cope with seasonal variation in space and time. Why run the risks of dependency on one species or even a cultivar when the risk of failure would increase? It is this aspect that suggests that monocultivar dependency or specialized food production on a yearly basis will initially be a nonadaptive strategy in dealing with seasonal constraints and environmental diversity. Instead, the early use of starchy plants such as maize, grasses, and potentially other domesticates would have been on a seasonal basis and probably not as a dominant food staple. It is the seasonality (dry season) of the resource that is the important factor explaining the attraction of hunter-gatherers to it and the development of social and economic strategies geared toward its use.

In synthesis, San Jacinto 1 has yielded evidence of some of the preconditions expected in models on the origins of food production. Highly localized resources were found along the stream floodplain. Hunter-gatherer groups who had a restricted territory utilized these resources. However, their movements remained somewhat mobile and artifact assemblage and feature distribution at the site indicate that they utilized logistic mobility strategies to obtain needed resources. Starchy seed resources were collected and processed in an intensive manner, as indicated by the abundant ground stone lithics and earth oven features recovered. Resource availability and site use were also highly seasonal, as indicated by the stratigraphy and identified ecofactual remains. Labor-intensive changes to the landscape itself are not in evidence. Instead, intensification of strategies appears to have been directed specifically at the plant resources themselves (harvesting). Plant availability was limited and localized in both space and time thereby necessitating both social and economic strategies that were early stages in the process that resulted in food production.

THE ORIGIN OF POTTERY IN HUNTER-GATHERER SOCIETIES

As has been demonstrated, the presence of pottery at San Jacinto 1 does not indicate sedentism. As a consequence, it would be good for future research not to rely on this traditionally assumed relationship. It appears to be much more productive to look at pottery in terms of its use as a tool leading to or helping with social and economic intensification of group interactions. This focus is needed because it appears that the origins of pottery production in this case are not linked to sedentism per se but to an increase in social interactions within or between groups who have restricted or reduced territoriality. As seen, this spatial-temporal territoriality is an adaptation to highly localized and seasonal resource availability that requires scheduling, monitoring, and intensive processing.

It is in this context that pottery first comes into play. Its use can be interpreted as involving a role either in economic intensification or in social intensification (Clark and Gosser 1995; Reid 1989; Rice 1999; Sampson 1988; Sassaman 1993). In the case of economic intensification pottery would be utilized for processing and cooking bulky foods, being involved in the survival of the group in basically economic terms. A role in social intensification, on the other hand, would be indicated, first, by functions related to group interactions such as serving or fermentation and, second, by symbolic accouterments that might indicate group identities (see also Dillehay 1998:38–41; Dillehay et al. 2003). Survival here takes on a more social/political/symbolic aspect whereby adaptation requires innovative ways to deal with other people and not just with getting enough food to fill one's stomach.

Some have tied the origin of pottery to the "feasting model" used to explain the origin of agriculture and the rise of economic and social inequality in hunter-gatherer groups and food producers (Hayden 1990). In this model pottery is not tied to sedentism but forms part of a different set of relations. Pottery is seen as one artifact that developed initially as a prestige item in the context of social inequality. Pottery may play such a role today, for example, with the display of decorative porcelain. However, can the use of such an item for prestige be the main reason people began producing pottery? The answer is no, because feasting models cannot be proved or disproved. If we want to think in terms of an activity such as feasting, the origins of pottery are better understood in the context of social obligations described very well by Marcel Mauss (1967) in terms of gift giving. The data from San Jacinto 1 do indicate that pottery at the site was not used for economic intensification in the form of cooking vessels (Oyuela-Caycedo 1993, 1995b; Pratt 1999a, 1999b). The pottery sherds at the site were not found in association with the fire-cracked rocks that were the predominant means of cooking in the earth ovens. The pottery also did not reveal signs of burning by being placed into fires for cooking. Further, it is not likely to have been used for storage containers considering that all the material corresponds to small vessels. Fermentation of large quantities of something is also unlikely, for the same reason of small vessel volume. The highly decorated characteristics of the fiber-tempered pottery speak loudly of the transmission of a symbolic message that escapes our cognition today. When fiber-tempered pottery was replaced by sand-tempered pottery, the decorative nature never returned to the reproduction of that symbolic message seen in the iconographic representations found on fiber-tempered pottery (Figures 6.1 through 6.6). By process of elimination then, social uses, such as the serving possibly of already fermented beverages, seem to be the likeliest reason for this early fiber-tempered pottery.

At San Jacinto 1, if pottery was a prestigious artifact used for serving, one has to ask, why serve in such an object when the activities performed at the site were those of a task group? If social festivities did occur at the site, they may have been limited to the members of the group and did not involve neighboring groups. It would be more logical to expect that the display of pottery as a prestigious item would occur at the base camp where dances and other social activities with neighboring bands would take place. On the other hand, greeting ceremonies and gift exchanges could occur at special-purpose sites away from the base camps when different groups first encounter each other or when related members are called upon to perform reciprocal labor exchanges. Group identity as opposed to prestige might be promoted or solidified in such a context based on the structural similarities in the diverse iconography of lug decoration. The areas where this would occur most likely would be locations of resource availability and overlapping territories as opposed to base camps of one group or another, as groups generally first meet at the borders or edges of their home ranges and not in the core areas (Peterson 1975:62; Wittenberger 1981:249). Pottery could also have been used to serve special foods such as hallucinogenic or alcoholic beverages during activities that were restricted to the task group with no necessary participation of any

Figure 6.1. Anthropomorphic representation in fiber-tempered pottery from San Jacinto 1 (E23N35, stratum 12, Level 16–23). Collection of the Museo Nacional de Colombia, Bogotá (photo by Vic Krantz).

Figure 6.2. Anthropomorphic representation in fiber-tempered pottery from San Jacinto 2 (trench 1, Level 10–20). Collection of the Museo Nacional de Colombia, Bogotá (photo by Vic Krantz).

Figure 6.3. Anthropomorphic representation in fiber-tempered pottery from Puerto Hormiga. Collection of the Museo Nacional de Colombia, Bogotá (photo by Vic Krantz).

Figure 6.4. Lug fragment from a San Jacinto 1 bowl (E24N40, stratum 9, Level 0–10). Collection of the Museo Nacional de Colombia, Bogotá (photo by Vic Krantz).

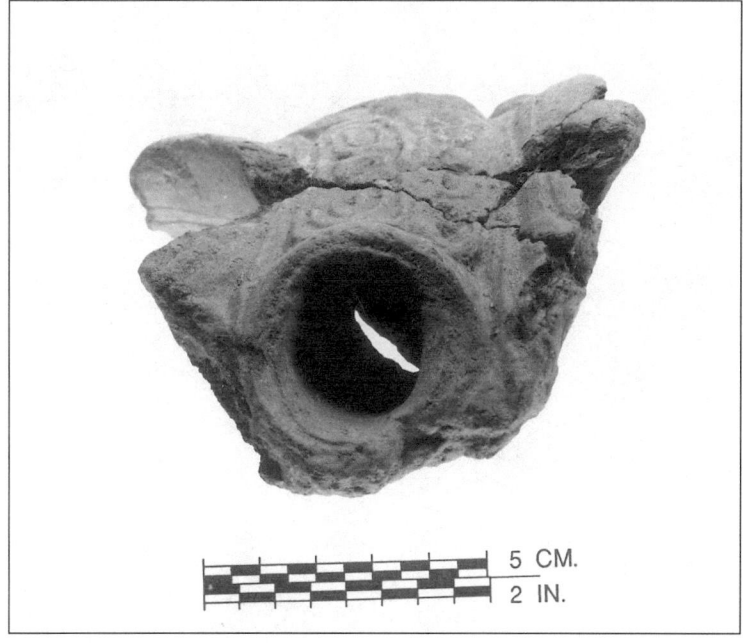

Figure 6.5. Fragment of a fiber-tempered pottery lug from a surface collection at San Jacinto 2. The globular vessel had a mouth diameter of approximately 8 cm. Top, top view; bottom, lateral view.

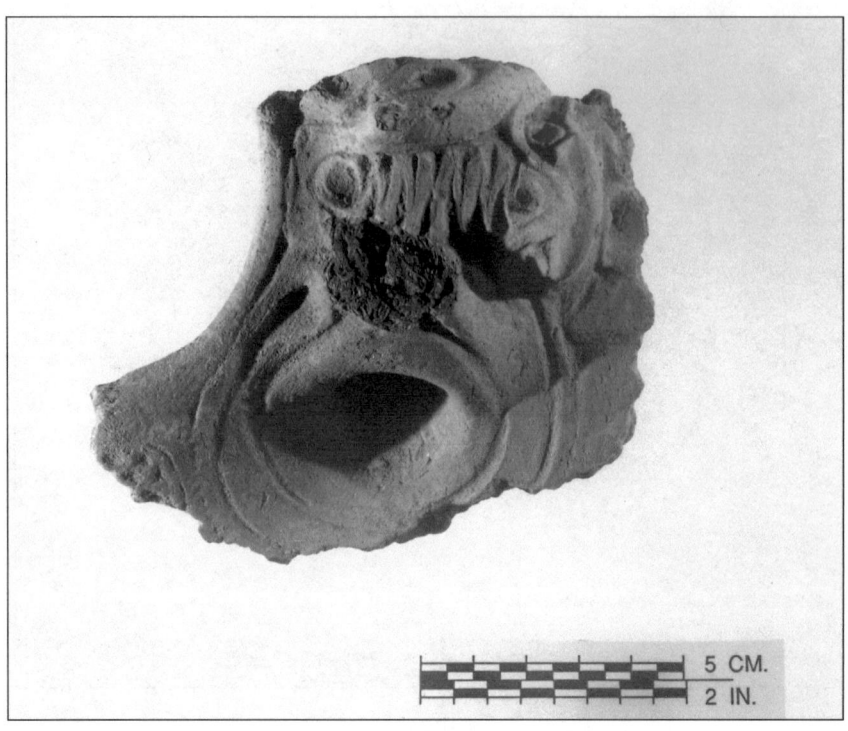

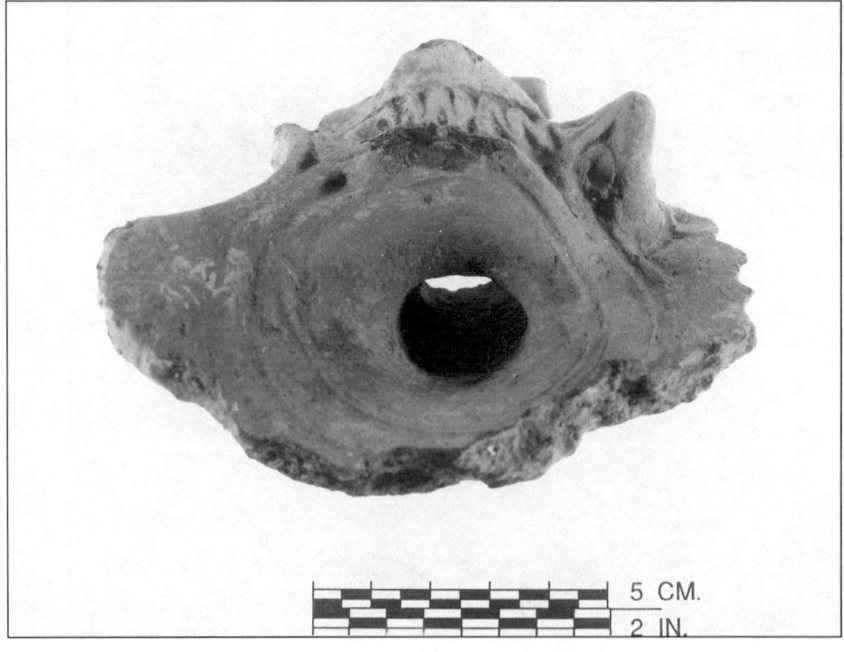

Figure 6.6. Fragment of a fiber-tempered pottery zoomorphic lug from a surface collection at San Jacinto 2. The globular vessel had a diameter of approximately 14 cm. Top, Top view; bottom, lateral view.

neighbors. In these latter two cases pottery would have a restricted presence in the archaeological record, as is observed at San Jacinto 1.

Could pottery serve in the symbolic transmission of identity? Perhaps the answer lies in the natural properties of the medium of clay itself and the context in which pottery first occurs. Hypothetically, the natural pliability of clay could have led to a potential means to differentiate group identity (Rice 1999:11–14). The differentiation of group identities would be important in the context of spatial-temporal territoriality. In this scenario group identity becomes useful because localized resources require the group over time to lay a claim to the resource and the territory where it is found. This need for "ownership" must be tied to the attractiveness of the resources being utilized and to the pull of other groups to the same locations in space and time.

To identify territory and claim use of it, symbolic means are required. The elaborate modeling of zoomorphic caricatures on the borders and handles of the pottery recovered from San Jacinto 1 could be interpreted to be examples of symbolic means of differentiating group identity. The use of the mollusk opercula to make beads for personal adornment may also have been a means of differentiating "us from them." Such differentiation may have been an early step toward marking territory and claiming ownership by utilizing symbols linked to the physical presence of the group itself as opposed to the outlining of territorial borders by use of more "conventional" means (i.e., petroglyphs). These types of symbolic tools would have been necessary, for instance, in situations in which the important feature was not continuously seen or available on the landscape. Seasonally available resources that "disappear" for parts of the year fit into this scenario and can be placed in contrast to permanent spatial landforms where markers of territory can be left on a year-round basis. In any case, the groups occupying San Jacinto 1 came upon an innovative tool to serve food and/or drink that could be modeled into symbols, the meaning of which can only be interpreted today by looking at the context of site use.

CONCLUSION

In conclusion, the archaeological site of San Jacinto 1 indicates that groups of hunter-gatherers utilized a favored point bar located on the San Jacinto stream in northern South America from 6000 to 5200 B.P. San Jacinto 1 can be classified as a special-purpose site within the logistic mobility site types. The hunter-gatherer groups had reduced mobility and restricted territoriality and utilized logistic strategies whereby persons of the group were sent to specific locations along the floodplain to obtain resources or to perform tasks at the appropriate time of year. The environment during the site's occupations was most likely drier than today with between 500 and 1,000 mm of precipitation per year and with a dry season that could have lasted from 5 to 7.5 months per year. Starchy seed resources were used at the site only on a seasonal basis during the dry season in this region of the world and were highly localized along the floodplain. Few changes to the landscape were required to utilize these resources.

The occupants at San Jacinto 1 were making and utilizing pottery at this early date for all intents and purposes as a form of serving vessel or possibly for use in fermentation. No evidence of direct cooking was found on the pottery fragments recovered. The specific resources that appear to have been utilized to make the fiber of the pottery were grasses. Based on the large numbers of ground stone lithics recovered, seed resources were most likely ground to make a flour or mush and wrapped in grass or Marantaceae leaves for cooking or steaming in the earth oven features that were also recovered at the site in abundance. These features were probably used as kilns in pottery making, as well. Plants such as arrowroot, purslane, and fruits of the Sapotaceae family may also have been eaten at the site, while other plants may have been utilized for fibers or medicinal/ritual purposes. No evidence of storage was recovered. Mollusks were also eaten at the site and the opercula of *Neocyclotus* were used to make beads.

The occupants at San Jacinto 1 focused upon seasonal resources that necessitated both logistic mobility strategies and strategies leading toward the intensified processing (harvesting) and use of these resources. This process did not at this stage involve labor-intensive changes to the landscape itself but instead appears to have been focused on the collection of the resources. It was, however, a precursor to both the advent of full-scale food production and agriculture and possibly to population growth, as additional labor would have been required to process the resources at the time of collection.

The results from San Jacinto 1 broaden our understanding of the complexity in adaptations of the people of the tropical lowlands to environmentally changing conditions. For the first time we have one site located in a context that is usually underrepresented in the archaeological record as a result of its low visibility on an active floodplain. The recognition of one kind of site with seasonal occupations (dry season) and a redundancy of activities performed reveals the importance of recognizing the problem of seasonal and landscape variation and its relationship to the archaeological assemblage of changing technologies and social strategies of mobile hunter-gatherers in the tropics.

Appendix 1

DESCRIPTION OF STRATIGRAPHY

Stratum 1: This soil has in the past been subject to mechanical cultivation for agricultural production. After the augering was completed, part of this stratum was removed from the area by a bulldozer for the construction of a new urban development project. This soil corresponds to the organic-mineral layer. The color variation is between black (5Y 2.5–3/2–3), very dark grayish brown, and grayish brown (10YR 3–4/2–4). The soil texture is clay. At times this well-developed soil has evidence of charcoal particles from the cleaning practices of slash and burn in the past years. The soil during the dry period has cracks that can pass to the next stratum. During the rainy period, because of the texture of the soil, water does not filtrate to the next stratum and mainly runs over the surface to the drainage system. In some areas with small depressions, ponds of water are formed. The major source of the origin of this soil seems to be back-flooding episodes with a low sedimentation rate that favors the development of the organic layer.

Stratum 2: This soil is a transitional soil located below stratum 1 and above stratum 3 or 4. It extends over the alluvial zone. Soil color is dark yellowish brown (10YR 4/4–6). The soil texture is mainly clay loam with a basic acidity and low content of organic material (.2 percent).

Stratum 3: This sediment is a horizontal stratigraphic facies that extends over part of the alluvial plain. It is located below stratum 2 and above stratum 4. Color variation fluctuates from a dark yellowish brown (10YR 4/4–6) to yellowish brown (10YR 5/6–8). Texture is sandy loam. The chemical characteristics of this soil indicate the lowest values of exchange properties of carbon, calcium, magnesium, potassium, and sodium (see Appendix 2). This can be interpreted as an indication of washed sands. Considering these characteristics and the homogeneous texture of the layer, this stratum is interpreted as being the product of a single and fast depositional sheet flooding episode from a more distant area of a terminal alluvial fan or fans. This phenomenon seems to explain the accretion in part of the alluvial area and the buried paleosol of stratum 4.

Stratum 4: This paleosol is registered in all of the augered areas and is located below the stratigraphic facies of stratum 3 or 2 and above stratum 5. This stratum has an abrupt separation from the above layers. The color variation is between black and very dark gray (5Y 2.5–3/1 and 10YR 2–3/1). This well-developed clay soil has a high content of phosphates (50 parts per thousand) possibly resulting from human activity.

Ferrous oxides are present. Small fragments of sand-tempered pottery were recovered from cores E0N0, E25N50, and E25N0, in all cases at a depth between 1.50 and 1.60 m, close to stratum 5. This soil is interpreted as having been formed during low depositional conditions that favored the development of the soil. The source of the deposited material seems to be related to the same or similar conditions as those observed in the present that led to the formation of stratum 1.

Stratum 5: This stratum is an anthropic soil that has an unknown distribution and may even be located outside of the alluvial sediment range. It is located below stratum 4 and above stratum 6. Color variation is between very dark gray and dark brown (10YR 3–4/1–3). Soil texture is clay, more similar to that of stratum 1 than stratum 4 (see Figure 3.4 and Appendix 2). The main characteristic of this soil is the association of cultural material like sherds. These pottery fragments were found in cores E25N15, E25N40, E25N30, E15N40, E25N50, and E25N75. Evidence of cultural features (burned soils) was recognized in E25N0 and E25N25. The origin of this soil seems to be similar to that of stratum 4.

Stratum 6: This soil extends throughout the alluvial plain and is located below stratum 5 and above stratum 7. The color variation is from very dark gray (10YR 3/1) to dark brown (10YR 3/3). The texture of the soil is clay. It is possible that the development of this organic soil is the result of slow depositional conditions similar to those detected in the present.

Stratum 7: This soil extends throughout the area of the alluvial plain. It is located below stratum 5 and above the anthropic soil of stratum 9 and the alluvial sediment of stratum 8. This is the thickest layer encountered. The color variation goes from dark yellowish brown at the top (10YR 4/4–6) to yellowish brown (10YR 5/4–8) at the bottom. The clay texture of the sediment has as a main chemical characteristic the presence of caliche nodules (CaO_3), which form horizons. The possible formation process of this clay layer can be interpreted as being the result of a constant and stable alluvial depositional environment. The grain size analysis suggests that this layer was formed as a result of constant back-flooding far from the actual water channel conditions and occurring during a long period of time. The rate of sedimentation was relatively high and did not permit the development of an organic soil.

Stratum 8: This stratigraphic facies extends over part of the alluvial zone and is located below stratum 7 and above stratum 9 and stratum 25. It gives the impression of covering the areas surrounding the anthropic site as well as covering the site itself in some places. This layer is not horizontal as were the others described before. Color variation is from yellowish brown (10YR 5/4–6) to dark brown or dark yellowish brown (10YR 4/3–6). This soil is mainly recognized by having a sandy clay loam soil texture. It also has as a chemical characteristic a high salinity value (electric conductivity 4.54 milliohms/cm) with a sodium saturation of 11 percent, permitting the classification of this soil as moderately salty (S1). This salinity classification makes it similar only to the soil of stratum 25 (see Figure 3.4 and Appendix 2). The texture, the chemical characteristics, and the location of this soil are interpreted as indicating a refill material, alluvial in origin and located relatively close to a stream channel. This

Description of Stratigraphy

stream channel deposited the material, filling the depressions of the area, and later produced a floodplain where the upper strata could develop in horizontal form.

Stratum 9: This anthropic soil has a discrete spatial distribution in an oval form. It is located below stratum 8 in one of the cores (E15N15) (during the excavation this soil was noted as occurring below stratum 8 thus confirming the initial observation) and in most of the area is above stratum 10. During the augering this stratum was encountered in eight cores. The color variation is between dark brown (10YR 3/3) and yellowish brown (10YR 5/4). The texture of the soil is clay and it has the highest content of phosphorus (460 ppm) of all strata. This layer is the first one where charcoal, shell remains, microflakes, and fiber-tempered sherds were recovered from most of the cores. The origin of the soil is mainly from anthropic activities and alluvial soils.

Stratum 10: This is also an anthropic soil and has a discrete and similar spatial distribution to that of stratum 9. It was observed in eight cores. It is always located below stratum 9 and above stratum 11 or stratum 12. The color variation is from very grayish brown (10YR 3/2–3) to dark brown (10YR 4/3). The clay-textured soil shows evidence of a high content of phosphorus (160 ppm), the result of human activity. As in the soil above, stratum 10 revealed cultural material as well as indications of features. Two of the auger perforations were interrupted in this layer as the result of encounters with rock artifacts located in features (E25N15 and E25N40). The last feature was confirmed during the excavation. The origin of this stratum is from human activity and alluvial deposition.

Stratum 11: This is an alluvial sediment facies that separates the anthropic soils of stratum 10 from those of stratum 12 in some places. Its distribution is limited to two of the cores (E25N25, E15N30). With the excavation the distribution was better delimited. The color is mainly dark yellowish brown (10YR 4/6) and the texture is of sandy clay loam. Noncultural material is associated with this sediment. It is similar in its process of formation to that of the other sandy clay loam sediments that form the lower fluvial strata 13, 15, 17, and 19. This stratum, however, appears to have been closest to the source of the fluvial flooding episodes, that being the stream channel.

Stratum 12: The extent of this discrete anthropic stratum is smaller than that of stratum 10. It was detected in five of the eight cores. It is located in general below anthropic stratum 10 or in some cases the noncultural stratum 11 and above stratum 13 or stratum 25. The color is very dark grayish brown (10YR 3/2) with a clay loam soil texture. As a chemical characteristic this stratum has a high content of phosphorus (280 ppm). Evidence of features was discovered during the augering. In addition, it was possible to recover cultural material at this time. The interpretation of the origin of the soil is alluvial with chemical alteration resulting from human activity.

Stratum 13: This stratum extends over a limited space smaller than that noted for stratum 12 (it was detected in four cores). It is always located below stratum 12 and above stratum 14. The color of the soil is yellowish brown (10YR 5/6). The sediments have a sandy clay loam texture. No cultural material is present. The formation and origin of the sediment are closely related to fluvial deposition as demonstrated for strata 11, 17, and 19.

Stratum 14: This anthropic soil extends over the same area as stratum 13 (four cores) in a form that indicated an inclined soil with a horizontal distribution reduced more than the anthropic soils of strata 9, 10, and 12. The soil is always located below stratum 13 and above strata 15 and 21 or stratum 25. The color of the sediment is dark brown (7.5YR 3/2). The soil texture is clay loam with a formation process related to human activity.

Stratum 15: This stratigraphic facies extends over an area and form similar to that of stratum 14 (four cores) and is always located below stratum 14 and above strata 16 and 21 (this last information is based on the excavation). The color is dark yellowish brown (10YR 4/4). The clay texture possibly originated from flooding with a low speed of sedimentation.

Stratum 16: This anthropic soil extends over a limited area and form similar to that of stratum 15 (four cores) and is always located below stratum 15 and above stratum 17. The color is black (2.5Y 2/0) and the texture is a clay loam that has as chemical characteristics the highest content of organic material of any stratum (3.76 percent) as well as the highest content of calcium (50.3 meq/100 g) (see Figure 3.4 and Appendix 2). The cultural characteristics of the soil indicate that its formation may be the result of the dumped organic garbage generated by the human occupation.

Stratum 17: This stratum extends over the same area as stratum 16 (four cores) and is located below stratum 16 and above stratum 18 or stratum 21. This dark yellowish brown (10YR 4/4) soil has a clay loam texture similar to that of stratum 16, the only difference being color and lack of organic material. The origin of the soil seems to be the result of its close proximity to the fluvial source, and no evidence of an origin from human activity is indicated.

Stratum 18: This anthropic soil extends over less of an area than that of stratum 17. During the augering it was located only in two of the cores (E15N15 and E25N25). This same pattern was observed for stratum 19. The layer is located below stratum 17 and above stratum 19 or 21. The color is black (2.5Y 2/0) with a sandy clay loam texture. The origin is related to human activity and fluvial material.

Stratum 19: This stratigraphic facies extends over an area similar to that of stratum 18 (two cores). It is always located below stratum 18 and above stratum 20 or stratum 21. The color is dark yellowish brown (10YR 4/4–6) with a sandy clay loam texture. As a chemical characteristic, this stratum has a low percentage of organic material (.04 percent) (see Figure 3.4 and Appendix 2). The sediment origin is fluvial.

Stratum 20: This stratum is the deepest anthropic soil encountered (two cores). It is always located below stratum 19 and above stratum 21 or stratum 25. The color variation is between black (2.5Y 2/0) and very dark gray (10YR 3/1). The texture of the soil is sandy clay loam. As a chemical characteristic, it has a significant amount of calcium (42.3 meq/100 g) (see Appendix 2). The stratum origin is related to human activities and dumping of garbage, in a similar manner to that of strata 12, 14, and 16. The origin of the soil is the same as that of stratum 18.

Stratum 21: This stratum was found in three of the cores (E25N25, E25N30, E25N50). The presence and absence of this stratum from the cores suggests a long oval spatial form for the overlying anthropic strata. Discovered during the augering, this

Description of Stratigraphy

sediment is always located below stratum 20 and stratum 10. During the excavation the stratum was confirmed as occurring below strata 10, 12, 15, 17, and 19 and above stratum 22 or stratum 23. The color of the sediment is yellowish brown (10YR 5/4–8) and the texture is sandy clay loam. As a chemical characteristic, it has a high content of phosphorus (124 ppm) (see Appendix 2) that is probably the result of human activity occurring above the stratum (in stratum 20). The origin of the sediment seems to be direct alluvial deposition.

Stratum 22: This stratigraphic facies extends over a smaller area than that of stratum 21 (two cores). It is located below stratum 21 and above stratum 23. The color is yellowish brown (10YR 5/6) with a sandy clay loam texture. The origin is alluvial.

Stratum 23: This stratum extends over a similar area to that of stratum 21 (three cores). It is located below stratum 21 or 22 and above the rock base of stratum 27 or above stratum 24 or 25. The evidence of the locations of the stratum above strata 24 and 25 comes from cores made inside the area excavated. The color variation registered from top to bottom of the layer is between yellowish brown (10YR 5/6) and dark yellowish brown (10YR 4/4). The clay loam texture has a fluvial origin.

Stratum 24: This stratigraphic facies extends only over a very small and limited area. It was detected only in the cores done inside the excavated area. It is located between strata 23 and 25. The color of the sediment is between dark yellowish brown (10YR 4/6) and yellowish brown (10YR 5/6). The loamy sand texture and grain size suggest a similar origin to the one described for stratum 3, that is, being deposited in one event of fluvial activity. This stratum also has the same chemical characteristics as those of stratum 3 (see Appendix 2).

Stratum 25: This stratum extends over the alluvial area and is located below stratum 23 or 24 and above stratum 26 or the rock layer stratum 27. The color variation is between dark yellowish brown and yellowish brown (10YR 4–5/4–6). The texture is sandy clay loam and the stratum has as a chemical characteristic a high salinity value (electric conductivity 5.32 milliohms/cm) with a sodium saturation of 12.6 percent, permitting it to be classified as moderately salty (S1) (see Appendix 2). The origin of this sediment seems to be fluvial and related also to water table fluctuations that affected its chemical characteristics.

Stratum 26: This stratum extends over the alluvial area. It is located below stratum 25 and above the rock layer stratum 27. The color variation is from yellowish brown (10YR 5/6) to brownish yellow (10YR 6/6–8). The texture is sandy clay loam. This sediment was in general found below the actual water table. The origin of the sediment seems to indicate fluvial formation.

Stratum 27: This stratum is a rock layer of cobbles and pebbles distributed over all of the cored area. Samples of it were not recovered but it was observed and detected during the augering by its halting the perforations in most of the cores. The rock layer was observed in the stream at different points in the actual channel cut. This stratum seems to yield evidence of the ancient streambed of the meandric system.

Appendix 2

Chemical and Physical Characteristics of Soils

Stratum	Sand (%)	Silt (%)	Clay (%)	pH	HU (%)	CCC (meq/100 g)	BT (meq/100 g)	Ca (meq/100 g)	Mg (meq/100 g)	K (meq/100 g)	Na (meq/100 g)	SK (%)	C (%)	P (ppm)	EC (milli-ohms/cm)	SNa (%)
1	26	30	44	6.9	5.3	24.4	32.4	26.3	5.3	0.5	0.3	2	1.09	16	0	0
2	46	24	30	7	2.6	18	19	15.6	2.9	0.2	0.3	1.1	0.2	8	0	0
3	66	16	18	7.1	2.6	9.4	11.2	10.1	0.8	0.1	0.2	1.1	0.08	15	0	0
4	34	22	44	7.4	4.7	29.9	33.2	27.4	4.8	0.5	0.5	1.7	0.48	50	0	0
5	24	32	44	7.6	4.7	26.4	27.7	22.7	4.7	0.3	0.5	1.1	1.09	16	0	0
6	22	30	48	7.4	4.2	27.1	28.9	23.1	4.8	0.3	0.7	1.1	0.24	14	0	0
7	24	34	42	7.9	4.2	24.2	34.3	29.2	3.8	0.3	1	1.2	0.08	43	0.95	0
8	50	20	30	8	2	15.5	30.7	24.9	3.9	0.2	1.7	1.3	0.05	14	4.54	11
9	30	26	44	8.2	3.1	25.6	34.3	28	4.9	0.3	1.1	1.2	0.24	460	0.68	0
10	32	26	42	8.2	3.7	28.2	44	39.8	3.7	0.4	1.1	1.4	0.91	160	0.86	0
11	50	20	30	8.1	2	15.1	35	30.6	3.1	0.2	1.1	1.3	0.08	90	2.15	0
12	42	24	34	8.1	3.1	23.9	42.6	36.7	4.3	0.3	1.3	1.3	0.95	280	1.89	0
13	50	22	28	8.1	1.5	15.4	30.7	26.2	3.2	0.2	1.1	1.3	0.1	98	3.57	0
14	46	22	32	8	3.7	29	53.6	45.6	5.6	0.2	2.2	0.7	1.67	27	3.79	0
15	28	26	46	8	4.2	20.8	39.2	30.8	5.8	0.2	2.4	1	0.09	41	1.6	0

Stratum	Sand (%)	Silt (%)	Clay (%)	pH	HU (%)	CCC (meq/100 g)	BT (meq/100 g)	Ca (meq/100 g)	Mg (meq/100 g)	K (meq/100 g)	Na (meq/100 g)	SK (%)	C (%)	P (ppm)	EC (milliohms/cm)	SNa (%)
16	44	26	30	8	4.7	45.6	59.4	50.3	7.1	0.2	1.8	0.4	3.76	46	2.69	0
17	38	26	36	8.1	2	11	36.4	30.6	3.5	0.1	2.2	0.9	0.15	65	1.6	0
18	58	18	24	8	2	18.4	38.9	31.8	4.9	0.2	2	1.1	0.31	67	4.31	0
19	48	18	34	8.1	2	14.7	29	14.9	2.4	0.1	1.6	0.7	0.04	34	1.9	0
20	54	18	28	8	2.6	19.3	49.4	42.3	4.9	0.2	2.1	1	0.83	11	7.81	0
21	64	14	22	8.2	1.5	12.6	24.3	20.3	3	0.2	0.8	1.6	0.13	124	1.01	0
22	60	18	22	8.2	1	12.1	26.7	22.2	3.2	0.2	1.1	1.7	0.28	16	1.51	0
23	36	30	34	8.2	2.6	17.6	31.8	26.5	3.5	0.2	1.6	1.1	0.1	13	1.47	0
24	76	10	14	8.3	1.5	7.7	20.4	17.3	2	0.1	1	1.3	0.1	41	1.74	0
25	48	24	28	8.1	2	14.3	34.7	27.5	5.3	0.1	1.8	0.7	0.1	12	5.32	12.6
26	48	22	30	8.3	2	14.7	33.5	27.5	4.5	0.2	1.3	1.4	0.08	8	2.36	8.8

HU = Humidity, CCC = exchange properties of carbon, BT = bases, Ca = calcium, Mg = magnesium, K = potassium, Na = sodium, SK = percent saturation of potassium, C = organic carbon, P = phosphorus, EC = electric conductivity, SNa = salinity (percent saturation of sodium).

Notes

CHAPTER 1: INTRODUCTION

1. Debate over the early dates of the pottery from Santarem, Brazil, as reported in Roosevelt et al. (1991) has occurred. For a discussion of possible problems with these results and other information on the site see Räsänen et al. (1991), Roosevelt (1995), and Simoes (1981). A more detailed critique on the pottery is found in Meggers (1997:27–32) and Williams (1997). For a reply to these critiques see Roosevelt (1997).

CHAPTER 2: THE THEORETICAL FRAMEWORK

1. The contribution of the model of foragers-collectors proposed by Binford (1978, 1980) has been discussed to some extent and seems to be the most accepted model of those offered by archaeology (see Ebert 1992; Kelly 1995; Price and Brown 1985; Thomas 1983). The initial model has also suffered the process of modification, with variations generated. One such variation is the "traveler and processors" model (see Bettinger 1991:100–103).

Different authors have recognized some problems in Binford's model of mobility but no enlightening alternative has been offered of a more appealing model. Some of the critiques, for example, relate to the ethnographic basis of the model. Humphreys (1987) argues in relation to the case of South African groups that the study of seasonal mobility is not viable (1) because of the range of environmental variation that exists in time at any point and (2) because the seasonal mobility of the hunter-gatherers from South Africa is not supported by the historical data. Lee (1972) argues that average annual rainfall has little meaning. This average is defined in terms of comparison of a year-to-year variation that is true, but the monthly variation year-by-year of rain implies strong unpredictability. The environmental variation is so complex that it is a delusion to argue for the lack of environmental incongruity in time or space, especially in the long term. Another set of critiques is summarized by Preucel (1990:12–13), who notes that the role of logistical mobility and effective temperature is overly deterministic and biased by different population densities in the temperate settings. Another critique is that the model is typological and oversimplifies the mobility variations that hunter-gatherers have. The last and most frequent critique is that the correlation between the archaeological evidence and the model is not so clear (for a more intensive critique, see Bettinger 1991).

2. Shell- and sand-tempered pottery can withstand direct heat better than can

fiber-tempered vessels and may be interpreted as indicating a function involved in cooking (Barnett and Hoopes 1995; Pratt 1999a, 1999b; Raymond et al. 1998; Rice 1999).

CHAPTER 3: THE STRATA AND FEATURES

1. More detailed information on soil composition and stratigraphy is presented in Oyuela-Caycedo 1993.

CHAPTER 4: THE POTTERY AND LITHICS

1. Do these expectations hold when we approach the equatorial line? In the case of northwestern South America, expedient flaked technology is present from the early Paleoindian components of El Abra and Tequendama in the highlands (Correal 1986; Hurt 1977) up almost until the Conquest. Does this also hold true for the lowlands of northern Colombia? Unfortunately, the lack of research in the lowlands on the Paleoindian and Archaic periods limits a response to this question. However, by examining the case of San Jacinto 1 and other sites in the lowlands such as Puerto Hormiga and Monsú, certain changes can be discerned that appear to be related to expedient technology and a greater emphasis on plant gathering and wild or cultivated plant harvesting. The following looks at the lithic technologies recovered from Puerto Hormiga and Monsú in comparison with the variation observed in the lithic technology at San Jacinto 1.

Both Puerto Hormiga and Monsú were excavated by G. Reichel-Dolmatoff and Alicia Dussan; they are respectively characterized as a shell midden and a mound (Reichel-Dolmatoff 1965b). Reichel explains this variation in archaeological deposition as being related to climatic changes as well as to a more diversified exploitation of different microenvironments close to Monsú. Puerto Hormiga dates between 5050 and 4150 B.P. and Monsú between 4650 and 4250 B.P., the Monsú phase (see Table 1.4) (uncorrected dates; for regional internal and external chronological analysis, see Hoopes 1992, 1994). These two sites are located relatively close to each other but their artifactual contents reflect different kinds of camps (Reichel-Dolmatoff 1965a, 1965b, 1971, 1985, 1986). Both are characterized by having an expedient tool technology, and both sites have been interpreted as camps of collectors. Importantly, no hard evidence for indicators of food production exists, while the most common processing technology consists of grinding and pounding tools. None of these artifacts shows any indication of a major investment in the manufacturing process; the only artifact that reveals such investment is pottery. Pottery is much more abundant than lithic artifacts at both sites.

At Monsú, 6,433 lithics without evidence of modification by manufacture were excavated and only 3.1 percent of these show evidence of modification by use. There is no mention of fire-cracked rocks or features related to cooking activities. However, it is likely that the unmodified stones were fire-cracked rocks and other expedient tools unrecognized by traditional forms of artifact classification, where form equals func-

Notes

tion with little analysis of use-wear patterns or recognition of other diagnostic attributes such as thermal alteration. The Reichels, however, did recognize the importance of unmodified rocks found at the sites since they included this category with the number of such artifacts and the kinds of material used for their manufacture. These data confirm the observation that most of the tools used by the people who reoccupied Monsú were manufactured with an expedient strategy in which only a few of the items, such as grinding plates, metates and mortars, hand mills, axes, and nutcrackers, had a clear use and function. For flaked stone technology only a very small number of artifacts (58 items) was recovered. As a rule, these indicate opportunistic battering and flake removal. Pottery at Puerto Hormiga and Monsú is abundant or highly visible, which implies changes in subsistence processing techniques that seem to be unrelated to what has been observed inland at San Jacinto.

One significant difference in technology occurred at Monsú during the last period (Barlovento). This was an emphasis on the use of *Strombus gigas* celts. A total of 51 shell celts were recovered and classified in two types. One type is interpreted as having been used for hardwood work such as canoe manufacture and also for the extraction of starch from palms. The second type of artifact reveals evidence of vertical use-wear. This is interpreted as evidence of the use of the end part as a digging stick (see Reichel-Dolmatoff and Dussan 1955). This shift to the production of a new tool must be related to new strategies of subsistence. It may be related to an increase in the exploitation of rhizomes, but only through a comparison with other artifactual evidence can this be clarified.

Strombus gigas tools have a wide distribution in the Caribbean up to Florida, but little is known of their subsistence context (relationship to features). It is possible to consider these celts as a curated technology (Keegan 1984), but it seems that the discard rate was very high in contrast to that of any other lithic tool found in previous periods or in the same phase. This could suggest that during the Barlovento Period this location was a temporary camp with intensification in procurement of foods from palms such as Sago or extraction of roots, as Reichel's interpretation holds. Sufficient evidence does not exist to interpret the degree of mobility and seasonality.

CHAPTER 5: THE ECOFACTUAL REMAINS

1. The analyzed samples included 45 random samples from the floors (18 percent of total units excavated), 22 random samples from the features (12 percent of features floated), and 10 nonrandom samples of features ^{14}C dated and another feature (posthole) (5 percent of features floated). The random sample of features included 11 samples from the fire-pit or earth oven features (10 percent of these features); 7 samples from other feature types including samples from postholes, soils from lithic or snail accumulations, and walls of features (11 percent of these features); and 4 samples from stratum 5 (100 percent of these features) (Bonzani 1995:appendix 2).

2. A cupule is the "corneous depression on the cob from which two kernels are born" (Wagner 1986:112–114). The fragment from stratum 20 is illustrated in Figure 5.1a. Measurements are 9.9 × 6.4 × 3–3.4 mm (exterior width × fragment length ×

fragment thickness, see King 1987b:81–120, figs. 12 and 13 and table 5; also Benz 2001:2104; Blake and Cutler 2001:95; Wagner 1986:114). The angle of the sides is between 80 and 90 degrees. This fragment was dated by AMS to 5208 ± 28 B.P. with a carbon isotope ratio of $\delta^{13}C$ −23.6 (see Table 1.1). An example of a maize cupule fragment recovered from a historic period site in Kentucky is illustrated in Figure 5.1b for comparison. Dimensions of the cupule are 9.5 × 7.4 × 4.5 mm. The angle of the sides of this cupule is approximately 60 degrees. The term, parenchyma, is used herein for the highly fragmented carbonized remains of botanical origin from seeds, fruits, or tubers.

3. One unidentified seed fragment from stratum 10 also yielded evidence of the pericarp and the scar of the abscission layer (Figure 5.2a; see later in the text for definition of these structures). This fragment measures 3.3 × 2.4 × 2.0 mm (width × depth or length × thickness) (Wagner 1986). An example of a modern carbonized maize kernel with the scar of the abscission layer in evidence is illustrated in Figure 5.2b for comparison.

CHAPTER 6: SAN JACINTO 1 IN PERSPECTIVE

1. This is contrary to the argument that the factor that most heavily conditions grain size is rate of sedimentation or geomorphology rather than cultural process (Thomas 1983:438).

References Cited

Adair, Mary J.
    2003   Great Plains Paleoethnobotany. In *People and Plants in Ancient North America*, edited by Paul E. Minnis, pp. 258–346. Smithsonian Institution Press, Washington, D.C.

Aldenderfer, Mark
    1998   *Montane Foragers: Asana and the South-Central Andean Archaic.* University of Iowa Press, Iowa City.
    1999   Cronología y conexiones: evidencias preceramicas de Asana. *Boletín de Arqueología PUCP* 3:375–391.

Angulo Valdes, Carlos
    1978   *Arqueología de la Cienaga Grande de Santa Marta.* Banco de la Republica, Bogotá.
    1981   *La Tradición Malambo.* Banco de la Republica, Bogotá.
    1988   *Guajaro en la arqueología del norte de Colombia.* Fundación de Investigaciones Arqueológicas Nacionales, Bogotá.

Armit, Ian, and Bill Finlayson
    1995   Social Strategies and Economic Change: Pottery in Context. In *The Emergence of Pottery,* edited by William K. Barnett and John W. Hoopes, pp. 267–276. Smithsonian Institution Press, Washington, D.C.

Arnold, Philip J.
    2003   Early Formative Pottery from the Tuxtle Mountains and Implications for Gulf Olmec Origins. *Latin American Antiquity* 14(1):29–46.

Atley, S. P.
    1980   Radiocarbon Dating of Ceramic Materials: Progress and Prospects. *Radiocarbon* 22(3):987–993.

Barnett, William K., and John W. Hoopes
    1995   *The Emergence of Pottery.* Smithsonian Institution Press, Washington, D.C.

Barrau, Jacques, and Alice Peeters
    1972   Histoire et préhistoire de la préparation des aliments d'origine végétale: les techniques d'utilization de ces aliments chez les cueilleurs et les cultivateurs archaíques de l'australasie. *Société de Océanistes* 35(28):141–152.

Barthlott, W.
    1984   Microstructural Features of Seed Surfaces. In *Current Concepts in Plant Taxonomy,* edited by V. H. Heywood and D. M. Moore, pp. 95–105. Academic Press, New York.

Bartholomäus, Agnes, Alberto De la Rosa Cortés, Jaime Orlando Santos Gutiérrez, Luis Enrique Acero Duarte, and Werner Moosbrugger
    1990   *El manto de la tierra: flora de los Andes.* Corporación Autónoma Regional de las Cuencas de los Ríos Bogotá, Ubaté y Suárez, CAR. Ediciones Lerner Ltda., Bogotá.

Bartlett, A., E. Barghoorn, and B. Rainer
    1969   Fossil Maize from Panama. *Science* 165:389–390.

Bartram, Laurence E., Ellen M. Kroll, and Henry T. Bunn
    1991   Variability in Camp Structure and Bone Food Refuse Patterning at Kua San Hunter-Gatherer Camps. In *The Interpretation of Archaeological Spatial Patterning,* edited by Ellen M. Kroll and T. D. Price, pp. 77–148. Plenum Press, New York.

Bar-Yosef, Ofer, and Anna Belfer-Cohen
    1989   Origins of Sedentism and Farming Communities in the Levant. *Journal of World Prehistory* 3(4):447–498.
    1991   From Sedentary Hunter-Gatherers to Territorial Farmers in the Levant. In *Between Bands and States,* edited by Susan A. Gregg, pp. 181–202. Center for Archaeological Investigations, Occasional Papers No. 9, Southern Illinois University, Carbondale.
    1992   From Foraging to Farming in the Mediterranean Levant. In *Transition to Agriculture Prehistory,* edited by A. B. Gebauer and T. D. Price, pp. 21–48. Prehistory Press, Madison, Wisconsin.

Basgall, Mark E.
    1987   Resource Intensification among Hunter-Gatherers: Acorn Economies in Prehistoric California. In *Research in Economic Anthropology,* Vol. 9, edited by Barry L. Isaac, pp. 21–52. JAI Press, Greenwich, Connecticut.

Beadle, George W.
    1972   The Mystery of Maize. *Field Museum of Natural History Bulletin* 43(10):2–11.
    1980   The Ancestry of Corn. *Scientific American* 242:112–119.

Belfer-Cohen, Anna, and Ofer Bar-Yosef
    2000   Early Sedentism in the Near East: A Bumpy Ride to Village Life. In *Life in Neolithic Farming Communities: Social Organization, Identity and Differentiation,* edited by Ian Kuijt, pp. 19–37. Kluwer Academic, New York.

Benz, Bruce F.
    2001   Archaeological Evidence of Teosinte Domestication from Guilá Naquitz, Oaxaca. *Proceedings of the National Academy of Sciences* 98(4):2104–2106.

Berggren, Greta
    1969   *Atlas of Seeds,* Vol. 2, *Cyperaceae.* Swedish Natural Science Research Council, Stockholm.

Bettinger, Robert L.
    1991   *Hunter-Gatherers: Archaeological and Evolutionary Theory.* Plenum Press, New York.

Binford, Lewis R.
    1968   Post-Pleistocene Adaptations. In *New Perspectives in Archaeology,* edited by S. Binford and L. Binford, pp. 313–342. Aldine, Chicago.

1978   *Nunamiut Ethnoarchaeology.* Academic Press, Orlando, Florida.
1979   Organization and Formation Processes: Looking at Curated Technologies. *Journal of Anthropological Research* 35:255–273.
1980   Willow Smoke and Dogs' Tails: Hunter-Gatherer Settlement Systems and Archaeological Site Formation. *American Antiquity* 45(1):4–20.
1983   *Working at Archaeology.* Academic Press, Orlando, Florida.
1988   *In Pursuit of the Past.* Thames and Hudson, New York.
1989   *Debating Archaeology.* Academic Press, Orlando, Florida.
2001   *Constructing Frames of Reference: An Analytical Method for Archaeological Theory Building Using Ethnographic and Environmental Data Sets.* University of California Press, Berkeley.

Binford, Lewis R., Sally R. Binford, Robert Whallon, and Margaret Ann Hardin
1970   *Archaeology at Hatchery West.* Memoirs of the Society for American Archaeology, No. 24. *American Antiquity* 35(4).

Bird, Junius B., John Hyslop, and Milica Dimitrijevic Skinner
1985   *The Preceramic Excavations at Huaca Prieta, Chicama Valley, Peru.* Anthropological Papers of the American Museum of Natural History, Vol. 62, Part 1, New York.

Bischof, H.
1966   Canapote: An Early Ceramic Site in Northern Colombia—Preliminary Report. *Actas y Memorias del XXXVI Congreso Internacional de Americanistas* 1:483–491.

Blake, Leonard W., and Hugh C. Cutler
2001   *Plants from the Past.* University of Alabama Press, Tuscaloosa.

Boada, Ana Maria
2002   Personal verbal communication.

Bollong, Charles A., C. Garth Sampson, and Andrew B. Smith
1997   Khoikhoi and Bushman Pottery in the Cape Colony: Ethnohistory and Later Stone Age Ceramics of the South African Interior. *Journal of Anthropological Archaeology* 16:269–299.

Bonavia, Duccio
1982   *Precerámico peruano. Los Gavilanes. Mar, desierto, y oasis en la história del hombre.* Corporación Financiera de Desarrollo S.A. (COFIDE). Oficina de Asuntos Culturales; Instituto Arqueológico Alemán, Comisión de Arqueología General y Comparada. Editorial Ausonia-Talleres Gráficos S.A., Lima.

Bonavia, Duccio, and Alexander Grobman
1989   Andean Maize: Its Origins and Domestication. In *Foraging and Farming: The Evolution of Plant Exploitation,* edited by D. R. Harris and G. C. Hillman, pp. 456–470. Unwin Hyman, Boston.
1999   Revisión de las pruebas de la existencia de maiz preceramico de los Andes centrales. *Boletín de Arqueología PUCP* 3:239–261.

Bonner, John T.
1980   *The Evolution of Culture in Animals.* Princeton University Press, Princeton, New Jersey.

Bonzani, Renée M.
 1984   Plant Remains from Nuraghe Seruci. Manuscript, on file at the Department of Classics, Tufts University, Medford, Massachusetts.
 1992   Territorial Boundaries, Buffer Zones, and Socio-Political Complexity: A Case Study of the Nuraghi on the Island of Sardinia. In *Sardinia in the Mediterranean: A Footprint in the Sea. Studies in Sardinian Archaeology Presented to Miriam S. Balmuth,* edited by Robert H. Tykot and Tamsey K. Andrews, pp. 210–220. Monographs in Mediterranean Archaeology 3. Sheffield Academic Press, Sheffield.
 1995   Seasonality, Predictability and Plant Use Strategies at San Jacinto 1, Northern Colombia. Ph.D. dissertation, Department of Anthropology, University of Pittsburgh.
 1997   Plant Diversity in the Archaeological Record: A Means Toward Defining Hunter-Gatherer Mobility Strategies. *Journal of Archaeological Science* 24:1129–1139.
 1998   Learning from the Present: The Constraints of Seasonality on Foragers and Collectors. In *Advances in the Archaeology of the Northern Andes,* edited by Augusto Oyuela-Caycedo and J. Scott Raymond, pp. 20–35. Monograph 39, Institute of Archaeology, University of California, Los Angeles.
 1999   Medicinal Use of Plants in the Peasant Community of San Jacinto, Northern Colombia. *Caldasia* (Bogotá) 21(2):203–218.

Boserup, Ester
 1965   *The Conditions of Agriculture Growth.* Aldine, Chicago.

Braidwood, R. J.
 1953   Query to Symposium; Did Man Once Live by Beer Alone? *American Anthropologist* 55:515–516.

Braun, David P.
 1983   Pots as Tools. In *Archaeological Hammers and Theories,* edited by James Moore and Arthur Keene, pp. 107–134. Academic Press, New York.
 1987   Coevolution of Sedentism, Pottery Technology, and Horticulture in the Central Midwest, 200 B.C–A.D. 600. In *Emergent Horticultural Economies of the Eastern Woodlands,* edited by William F. Keegan, pp. 153–181. Center for Archaeological Investigations, Occasional Papers No. 7, Southern Illinois University, Carbondale.

Breure, Abraham S. H.
 1984   Survey of the Land Mollusca of the Sierra Nevada de Santa Marta, Colombia. In *La Sierra Nevada de Santa Marta (Colombia), Transecto Buritaca–La Cumbra,* edited by Thomas Van der Hammen and Pedro M. Ruiz, pp. 487–500. J. Cramer, Berlin.

Brochado, Jose Joaquim J. P.
 1984   *An Ecological Model of the Spread of Pottery and Agriculture into Eastern South America.* University Microfilms International, Ann Arbor, Michigan.

Bronson, Bennet
 1977   The Earliest Farming: Demography as Cause and Consequence. In *Origins of Agriculture,* edited by C. A. Reed, pp. 23–48. Mouton, The Hague.

Brooks, Mark J., and Kenneth E. Sassaman
1990 Point Bar Geoarcheology in the Upper Coastal Plain of the Savannah River Valley, South Carolina: A Case Study. In *Archaeological Geology of North America*, edited by Norman P. Lasca and Jack Donahue, pp. 183–197. Centennial Special Volume 4, Geological Society of America, Boulder, Colorado.

Brown, James A.
1986 Early Ceramics and Culture: A Review of Interpretations. In *Early Woodland Archaeology*, edited by Kenneth B. Farnsworth and Thomas E. Emerson, pp. 598–608. Center for American Archeology Press, Kampsville, Illinois.
1989 The Beginnings of Pottery as an Economic Process. In *What's New? A Closer Look at the Process of Innovation*, edited by Sander E. van der Leeuw and Robin Torrence, pp. 203–224. Unwin Hyman, Boston.

Brücher, Heinz
1989 *Useful Plants of Neotropical Origin and Their Wild Relatives*. Springer-Verlag, Berlin.

Bruhns, Karen
1994 *Ancient South America*. Cambridge University Press, Cambridge.

Buckler, Edward S. IV
1996 Personal verbal communication.

Buckler, Edward S. IV, Deborah M. Pearsall, and Timothy P. Holtsford
1998 Climate, Plant Ecology, and Central Mexican Archaic Subsistence. *Current Anthropology* 39(1):152–164.

Bullen, Ripley P.
1972 The Orange Period of Peninsular Florida. *The Florida Anthropologist* 25(2): 9–33.

Burger, Richard L.
1992 *Chavin and the Origin of Andean Civilization*. Thames and Hudson, London.

Cabrera, Gabriel, Carlos Franky, and Dany Mahecha
1999 *Los Nukak: nómadas de la Amazonia Colombiana*. Editorial Universidad Nacional, Bogotá.

Canal, David, and Núria Rovira
1999 La agricultura y la alimentación vegetal de la Edad del Hierro en la Cataluña Oriental. In *Els productes alimentaris d'origen vegetal a L'edat del Ferro de l'Europa Occidental: de la producció al consum*, edited by Ramon Buxó and Enriqueta Pons, pp. 139–150. Sèrie Monogràfica 18, Museu d'Arqueologia de Catalunya, Girona.

Cane, Scott
1989 Australian Aboriginal Seed Grinding and Its Archaeological Record: A Case Study from the Western Desert. In *Foraging and Farming: The Evolution of Plant Exploitation*, edited by D. R. Harris and G. C. Hillman, pp. 99–119. Unwin Hyman, Boston.

Cashdan, Elizabeth
1983 Territoriality among Human Foragers: Ecological Models and an Application to Four Bushman Groups. *Current Anthropology* 24(1):47–66.

1984   Effects of Food Production on Mobility in the Central Kalahari. In *From Hunters to Farmers*, edited by J. Desmond Clark and Steven A. Brandt, pp. 311–327. University of California Press, Berkeley.

1990   Introduction. In *Risk and Uncertainty in Tribal and Peasant Economies*, edited by Elizabeth Cashdan, pp. 1–16. Westview Press, Boulder, Colorado.

1992   Spatial Organization and Habitat Use. In *Evolutionary Ecology and Human Behavior*, edited by Eric Alden Smith and Bruce Winterhalder, pp. 237–266. Aldine de Gruyter, New York.

Cashdan, Elizabeth (editor)
1990   *Risk and Uncertainty in Tribal and Peasant Economies*. Westview Press, Boulder, Colorado.

Castañeda, Rafael Romero
1965   *Flora del centro de Bolívar*. Banco de la República, Bogotá.

Castetter, Edward F., and Willis H. Bell
1951   *Yuman Indian Agriculture*. University of New Mexico, Albuquerque.

Castro, Jaime Enrique
1993   La actividad de molienda en San Jacinto 1, los líticos de moler. Thesis project. Manuscript, on file, Departamento de Antropología, Universidad de Los Andes, Bogotá.

Cauvin, Jacques
2000a   *The Birth of the Gods and the Origins of Agriculture*. Cambridge University Press, Cambridge.
2000b   The Symbolic Foundations of the Neolithic Revolution in the Near East. In *Life in Neolithic Farming Communities: Social Organization, Identity and Differentiation*, edited by Ian Kuijt, pp. 235–252. Kluwer Academic, New York.

Cerling, Thure E.
1999   Paleorecords of C4 Plants and Ecosystems. In *C4 Plant Biology*, edited by Rowan F. Sage and Russell K. Monson, pp. 445–469. Academic Press, New York.

Clark, John E., and Michael Blake
1990   The Development of Early Formative Ceramics in the Soconusco, Chiapas, Mexico. Paper presented at the 55th Annual Meeting of the Society for American Archaeology, Las Vegas.

Clark, John E., and Dennis Gosser
1995   Reinventing Mesoamerica's First Pottery. In *The Emergence of Pottery*, edited by William K. Barnett and John W. Hoopes, pp. 209–222. Smithsonian Institution Press, Washington, D.C.

Clark, Phillip J., and Francis C. Evans
1954   Distance to Nearest Neighbor as a Measure of Spatial Relationships in Populations. *Ecology* 35:445–453.

Close, Angela E.
2000   Reconstructing Movement in Prehistory. *Journal of Archaeological Method and Theory* 7(1):49–77.

Cohen, Mark
 1977 *The Food Crisis in Prehistory.* Yale University Press, New Haven, Connecticut.
Collinson, J. D.
 1986 Alluvial Sediments. In *Sedimentary Environments and Facies,* 2nd ed., edited by H. G. Reading. Blackwell Scientific, Boston.
Cooke, Richard
 1984 The "Proyecto Santa Maria": A Multidisciplinary Analysis of Prehistoric Adaptations to a Tropical Watershed in Panama. In *Recent Developments in Isthmian Archaeology,* edited by Frederick W. Lange, pp. 3–30. BAR International Series 212. British Archaeological Reports, Oxford.
 1992a Prehistoric Nearshore and Littoral Fishing in the Eastern Tropical Pacific: An Ichthyological Evaluation. *Journal of World Prehistory* 6(1):1–41.
 1992b Etapas tempranas de la produccion de alimentos vegetales en la Baja Centroamerica y partes de Colombia (Region Historica Chibcha-Choco). *Revista de Arqueología Americana* 6:35–70.
Cooke, Richard, and Anthony J. Ranere
 1992a The Origin of Wealth and Hierarchy in the Central Region of Panama (12000–2000 B.P.). In *Wealth and Hierarchy in the Intermediate Area,* edited by Frederick W. Lange, pp. 243–316. Dumbarton Oaks Research Library and Collection, Washington, D.C.
 1992b Prehistoric Human Adaptation to the Seasonally Dry Forest of Panama. *World Archaeology* 24(1):114–133.
Correal Urrego, G.
 1986 Apuntes sobre el medio ambiente Pleistocénico y el hombre prehistórico en Colombia. In *New Evidence for the Peopling of the Americas,* edited by A. L. Bryan, pp. 115–131. Center for the Study of Early Man, University of Maine, Orono.
Cowgill, George L.
 1975 On Causes and Consequences of Ancient and Modern Population Changes. *American Anthropologist* 77:504–525.
Crown, Patricia L., and W. H. Wills
 1995 Economic Intensification and the Origins of Ceramic Containers in the American Southwest. In *The Emergence of Pottery,* edited by William K. Barnett and John W. Hoopes, pp. 241–256. Smithsonian Institution Press, Washington, D.C.
Cruz-Uribe, Kathryn
 1988 The Use and Meaning of Species Diversity and Richness in Archaeological Faunas. *Journal of Archaeological Science* 15:179–196.
Cuadros Villalobos, Hermes
 1992 Personal verbal communication.
Damp, Jonathan E.
 1984a Architecture of the Early Valdivia Village. *American Antiquity* 49(3):573–585.
 1984b Environmental Variation, Agriculture, and Settlement Processes in Coastal Ecuador (3300–1500 B.C.). *Current Anthropology* 25(1):106–112.

1988   La primer ocupación Valdivia de Real Alto: patrones economicos, arquitectonicos e ideologicos. Biblioteca Ecuatoriana de Arqueología, Quito, Ecuador.

Damp, J., D. Pearsall, and L. Kaplan
1981   Beans for Valdivia. *Science* 212(4496):811–812.

Damp, J., and L. Patricia Vargas S.
1995   The Many Contexts of Early Valdivia Ceramics. In *The Emergence of Pottery*, edited by William K. Barnett and John W. Hoopes, pp. 157–168. Smithsonian Institution Press, Washington, D.C.

Dawkins, Richard
1976   *The Selfish Gene.* Oxford University Press, Oxford.

DeFrance, Susan D., William F. Keegan, and Lee A. Newsom
1996   The Archaeobotanical, Bone Isotope, and Zooarchaeological Records from Caribbean Sites in Comparative Perspective. In *Case Studies in Environmental Archaeology*, edited by Elizabeth J. Reitz, Lee A. Newsom, and Sylvia J. Scudder, pp. 289–304. Plenum Press, New York.

Dering, Phil
1999   Earth-Oven Plant Processing in Archaic Period Economies: An Example from a Semi-Arid Savannah in South-Central North America. *American Antiquity* 64(4):659–675.

Descola, Philippe
1996   *In the Society of Nature: A Native Ecology in Amazonia.* Cambridge University Press, Cambridge.

DeWet, J. M. J.
1975   Evolutionary Dynamics of Cereal Domestication. *Bulletin of the Torrey Botanical Club* 102(6):307–312.
1981   Grasses and the Culture History of Man. *Annual Missouri Botanical Garden* 68:87–104.

Dillehay, Tom D.
1998   La organización dual en los Andes: el problema y la metodología de investigación en el Caso de San Luis, Zaña. *Boletín de Arqueología PUCP* 2:37–60.
2000   *The Settlement of the Americas.* Basic Books, Perseus Book Group, New York.

Dillehay, Tom D., and Jack Rossen
2002   Plant Food and Its Implications for the Peopling of the New World: A View from South America. *Memoirs of the California Academy of Sciences* 27:237–253.

Dillehay, Tom D., Jack Rossen, Greg Maggard, Kary Stackelbeck, and Patricia Netherly
2003   Localization and Possible Social Aggregation in the Late Pleistocene and Early Holocene on the North Coast of Perú. *Quaternary International* 109-110:3–11.

Doebley, John
1990a   Molecular Evidence and the Evolution of Maize. In *New Perspectives on the Origin and Evolution of New World Domesticated Plants,* edited by Peter K. Bretting, pp. 6–27. *Economic Botany* 44 (Supplement).

Doorman, F.
  1982   A Matter of Taste as a Matter of Fact: The Socioeconomic Context of Technological Change among Cassava Cultivators in a Northern Colombian Village. In *Man & Manioc*, Vol. 1, *Case Studies in Cassava Cultivators*, edited by L. Box and F. Doorman, pp. 77–111. Mededelingen van de Vakgroepen Sociologie van de Landbouwhogeschool, No. 3, Agricultural University, Wageningen, The Netherlands.

Dyson-Hudson, Rada, and Eric Alden Smith
  1978   Human Territoriality: An Ecological Reassessment. *American Anthropologist* 80:21–41.

Ebert, James I.
  1992   *Distributional Archaeology*. University of New Mexico Press, Albuquerque.

Eerkens, Jelmer W., Hector Neff, and Michael D. Glascock
  2002   Ceramic Production among Small-Scale and Mobile Hunters and Gatherers: A Case Study from the Southwestern Great Basin. *Journal of Anthropological Archaeology* 21:200–229.

Emerson, Thomas E., and Dale L. McElrath
  1983   Settlement-Subsistence Model of the Terminal Late Archaic Adaptation in the American Bottom, Illinois. In *Archaic Hunters and Gatherers in the American Midwest*, edited by James L. Phillips and James A. Brown, pp. 219–240. Academic Press, Orlando, Florida.

Engel, Frederic Andre
  1970   Exploration of the Chilca Canyon, Peru. *Current Anthropology* 11(1):55–58.
  1973   New Facts about Pre-Columbian Life in the Andean Lomas. *Current Anthropology* 14(3):271–280.

Eubanks, Mary
  1995   A Cross between Two Maize Relatives: *Tripsacum dactyloides* and *Zea diploperennis* (Poaceae). *Economic Botany* 49(2):172–182.

Feldman, Robert A.
  1985   Preceramic Corporate Architecture: Evidence for the Development of Non-Egalitarian Social Systems in Peru. In *Early Ceremonial Architecture in the Andes*, edited by Christopher B. Donnan, pp. 71–92. Dumbarton Oaks, Washington, D.C.

Ferring, Reid C.
  1986   Rates of Fluvial Sedimentation: Implications for Archaeological Variability. *Geoarchaeology* 1(3).

Fish, Suzanne K., Paul R. Fish, and John H. Madsen
  1992   Evidence for Large-Scale Agave Cultivation in the Marana Community. In *The Marana Community in the Hohokam World*, edited by Suzanne K. Fish, Paul R. Fish, and John H. Madsen, pp. 73–87. University of Arizona Press, Tucson.

Fitzhugh, Ben
  2001   Risk and Invention in Human Technological Evolution. *Journal of Anthropological Archaeology* 20:125–167.

Flannery, Kent V.
 1973   The Origins of Agriculture. *Annual Review of Anthropology* 2:271–310.
Flannery, Kent V. (editor)
 1986   *Guilá Naquitz: Archaic Foraging and Early Agriculture in Oaxaca, Mexico.* Academic Press, New York.
Flannery, Kent V., and Joyce Marcus
 1994   *Early Formative Pottery of the Valley of Oaxaca, Mexico.* Memoirs of the Museum of Anthropology No. 27, University of Michigan, Ann Arbor.
Fonseca Zamora, Oscar M.
 1998   La cerámica temprana de Costa Rica en el contexto del área histórica Chibchoide (4000–2500 A.P.). *Revista de Arqueología Americana* 13:41–68.
Food and Agriculture Organization of the United Nations
 1986   *Food and Fruit-Bearing Forest Species. 3: Examples from Latin America.* Food and Agriculture Organization of the United Nations, Rome.
Ford, R. I.
 1985   The Process of Plant Food Production in Prehistoric North America. In *Prehistoric Food Production in North America,* edited by Richard I. Ford, pp. 1–18. Anthropological Papers No. 75, Museum of Anthropology, University of Michigan, Ann Arbor.
Fortier, Andrew C.
 1983   Settlement and Subsistence at the Go-Kart North Site: A Late Archaic Titterington Occupation in the American Bottom, Illinois. In *Archaic Hunters and Gatherers in the American Midwest,* edited by James L. Phillips and James A. Brown, pp. 243–260. Academic Press, Orlando, Florida.
Frison, George C.
 1983   Stone Circles, Stone-Filled Fire Pits, Grinding Stones and High Plains Archaeology. *Plains Anthropologist* 28(102):81–91.
 1991   *Agate Basin Prehistoric Hunters of the High Plains.* Academic Press, Orlando, Florida.
Gamble, Clive, and William A. Boismier
 1991   *Ethnoarchaeological Approaches to Mobile Campsites.* International Monographs in Prehistory, Ann Arbor, Michigan.
García Barriga, Hernando
 1992   *Flora medicinal de Colombia. Tomo I, II, III.* 2nd ed. Tercer Mundo Editores, Bogotá.
Gardner, Paul S.
 1997   The Ecological Structure and Behavioral Implications of Mast Exploitation Strategies. In *People, Plants, and Landscapes: Studies in Paleoethnobotany,* edited by Kristen Gremillion, pp. 161–178. University of Alabama Press, Tuscaloosa.
Gaut, Brandon S., and Michael T. Clegg
 1993   Molecular Evolution of the *Adh1* Locus in the Genus *Zea. Proceedings of the National Academy of Sciences* 90:5095–5099.

Gebhard, R., Y. El-Hage, F. E. Wagner, U. Wagner, H. Bischof, J. Riederer, and A. M. Wippern
- 1988/ Early Ceramics from Canapote, Colombia, Studied by Physical Methods. In
- 1989 *Paleoetnologica* (Buenos Aires) 5:17–34.

Gentry, Alwyn H.
- 1993 *A Field Guide to the Families and Genera of Woody Plants of Northwest South America (Colombia, Ecuador, Peru).* Conservation International, Washington, D.C.

Gifford-Gonzalez, Diane, Kathlyn M. Stewart, and Natalia Rybczynski
- 1999 Human Activities and Site Formation at Modern Lake Margin Foraging Camps in Kenya. *Journal of Anthropological Archaeology* 18:397–440.

Gil, Adolfo F.
- 2003 *Zea mays* on the South American Periphery: Chronology and Dietary Importance. *Current Anthropology* 44(2):295–299.

Gladfelter, Bruce
- 1985 On the Interpretation of Archaeological Sites in Alluvial Settings. In *Archaeological Sediments in Context,* Vol. 1, edited by Julie K. Stein and William R. Farrand, pp. 41–52. Center for the Study of Early Man, University of Maine, Orono.

Gonçalves, Marco Antonio
- 2001 *O mundo inacabado: açao e criaçao em uma cosmologia Amazônica. Etnografia Piraha.* Editora Universidade Federal do Rio de Janeiro, Rio de Janeiro.

Gorecki, Paul P.
- 1991 Horticulturalists as Hunter-Gatherers: Rock Shelter Usage in Papua New Guinea. In *Ethnoarchaeological Approaches to Mobile Campsites: Hunter-Gatherer and Pastoralist Case Studies,* edited by Clive Gamble, pp. 237–262. International Monographs in Prehistory, Ann Arbor, Michigan.

Gould, Richard A., and John E. Yellen
- 1987 Man the Hunted: Determinants of Household Spacing in Desert and Tropical Foraging Societies. *Journal of Anthropological Archaeology* 6:77–103.

Grayson, Donald K., and David Hurst Thomas
- 1983 Seasonality at Gatecliff Shelter. In *The Archaeology of Monitor Valley 2. Gatecliff Shelter,* edited by David Hurst Thomas, pp. 434–438. Anthropological Papers of the American Museum of Natural History, Vol. 59, Part 1, New York.

Gregg, Susan A.
- 1991 Indirect Food Production, Mutualism and the Archaeological Visibility of Cultivation. In *Between Bands and States,* edited by Susan A. Gregg, pp. 203–215. Center for Archaeological Investigations, Occasional Papers No. 9, Southern Illinois University, Carbondale.

Gremillion, Kristen J.
- 2002 Foraging Theory and Hypothesis Testing in Archaeology: An Exploration of Methodological Problems and Solutions. *Journal of Anthropological Archaeology* 21:142–164.

2004 Seed Processing and the Origins of Food Production in Eastern North America. *American Antiquity* 69(2):215–233.

Grieder, T., A. Bueno, E. Earle Smith, Jr., and R. Malina
1988 *La Galgada, Peru: A Preceramic Culture in Transition.* University of Texas Press, Austin.

Griffin, John W.
1972 Fiber-Tempered Pottery in the Tennessee Valley. *The Florida Anthropologist* 25(2):34–36.

Guccione, M. J., R. H. Laggerty II, and L. Scott Cummings
1988 Environmental Constraints of Human Settlement in an Evolving Holocene Alluvial System, the Lower Mississippi Valley. *Geoarchaeology* 3(1):65–84.

Halstead, Paul, and John O'Shea
1989 A Friend in Need Is a Friend Indeed: Social Storage and the Origins of Social Ranking. In *Bad Year Economics: Cultural Responses to Risk and Uncertainty,* edited by John O'Shea and Paul Halstead, pp. 123–126. Cambridge University Press, New York.

Hard, Robert J., and William L. Merrill
1992 Mobile Agriculturalists and the Emergence of Sedentism: Perspectives from Northern Mexico. *American Anthropologist* 94:601–620.

Harlan, J. R.
1989 Wild-Grass Seed Harvesting in the Sahara and Sub-Sahara of Africa. In *Foraging and Farming: The Evolution of Plant Exploitation,* edited by D. R. Harris and G. C. Hillman, pp. 79–98. Unwin Hyman, London.
1992a *Crops and Man.* 2nd ed. American Society of Agronomy, Madison, Wisconsin.
1992b Indigenous African Agriculture. In *The Origins of Agriculture: An International Perspective,* edited by C. Wesley Cowan and Patty Jo Watson, pp. 59–70. Smithsonian Institution Press, Washington, D.C.
1993 The Tropical African Cereals. In *The Archaeology of Africa: Food, Metals, and Towns,* edited by Thurstan Shaw, Paul Sinclair, Bassey Andah, and Alex Okpoko, pp. 53–60. Routledge, New York.
1999 Harvesting of Wild-Grass Seed and Implications for Domestication. In *Prehistory of Agriculture: New Experimental and Ethnographic Approaches,* edited by Patricia C. Anderson, pp. 1–5. Monograph 40, Institute of Archaeology, University of California, Los Angeles.

Harney, W. E.
1951 Australian Aboriginal Cooking Methods. *Mankind* 4(6):242–246.

Harrington, H. D.
1977 *How to Identify Grasses and Grasslike Plants (Sedges and Rushes).* Swallow Press, Athens, Ohio.

Harris, David R.
1972 The Origin of Agriculture in the Tropics. *American Scientist* 60:181–193.
1980 Commentary: Human Occupation and Exploitation of Savanna Environments. In *Human Ecology in Savanna Environments,* edited by David R. Harris, pp. 31–39. Academic Press, New York.

1996a   Domesticatory Relationships of People, Plants and Animals. In *Redefining Nature: Ecology, Culture, and Domestication,* edited by Roy Ellen and Katsuyoshi Fukui, pp. 437–463. Berg, Washington, D.C.

1996b   Introduction: Themes and Concepts in the Study of Early Agriculture. In *The Origins and Spread of Agriculture and Pastoralism in Eurasia,* edited by David R. Harris, pp. 1–11. Smithsonian Institution Press, Washington, D.C.

Hart, John P.

1999   Maize Agriculture Evolution in the Eastern Woodlands of North America: A Darwinian Perspective. *Journal of Archaeological Method and Theory* 6(2):137–180.

Hassan, Frekri A.

1985   Fluvial Systems and Geoarchaeology in Arid Lands: With Examples from North Africa, the Near East and the American Southwest. In *Archaeological Sediments in Context,* Vol. 1, edited by Julie K. Stein and William R. Farrand, pp. 53–68. Center for the Study of Early Man, University of Maine, Orono.

Hastorf, Christine A.

1994   The Changing Approaches to Maize Research. In *History of Latin American Archaeology,* edited by Augusto Oyuela-Caycedo, pp. 139–154. Worldwide Archaeology Series 15, Avebury, Aldershot.

1999a   Cultural Implications of Crop Introductions in Andean Prehistory. In *The Prehistory of Food: Appetites for Change,* edited by C. Gosden and J. Hather, pp. 35–58. Routledge, New York.

1999b   Recent Research in Paleoethnobotany. *Journal of Archaeological Research* 7(1):55–103.

Hather, John

1993   *An Archaeobotanical Guide to Root and Tuber Identification,* Vol. I, *Europe and South West Asia.* Oxbow Monograph 28, The Short Run Press, Exeter.

2000   *Archaeological Parenchyma.* Archetype Publications, London.

Hawkes, Kristen, Kim Hill, and James F. O'Connell

1982   Why Hunters Gather: Optimal Foraging and the Ache of Eastern Paraguay. *American Ethnologist* 9:379–398.

Hayden, Brian

1990   Nimrods, Piscators, Pluckers, and Planters: The Emergence of Food Production. *Journal of Anthropological Archaeology* 9(1):31–69.

1995   The Emergence of Prestige Technologies and Pottery. In *The Emergence of Pottery,* edited by William K. Barnett and John W. Hoopes, pp. 257–265. Smithsonian Institution Press, Washington, D.C.

2001   Fabulous Feasts: A Prolegomenon to the Importance of Feasting. In *Feasts: Archaeological and Ethnographic Perspectives on Food, Politics, and Power,* edited by Michael Dietler and Brian Hayden, pp. 23–64. Smithsonian Institution Press, Washington, D.C.

Healey, Chris

1990   Hunting Horticulturalists: The Demographics of Productivity. In *Hunters-*

Gatherers Demography: Past and Present, edited by Betty Meehan and Neville White, pp. 139–148. University of Sydney, Sydney.

Heidke, James M., and Judith A. Habicht-Mauche
  1998 The First Occurrences and Early Distribution of Pottery in the North American Southwest. *Revista de Arqueología Americana* 14:65–99.

Henry, Donald O.
  1992 *From Foraging to Agriculture: The Levant at the End of the Ice Age.* University of Pennsylvania Press, Philadelphia.

Hernández, Alicia, Humberto Lagiglia, and Adolfo Gil
  1999– El registro arqueobotánico en el sitio "Agua de los Caballos-1" (San Rafael,
  2000   Mendoza). *Anales de Arqueología y Etnología* 54-55:181–203.

Herrera, Luisa Fernanda, Ines Cavelier, Camilio Rodriguez, and Santiago Mora
  1992 The Technical Transformation of an Agricultural System in the Colombian Amazon. *World Archaeology* 24(1):98–113.

Hillman, G. C.
  1989 Late Palaeolithic Plant Foods from Wadi Kubbaniya in Upper Egypt: Dietary Diversity, Infant Weaning, and Seasonality in a Riverine Environment. In *Foraging and Farming: The Evolution of Plant Exploitation,* edited by D. R. Harris and G. C. Hillman, pp. 207–239. Unwin Hyman, London.
  1996 Late Pleistocene Changes in Wild Plant-Foods Available to Hunter-Gatherers of the Northern Fertile Crescent: Possible Preludes to Cereal Cultivation. In *The Origins and Spread of Agriculture and Pastoralism in Eurasia,* edited by David R. Harris, pp. 159–203. Smithsonian Institution Press, Washington, D.C.

Hillman, G. C., S. M. Colledge, and D. R. Harris
  1989 Plant-Food Economy during the Epipalaeolithic Period at Tell Abu Hureryra, Syria: Dietary Diversity, Seasonality, and Modes of Exploitation. In *Foraging and Farming: The Evolution of Plant Exploitation,* edited by D. R. Harris and G. C. Hillman, pp. 240–268. Unwin Hyman, London.

Holldobler, Bert, and Edward O. Wilson
  1990 *The Ants.* Harvard University Press, Cambridge, Massachusetts.

Hoopes, John W.
  1992 Early Formative Cultures in the Intermediate Area: A Background to the Emergence of Social Complexity. In *Wealth and Hierarchy in the Intermediate Area,* edited by Frederick W. Lange, pp. 43–84. Dumbarton Oaks Research Library and Collection, Washington, D.C.
  1994 Ford Revisited: A Critical Review of the Chronology and Relationships of the Earliest Ceramic Complexes in the New World, 6000–1500 B.C. *Journal of World Prehistory* 8:1–50.

House, John H., and James W. Smith
  1975 Experiments in Replication of Fire-Cracked Rock. In *The Cache River Archaeological Project,* edited by Michael B. Schiffer and John H. House, pp. 75–80. Research Series 8, Arkansas Archeological Survey, Fayetteville.

Human Rights Watch
1998   *War Without Quarter: Colombia and International Humanitarian Law.* Human Rights Watch, New York.

Humphreys, A. J. B.
1987   Prehistoric Seasonal Mobility: What Are We Really Achieving? *South African Archaeological Bulletin* 42(145):34–38.

Hunt, S.
1976   The Gastropod Operculum: A Comparative Study of the Composition of Gastropod Opercular Proteins. *Journal of Mollusca Studies* 42:251–260.

Hunter, Andrea A.
1992   Utilization of *Hordeum pusillum* (Little Barley) in the Midwest United States: Applying Rindos' Co-evolutionary Model of Domestication. Unpublished Ph.D. dissertation, University of Missouri-Columbia.

Hurt, Wesley R.
1977   The Edge-Trimmed Tool Tradition of Northwest South America. In *For the Director: Research Essays in Honor of James B. Griffin,* edited by Charles E. Cleland, pp. 268–294. Anthropological Papers No. 61, Museum of Anthropology, University of Michigan, Ann Arbor.

Iltis, Hugh H.
2000   Homeotic Sexual Translocations and the Origin of Maize (*Zea mays,* Poaceae): A New Look at an Old Problem. *Economic Botany* 54(1):7–42.

Ingold, Tim
1983   The Significance of Storage in Hunting Societies. *Man* 18(3):553–571.
1996   Growing Plants and Raising Animals: An Anthropological Perspective on Domestication. In *The Origins and Spread of Agriculture and Pastoralism in Eurasia,* edited by David R. Harris, pp. 12–24. Smithsonian Institution Press, Washington, D.C.

Ingold, Tim, David Riches, and James Woodburn (editors)
1991   *Hunters and Gatherers: History, Evolution and Social Change.* Berg, New York.

Instituto Geografico "Agustín Codazzí"
1975   *Estudio general de suelos de los municipios de Carmen de Bolívar, San Jacinto, San Juan Nepomuceno, Zambrano, El Guamo y Cordoba (Departamento de Bolívar).* Bogotá.

Isely, Duane
1947   *Investigations in Seed Classification by Family Characteristics.* Research Bulletin 351, Agricultural Experiment Station, Iowa State College of Agriculture and Mechanic Arts, Ames, Iowa.

Jaenicke-Després, Viviane, Ed S. Buckler, Bruce D. Smith, M. Thomas, P. Gilbert, Alan Copper, John Doebley, and Svante Pääbo
2003   Early Allelic Selection in Maize as Revealed by Ancient DNA. *Science* 302:1206–1208.

Jenkins, Ned J., David H. Dye, and John A. Walthall
1986   Early Ceramic Development in the Gulf Coastal Plain. In *Early Woodland*

Archaeology, edited by Kenneth B. Farnsworth and Thomas E. Emerson, pp. 546–563. Center for American Archeology Press, Kampsville, Illinois.

Johannessen, Sissel, and Christine A. Hastorf (editors)
- 1994 *Corn and Culture in the Prehistoric New World.* Westview Press, San Francisco.

Johnson, Allen
- 2003 *Families of the Forest: The Matsigenka Indians of the Peruvian Amazon.* University of California Press, Berkeley.

Johnson, Patti J.
- 1978 Patwin. In *California,* edited by Robert F. Heizer, pp. 350–360. Handbook of North American Indians, Vol. 8, Smithsonian Institution, Washington, D.C.

Jones, Rhys, and Betty Meehan
- 1989 Plant Foods of the Gidjingali: Ethnographic and Archaeological Perspectives from Northern Australia on Tuber and Seed Exploitation. In *Foraging and Farming: The Evolution of Plant Exploitation,* edited by D. R. Harris and G. C. Hillman, pp. 120–135. Unwin Hyman, Boston.

Jones, Samuel B., Jr., and Arlene E. Luchsinger
- 1986 *Plant Systematics.* 2nd ed. McGraw-Hill, New York.

Katz, S. H., M. L. Hediger, and L. A. Valleroy
- 1974 Traditional Maize Processing Techniques in the New World. *Science* 184:765–773.

Katzenberg, M. A., S. R. Saunders, and S. Abonyi
- 2001 Bone Chemistry, Food, and History: A Case Study from 19th-Century Upper Canada. In *Biogeochemical Approaches to Paleodietary Analysis,* edited by S. H. Ambrose and M. A. Katzenberg, pp. 1–22. Kluwer Academic/Plenum Press, New York.

Keegan, William F.
- 1984 Pattern and Process in *Strombus gigas* Tool Replication. *Journal of New World Archaeology* 6(2):15–24.

Keeley, Lawrence H.
- 1982 Hafting and Retooling: Effects on the Archaeological Record. *American Antiquity* 47(4):798–808.

Kelly, R. L.
- 1995 *The Foraging Spectrum: Diversity in Hunter-Gatherer Lifeways.* Smithsonian Institution Press, Washington, D.C.

Kesarwani, Arun
- 1987 Sedentism: Problems and Issues. *Man and Environment* 11:67–77.

King, Frances B.
- 1987a The Evolutionary Effects of Plant Cultivation. In *Emergent Horticultural Economies of the Eastern Woodlands,* edited by William F. Keegan, pp. 51–66. Center for Archaeological Investigations, Occasional Papers No. 7, Southern Illinois University, Carbondale.
- 1987b Prehistoric Maize in Eastern North America: An Evolutionary Evaluation. Unpublished Ph.D. dissertation, University of Illinois, Urbana-Champaign.
- 1995 Personal written communication.

Koldehoff, Brad
　1987　The Cahokia Flake Tool Industry: Socioeconomic Implications for Late Prehistory in the Central Mississippi Valley. In *The Organization of Core Technology*, edited by Jay K. Johnson and Carol A. Morrow, pp. 151–185. Westview Press, Boulder, Colorado.

Kramer, Karen, and David Hurst Thomas
　1983　Ground Stone. In *The Archaeology of Monitor Valley 2. Gatecliff Shelter*, edited by David Hurst Thomas, pp. 231–239. Anthropological Papers of the American Museum of Natural History, Vol. 59, Part 1, New York.

Kuhn, Steven L.
　1989　Hunter-Gatherer Foraging Organization and Strategies of Artifact Replacement and Discard. In *Experiments in Lithic Technology*, edited by Daniel S. Amick and Raymond P. Mauldin, pp. 33–47. British Archaeological Reports, Oxford.

Kuijt, Ian
　2000　People and Space in Early Agricultural Villages: Exploring Daily Lives, Community Size, and Architecture in the Late Pre-Pottery Neolithic. *Journal of Anthropological Archaeology* 19:75–102.

Kuijt, Ian, and Nigel Goring-Morris
　2002　Foraging, Farming, and Social Complexity in the Pre-Pottery Neolithic of the Southern Levant: A Review and Synthesis. *Journal of World Prehistory* 16(4):361–440.

LaPena, Frank R.
　1978　Wintu. In *California*, edited by Robert F. Heizer, pp. 324–340. Handbook of North American Indians, Vol. 8, Smithsonian Institution, Washington, D.C.

Latas, Timothy W.
　1992　An Analysis of Fire-Cracked Rocks: A Sedimentological Approach. In *Deciphering a Shell Midden*, edited by Julie K. Stein, pp. 211–237. Academic Press, New York.

Lavallée, Daniéle
　1995　*The First South Americans: The Peopling of a Continent from the Earliest Evidence to High Culture*. University of Utah Press, Salt Lake City.

Lee, Richard
　1972　!Kung Spatial Organization: An Ecological and Historical Perspective. *Human Ecology* 1:125–147.

Legros, T.
　1990　Les premières céramiques Américaines. *Les Dossiers d'Archéologie* 145:60–63.

Le Roy Gordon, B.
　1983　*El Sinú: geografía humana y ecología*. Carlos Valencia Editores, Bogotá.

Linares, Olga F., and Anthony J. Ranere (editors)
　1980　*Adaptive Radiations in Prehistoric Panama*. Peabody Museum Monographs No. 5, Harvard University, Cambridge, Massachusetts.

Linares, Olga F., P. D. Sheets, and E. Rosenthal
　1975　Prehistoric Agriculture in Tropical Highlands. *Science* 187(4172):137–145.

Lippi, R. D., R. McK. Bird, and D. M. Stemper
 1984   Maize Recovered at La Ponga, an Early Ecuadorian Site. *American Antiquity* 49:118–124.
Long, A., B. F. Benz, D. J. Donahue, A. J. T. Jull, and L. J. Toolin
 1989   First Direct Dates on Early Maize from Tehuacán, Mexico. *Radiocarbon* 31:1035–1040.
Lopez, Carlos
 1998   Evidence of Late Pleistocene–Holocene Occupations in the Tropical Lowlands of the Middle Magdalena Valley. In *Advances in the Archaeology of the Northern Andes,* edited by Augusto Oyuela-Caycedo and J. Scott Raymond, pp. 1–9. Monograph 39, Institute of Archaeology, University of California, Los Angeles.
Lorenzo, José Luis
 1958   *Un sitio precerámico en Yanhuitlán, Oaxaca.* Instituto Nacional de Antropología e Historía, Dirección Prehistoria, Publ. 6, México, D.F.
Lovick, Steven K.
 1983   Fire-Cracked Rocks as Tools: Wear-Pattern Analysis. *Plains Anthropologist* 28(99):41–52.
Lowell, Julia C.
 1999   The Fires of Grasshopper: Enlightening Transformations in Subsistence Practices through Fire-Feature Analysis. *Journal of Anthropological Archaeology* 18:441–470.
Lurie, Rochelle
 1989   Lithic Technology and Mobility Strategies: The Koster Site Middle Archaic. In *Time, Energy, and Stone Tools,* edited by Robin Torrence, pp. 46–56. Cambridge University Press, Cambridge.
Lynch, Thomas F.
 1973   Harvest Timing, Transhumance, and the Process of Domestication. *American Anthropologist* 75(5):1254–1258.
Lynch, Thomas F., R. Guillespie, John A. J. Gowlett, and R. E. M. Hedges
 1985   Chronology of Guitarrero Cave, Peru. *Science* 229:864–867.
McClung de Tapia, Emily
 1992   The Origins of Agriculture in Mesoamerica and Central America. In *The Origins of Agriculture,* edited by C. Wesley Cowan and Patty Jo Watson, pp. 143–171. Smithsonian Institution Press, Washington, D.C.
MacDonald, Douglas H., and Barry S. Hewlett
 1999   Reproductive Interests and Forager Mobility. *Current Anthropology* 40(4):501–523.
McGimsey, Charles R. III
 1956   Cerro Mangote: A Preceramic Site in Panama. *American Antiquity* 22(2):151–161.
McGimsey, Charles R. III, Michael B. Collins, and Thomas W. McKern
 1986–1987   Cerro Mangote and Its Population. *Journal of the Steward Anthropological Society* 16(1-2):125–157.

McK. Bird, Robert
  1984 South American Maize in Central America? In *Pre-Columbian Plant Migration,* edited by Doris Stone, pp. 38–65. Peabody Museum of Archaeology and Ethnology, Harvard University, Cambridge, Massachusetts.

MacNeish, Richard S.
  1967 A Summary of the Subsistence. In *The Prehistory of the Tehuacán Valley,* Vol. 1, *Environment and Subsistence,* edited by D. Byers, pp. 290–309. University of Texas Press, Austin.
  1992 *The Origins of Agriculture and Settled Life.* University of Oklahoma Press, Norman.

MacNeish, Richard S., Melvin L. Fowler, Angel Garcia Cook, Frederick A. Peterson, Antoinette Nelken-Terner, and James A. Neely
  1972 *The Prehistory of the Tehuacan Valley: Excavations and Reconnaissance.* University of Texas Press, Austin.

MacNeish, Richard S., Antoinette Nelken-Terner, and Robert K. Vierra
  1980 Introduction. In *Prehistory of the Ayacucho Basin, Peru,* Vol. 3, *Non-Ceramic Artifacts,* edited by Richard S. MacNeish, Robert K. Vierra, Antoinette Nelken-Terner, and Carl J. Phagan, pp. 1–34. University of Michigan Press, Ann Arbor.

MacNeish, Richard S., R. K. Vierra, A. Nelken-Terner, R. Lurie, and A. Garcia-Cook
  1983 *Prehistory of the Ayacucho Basin, Peru,* Vol. 4. University of Michigan Press, Ann Arbor.

Mandel, Rolfe D.
  1992 Soils and Holocene Landscape Evolution in Central and Southwestern Kansas: Implications for Archaeological Research. In *Soils in Archaeology,* edited by Vance T. Holliday, pp. 41–100. Smithsonian Institution Press, Washington, D.C.

Marcos, Jorge
  1988 *Real Alto: la historia de un centro ceremonila Valdivia.* 2 vols. Biblioteca Ecuatoriana de Arqueología, Quito, Ecuador.

Marcus, Joyce
  1983 The Esperidon Complex and the Origins of the Oaxaca Formative. In *The Cloud People: Divergent Evolution of the Zapotec and Mixtec Civilizations,* edited by Kent V. Flannery and Joyce Marcus, pp. 42–43. Academic Press, New York.

Marean, Curtis W.
  1997 Hunter-Gatherer Foraging Strategies in Tropical Grasslands: Model Building and Testing in the East African Middle and Later Stone Age. *Journal of Anthropological Archaeology* 16:189–225.

Markgraf, Vera
  1989 Palaeoclimates in Central and South America Since 18,000 B.P. Based on Pollen and Lake-Level Records. *Quaternary Science Reviews* 8:1–24.

Martínez, Natàlia Alonso
  1999 La agricultura de la primera Edad del Hierro y de epoca Ibérica en el Llano Occidental Catalán: problemática y nuevas aportaciones. In *Els productes*

alimentaris d'origen vegetal a L'edat del Ferro de l'Europa Occidental: de la producció al consum, edited by Ramon Buxó and Enriqueta Pons, pp. 127–138. Sèrie Monogràfica 18, Museu d'Arqueologia de Catalunya, Girona.

Matsuoka, Y., Y. Vigouroux, M. M. Goodman, J. Sanchez, G. E. Buckler, and J. Doebley
 2002 A Single Domestication for Maize Shown by Multilocus Microsatellite Genotyping. *Proceedings of the National Academy of Sciences* 99:6080–6084.

Mauss, Marcel
 1967 *The Gift: Forms and Functions of Exchange in Archaic Societies.* W. W. Norton, New York.

Meggers, Betty J.
 1997 La cerámica temprana en América del Sur: invención independiente o difusión? *Revista de Arqueología Americana* 13:7–40.

Meggers, Betty J., C. Evans, and E. Estrada
 1965 *Early Formative Period of Coastal Ecuador: The Valdivia and Machalilla Phases.* Smithsonian Institution, Washington, D.C.

Mehrer, Mark W.
 1998 Early Pottery in Midwestern North America. *Revista de Arqueología Americana* 14:135–151.

Miller Rossen, Arlene
 1993 Phytolith Evidence for Early Cereal Exploitation in the Levant. In *Current Research in Phytolith Analysis: Applications in Archaeology and Paleoecology,* edited by Deborah M. Pearsall and Dolores R. Piperno, pp. 160–171. MASCA Research Papers in Science and Archaeology, Vol. 10, University of Pennsylvania Museum of Archaeology and Anthropology, Philadelphia.

Minnis, Paul E.
 1992 Earliest Plant Cultivation in the Desert Borderlands of North America. In *The Origins of Agriculture,* edited by C. Wesley Cowan and Patty Jo Watson, pp. 121–141. Smithsonian Institution Press, Washington, D.C.

Molist, Miguel
 n.d. Les structures de combustion au proche-orient Néolithique (10,000–3,700 B.C.). Thèse de Doctorat, University Lyon 2.

Monsalve, José G.
 1985 A Pollen Core from the Hacienda Lusitania. *Pro Calima* 4:40–44.

Montes Giraldo, J. J., and M. L. Rodriguez de Montes
 1975 *El maíz en el habla y la cultura popular de Colombia.* Publicaciones del Instituto Caro y Cuervo XXXIII, Bogotá.

Montgomery, F. H.
 1977 *Seeds and Fruits of Plants of Eastern Canada and Northeastern United States.* University of Toronto Press, Toronto.

Moran, Emilio F.
 1983 Mobility as a Negative Factor in Human Adaptability: The Case of South American Tropical Forest Populations. In *Rethinking Human Adaptation,* edited by Emilio F. Moran, pp. 117–135. Westview Press, Boulder, Colorado.

Morcote Ríos, Gaspar
 1996 Evidencia arqueobotánica de cultígenos presentes en grupos muiscas de la Sabana de Bogotá en los siglos VIII y XI. In *Bioantropología de la Sabana de Bogotá, siglos VIII al XIV D.C.,* edited by Braida Enciso and Monika Therrien, pp. 59–83. Instituto Colombiano de Antropología-ICAN, Colcultura, Bogotá.

Morey, Nancy Kathleen C.
 1975 *Ethnohistory of the Colombian and Venezuela Llanos.* Ph.D. dissertation, University of Utah. University Microfilms, Ann Arbor, Michigan.

Morse, Douglass H.
 1980 *Behavioral Mechanisms in Ecology.* Harvard University Press, Cambridge, Massachusetts.

Moseley, M.
 1975 *The Maritime Foundations of Andean Civilization.* Cummings, New York.
 1992 *The Incas and Their Ancestors.* Thames and Hudson, London.

Nelson, Margaret C.
 1991 The Study of Technological Organization. In *Archaeological Method and Theory,* Vol. 3, edited by M. B. Schiffer, pp. 57–100. University of Arizona Press, Tucson.

Neuffer, M. Gerald, Edward H. Coe, and Susan R. Wessler
 1997 *Mutants of Maize.* Cold Spring Harbor Laboratory Press, Plainview, New York.

Neusius, Sarah W.
 1986 Generalized and Specialized Resource Utilization during the Archaic Period: Implications of the Koster Site Faunal Record. In *Foraging, Collecting, and Harvesting: Archaic Period Subsistence and Settlement in the Eastern Woodlands,* edited by Sarah W. Neusius, pp. 117–143. Center for Archaeological Investigations, Occasional Papers No. 6, Southern Illinois University, Carbondale.

Newsom, Lee A.
 2002 Personal email communication.

Newsom, Lee A., and Kathleen A. Deagan
 1994 *Zea mays* in the West Indies: The Archaeological and Early Historical Record. In *Corn and Culture in the Prehistoric New World,* edited by Sissel Johannessen and Christine A. Hastorf, pp. 203–217. Westview Press, San Francisco.

Newsom, Lee A., and Jantien Molengraaff
 1999 Paleoethnobotanical Analysis. In *Archaeological Investigations on St. Martin (Lesser Antilles),* edited by Corinne L. Hofman and Menno L. P. Hoogland, pp. 229–247. Archaeological Studies, Leiden University, Leiden.

Newsom, Lee A., and Deborah M. Pearsall
 2003 Trends in Caribbean Island Archaeobotany. In *People and Plants in Ancient North America,* edited by Paul E. Minnis, pp. 347–412. Smithsonian Institution Press, Washington, D.C.

Norr, Lynette
 1984 Prehistoric Subsistence and Health Status of Coastal Peoples from the Panamanian Isthmus of Lower Central America. In *Paleopathology and the Origins of Agriculture,* edited by Mark N. Cohen and George J. Armelagos, pp. 463–490. Academic Press, Orlando, Florida.

O'Connell, James F.
 1987 Alyawara Site Structure and Its Archaeological Implications. *American Antiquity* 52(1):74–108.

Odell, George
 1998 Investigating Correlates of Sedentism and Domestication in Prehistoric North America. *American Antiquity* 63(4):553–568.

O'Shea, John M.
 1981 Coping with Scarcity: Exchange and Social Storage. In *Economic Archaeology: Toward an Integrated Approach,* edited by A. Sheridan and G. Bailey, pp. 167–183. British Archaeological Reports, Oxford.

Owen, Bruce
 1988 Population Pressure as an Explanation for Cultural Change. *Anthropology* 15:1–31.

Oyuela-Caycedo, Augusto
 1987 Dos sitios arqueologicos con degrasante de fibra vegetal en la Serrania de San Jacinto (Departamento de Bolívar). *Boletín de Arqueología* 2(1):5–26.
 1993 Sedentism, Food Production, and Pottery Origins in the Tropics: San Jacinto 1; A Case Study in the Sabana de Bolivar, Serrania de San Jacinto, Colombia. Unpublished Ph.D. dissertation, Department of Anthropology, University of Pittsburgh.
 1995a Review of MacNeish, Richard S. The Origins of Agriculture and Settled Life. *Hispanic American Historical Review* 75(3):453–454.
 1995b Rocks vs Clay: The Evolution of Pottery Technology in the Case of San Jacinto 1 (Colombia). In *The Emergence of Pottery,* edited by William K. Barnett and John W. Hoopes, pp. 133–144. Smithsonian Institution Press, Washington, D.C.
 1996 The Study of Collector Variability in the Transition to Sedentary Food Producers in Northern Colombia. *Journal of World Prehistory* 10(1):49–93.
 1998 Seasonality in the Tropical Lowlands of Northwest South America: The Case of San Jacinto 1, Colombia. In *Seasonality and Sedentism,* edited by Thomas R. Rocek and Ofer Bar-Yosef, pp. 165–179. Peabody Museum Bulletin 6, Peabody Museum of Archaeology and Ethnology, Harvard University, Cambridge, Massachusetts.
 2001 What Can the AAA Do for Indigenous People in Colombia? *Anthropology News* (American Anthropological Association) October 2001, p. 7.

Parry, William, and Robert L. Kelly
 1987 Expedient Core Technology and Sedentism. In *The Organization of Core Technology,* edited by Jay K. Johnson and Carol A. Morrow, pp. 285–304. Westview Press, Boulder, Colorado.

Parsons, James J.
- 1980 Europeanization of the Savanna Lands of Northern South America. In *Human Ecology in Savanna Environments*, edited by David R. Harris, pp. 267–289. Academic Press, New York.

Patiño, Victor Manuel
- 1967 *Plantas cultivadas y animales domesticos en America Equinoccial. Tomo III: Fibras, medicinas, miscelaneas.* Imprenta Departamental, Cali.
- 1990 *Historia de la cultura material en la América Equinoccial. Tomo I: Alimentación y alimentos.* Instituto Caro y Cuervo, Biblioteca "Ezequiel Uricoechea," Bogotá.

Pearsall, Deborah M.
- 1980 Pachamachay Ethnobotanical Report: Plant Utilization at a Hunting Base Camp. In *Prehistoric Hunters of the High Andes*, edited by John W. Rick, pp. 191–231. Academic Press, New York.
- 1988 *La producción de alimentos en Real Alto.* Biblioteca Ecuatoriana de Arqueología, Quito, Ecuador.
- 1989 Adaptation of Prehistoric Hunter-Gatherers to the High Andes: The Changing Role of Plant Resources. In *Foraging and Farming: The Evolution of Plant Exploitation*, edited by D. R. Harris and G. C. Hillman, pp. 318–332. Unwin Hyman, London.
- 1992 The Origins of Plant Cultivation in South America. In *The Origins of Agriculture*, edited by C. Wesley Cowan and Patty Jo Watson, pp. 173–205. Smithsonian Institution Press, Washington, D.C.
- 2000 *Paleoethnobotany: A Handbook of Procedures.* 2nd ed. Academic Press, New York.
- 2003 Plant Food Resources of the Ecuadorian Formative: An Overview and Comparison to the Central Andes. In *Archaeology of Formative Ecuador*, edited by J. Scott Raymond and Richard L. Burger, pp. 213–257. Dumbarton Oaks Research Library and Collection, Washington, D.C.

Pearsall, Deborah M., and Dolores R. Piperno
- 1990 Antiquity of Maize Cultivation in Ecuador: Summary and Reevaluation of the Evidence. *American Antiquity* 55(2):324–337.

Pearsall, Deborah M., Karol Chandler-Ezell, and James A. Zeidler
- 2004 Maize in Ancient Ecuador: Results of Residue Analysis of Stone Tools from the Real Alto Site. *Journal of Archaeological Science* 31(4):423–442.

Perez-Arbelaez, E.
- 1978 *Plantas utiles de Colombia.* Litografía Arco, Bogotá.

Peterson, N.
- 1972 Totemism Yesterday: Sentiment and Local Organization among the Australian Aborigines. *Man* 7:12–32.
- 1975 Hunter-Gatherer Territoriality: The Perspective from Australia. *American Antiquity* 77:53–68.

Phillips, James L., and Bruce G. Gladfelter
- 1983 The Labras Lake Site and the Paleogeographic Setting of the Late Archaic

in the American Bottom. In *Archaic Hunters and Gatherers in the American Midwest,* edited by James L. Phillips and James A. Brown, pp. 197–218. Academic Press, Orlando, Florida.

Pianka, Eric R.
1980   *Evolutionary Ecology.* Harper and Row, New York.

Pickersgill, Barbara, and Charles B. Heiser, Jr.
1978   Origins and Distribution of Plants Domesticated in the New World Tropics. In *Advances in Andean Archaeology,* edited by David L. Browman, pp. 133–165. Mouton, The Hague.

Pielou, E. C.
1959   The Use of Point-to-Plant Distances in the Study of the Patterns of Plant Populations. *Journal of Ecology* 47:607–613.

Pinder, David, Izumi Shimada, and David Gregory
1979   The Nearest-Neighbor Statistics: Archaeological Application and New Developments. *American Antiquity* 44(3):430–445.

Piperno, Dolores R.
1990   Archaeological Agriculture and Land Usage in the Amazon Basin, Ecuador. *Journal of Archaeological Science* 17:665–677.
1995   Letter to authors.
2001   On Maize and the Sunflower. *Science* 292:2260–2261.

Piperno, Dolores R., and H. K. Clarie
1984   Early Plant Use and Cultivation in the Santa Marta Basin, Panama: Data from Phytoliths and Pollen. In *Recent Developments in Isthmian Archaeology,* edited by Frederick W. Lange, pp. 85–122. BAR International Series 212. British Archaeological Reports, Oxford.

Piperno, Dolores R., and Kent V. Flannery
2001   The Earliest Archaeological Maize (*Zea mays* L.) from Highland Mexico: New Accelerator Mass Spectrometry Dates and Their Implications. *Proceedings of the National Academy of Sciences* 98(4):2101–2103.

Piperno, Dolores R., and Deborah M. Pearsall
1998   *The Origins of Agriculture in the Lowland Tropics.* Academic Press, San Diego.

Piperno, Dolores R., and Karen E. Stothert
2003   Phytolith Evidence for Early Holocene *Cucurbita* Domestication in Southwest Ecuador. *Science* 299:1054–1057.

Piperno, Dolores R., Karen H. Clary, Richard G. Cooke, Anthony J. Ranere, and Doris Weiland
1985   Preceramic Maize in Central Panama: Phytolith and Pollen Evidence. *American Anthropologist* 87:871–878.

Piperno, Dolores R., Anthony J. Ranere, Irene Holst, and Patricia Hansell
2000   Starch Grains Reveal Early Root Crop Horticulture in the Panamanian Tropical Forest. *Nature* 407:894–897.

Plazas, Clemencia, and Ana María Falchetti de Saenz
1981   *Asentamientos prehispanicos en el Bajo San Jorge.* Banco de la Republica, Bogotá.

1986   Cerámica arcaica en la Sabana de San Marcos. *Boletín de Arqueología* 2:16–23.
Plazas, Clemencia, Ana María Falchetti, Juanita Sáenz Samper, and Sonia Archila
1993   *La Sociedad Hidraulica Zenu.* Banco de la Republica, Bogotá.
Pohl, Richard W.
1968   *How to Know the Grasses.* 3rd ed. Wm. C. Brown, Dubuque, Iowa.
Pollock, Nancy J.
1985   On Food Storage among Hunter-Gatherers: Pacific Island Societies. *Current Anthropology* 26(4):540–541.
Pool, Christopher A.
2000   Why a Kiln? Firing Technology in the Sierra de Los Tuxtlas, Veracruz (Mexico). *Archaeometry* 42(1):61–76.
Pratt, Jo Ann F.
1999a   Determining the Function of One of the New World's Earliest Pottery Assemblages: The Case of San Jacinto, Colombia. *Latin American Antiquity* 10(1):71–85.
1999b   Editors Corner Corrections. *Latin American Antiquity* 10(2):104–106.
Preucel, Robert W., Jr.
1990   *Seasonal Circulation and Dual Residence in the Pueblo Southwest.* Garland, New York.
Price, Douglas T., and James A. Brown
1985   Aspects of Hunter-Gatherer Complexity. In *Prehistoric Hunter-Gatherers: The Emergence of Cultural Complexity,* edited by T. Douglas Price and James A. Brown, pp. 3–20. Academic Press, Orlando, Florida.
Purseglove, J. W.
1972   *Tropical Crops. Monocotyledons.* Longman, London.
Rafferty, Janet E.
1985   Archaeological Record on Sedentariness: Recognition, Development, and Implications. In *Advances in Archaeological Method and Theory,* Vol. 8, edited by Michael Schiffer, pp. 113–156. Academic Press, New York.
Rambo, Terry A.
1991   The Study of Cultural Evolution. In *Profiles in Cultural Evolution,* edited by T. Rambo and K. Gillogly, pp. 23–109. Anthropological Papers No. 85, Museum of Anthropology, University of Michigan, Ann Arbor.
Ranere, Anthony J.
1975   Toolmaking and Tool Use among the Preceramic Peoples of Panama. In *Lithic Technology: Making and Using Stone Tools,* edited by Earl Swanson, pp. 173–209. Mouton, The Hague.
1980   Preceramic Shelters in the Talamanca Range. In *Adaptive Radiations in Prehistoric Panama,* edited by Olga F. Linares and Anthony J. Ranere. Peabody Museum Monographs No. 5, Harvard University, Cambridge, Massachusetts.
Räsänen, Matti E., Jukka S. Salo, and Högne Jungnet
1991   Holocene Floodplain Lake Sediments in the Amazon: C-14 Dating and Paleoecological Use. *Quaternary Science Reviews* 10(4):363–373.

Raymond, J. Scott
 1988   Subsistence Patterns during the Early Formative in the Valdivia Valley, Ecuador. In *Diet and Subsistence: Current Archaeological Perspectives*, edited by B. V. Kennedy and G. M. Lemoine, pp. 159–163. Proceedings of the 19th Annual Chacmool Conference, University of Calgary Archaeological Association, Calgary, Canada.
 1993   Ceremonialism in the Early Formative of Ecuador. In *El Mundo Ceremonial Andino*, edited by Luis Millones and Yoshio Onuki, pp. 25–43. Senri Ethnological Studies No. 37, National Museum of Ethnology, Osaka.
 1998   Beginnings of Sedentism in the Lowlands of Northwestern South America. In *Advances in the Archaeology of the Northern Andes*, edited by Augusto Oyuela-Caycedo and J. Scott Raymond, pp. 10–19. Monograph 39, Institute of Archaeology, University of California, Los Angeles.
 2003   Social Formations in the Western Lowlands of Ecuador during the Early Formative. In *Archaeology of Formative Ecuador*, edited by J. Scott Raymond and Richard L. Burger, pp. 33–67. Dumbarton Oaks Research Library and Collection, Washington, D.C.

Raymond, J. Scott, and Richard L. Burger (editors)
 2003   *Archaeology of Formative Ecuador*. Dumbarton Oaks Research Library and Collection, Washington, D.C.

Raymond, J. Scott, Jorge G. Marcos, and Donald W. Lathrap
 1980   Evidence of Early Formative Settlement in the Guayas Basin, Ecuador. *Current Anthropology* 21(5).

Raymond, J. Scott, Augusto Oyuela-Caycedo, and Patrick Carmichael
 1994   Una comparación de las tecnologías de la cerámica temprana de Ecuador y Colombia. In *Tecnología y organización de la producción cerámica prehispánica en Los Andes*, edited by Izumi Shimada, pp. 33–52. Pontificia Universidad Católica del Perú: Fondo Editorial, Lima.
 1998   The Earliest Ceramic Technologies of the Northern Andes: A Comparative Analysis. In *Andean Ceramics: Technology, Organization, and Approaches*, edited by Izumi Shimada, pp. 153–172. MASCA Research Papers in Science and Archaeology, Supplement to Vol. 15, University of Pennsylvania Museum of Archaeology and Anthropology, Philadelphia.

Reichel-Dolmatoff, Gerardo
 1954   Conchales de la Costa Caribe de Colombia. *XXXI Congresso Internacional de Americanistas* 2:619–626.
 1961   The Agricultural Basis of the Sub-Andean Chiefdoms of Colombia. In *The Evolution of Horticultural Systems in Native South America: Causes and Consequences. A Symposium*, edited by Johannes Wilbert, pp. 83–100. Sociedad de Ciencias Naturales La Salle, Caracas.
 1965a *Colombia*. Frederick A. Praeger, New York.
 1965b *Excavaciones Arqueológicas en Puerto Hormiga, Departamento de Bolívar*. Ediciones de la Universidad de Los Andes, Antropologia 2, Bogotá.
 1971   Early Pottery from Colombia. *Archaeology* 24(4):338–345.

1982 Colombia indigena: periodo prehispanico. In *Manual de historia de Colombia,* pp. 33–115. Procultura S.A., Bogotá.
1985 *Monsú: un sitio arqueológico.* Banco Popular, Bogotá.
1986 *Arqueología de Colombia: un texto introductorio.* Fundación Segunda Expedición Botanica, Bogotá.
1991 *Arqueología del Bajo Magdalena: estudio de la cerámica de Zambrano.* Banco Popular-Colcultura, Bogotá.

Reichel-Dolmatoff, Gerardo, and Alicia Dussan de Reichel-Dolmatoff
1955 Excavaciones Arqueologicas en los conchales de la Costa de Barlovento. *Revista Colombiana de Antropología* 4:247–272.
1956 Momil: Excavaciones en el Sinu. *Revista Colombiana de Antropologia* 5:109–333.

Reid, Kenneth C.
1984a Fire and Ice: New Evidence for the Production and Preservation of Fiber-Tempered Pottery in the Mid-Latitude Lowlands. *American Antiquity* 49(1):55–76.
1984b *Nebo Hill and Late Archaic Prehistory on the Southern Prairie Peninsula.* University of Kansas Publications in Anthropology No. 15, Lawrence.
1989 A Material Science Perspective on Hunter-Gatherer Pottery. In *Pottery Technology: Ideas and Approaches,* edited by Gordon Bronitsky, pp. 167–180. Westview Press, Boulder, Colorado.

Reineck, H. E., and I. B. Singh
1975 *Depositional Sedimentary Environments.* Springer-Verlag, New York.

Renfrew, Jane
1973 *Paleoethnobotany: The Prehistoric Food Plants of the Near East and Europe.* Columbia University Press, New York.

Rice, Prudence M.
1999 On the Origins of Pottery. *Journal of Archaeological Method and Theory* 6(1):1–54.

Rindos, David
1984 *The Origins of Agriculture: An Evolutionary Perspective.* Academic Press, Orlando, Florida.

Rival, Laura M.
2002 *Trekking Through History: The Huaorani of Amazonian Ecuador.* Columbia University Press, New York.

Rocek, Thomas R., and Ofer Bar-Yosef (editors)
1998 *Seasonality and Sedentism: Archaeological Perspectives from Old and New World Sites.* Peabody Museum Bulletin 6, Peabody Museum of Archaeology and Ethnology, Harvard University, Cambridge, Massachusetts.

Rodríguez Ramirez, Camilo
1988 Las tradiciones alfareras tempranas en las Llanuras del Caribe Colombiano. *Boletín de Arqueología, Banco de la Republica* (Bogotá) 3(2):26–40.
1995 Sites with Early Ceramics in the Littoral of Colombia: A Discussion of Periodization and Typologies. In *The Emergence of Pottery,* edited by William K.

Barnett and John W. Hoopes, pp. 145–156. Smithsonian Institution Press, Washington, D.C.

Rodríguez-T., Elkin
2001   Diversificación de cultivos o formas de producción: datos sobre actividades económicas de subsistencia prehispánicas en el valle medio del Río Otún (Risaralda). In *Memorias del simposio pueblos y ambientes: una mirada al pasado precolombino,* edited by Gaspar Morcote, pp. 189–223. Colección Memorias No. 10, Academia Colombiana de Ciencias Exactas, Físicas y Naturales, Bogotá.

Roosevelt, Anna Curtenius
1980   *Parmana: Prehistoric Maize and Manioc Subsistence along the Amazon and Orinoco.* Academic Press, Orlando, Florida.
1984   Population, Health and the Evolution of Subsistence. In *Paleopathology and the Origins of Agriculture,* edited by Mark N. Cohen and George J. Armelagos, pp. 559–583. Academic Press, Orlando, Florida.
1989   Resource Management in Amazonia before the Conquest: Beyond Ethnographic Projection. *Advances in Economic Botany* 7:30–62.
1995   Early Pottery in the Amazon: Twenty Years of Scholarly Obscurity. In *The Emergence of Pottery,* edited by William K. Barnett and John W. Hoopes, pp. 115–131. Smithsonian Institution Press, Washington, D.C.
1997   The Demise of the Alaka Initial Ceramic Phase Has Been Greatly Exaggerated: Response to D. Williams. *American Antiquity* 62(2):353–364.

Roosevelt, Anna Curtenius, R. A. Housley, M. Imazio Da Silveira, S. Maranca, and R. Johnson
1991   Eight Millennium Pottery from a Prehistoric Shell Midden in the Brazilian Amazon. *Science* 254:1621–1624.

Rosenberg, Michael
1998   Cheating at Musical Chairs: Territoriality and Sedentism in an Evolutionary Context. *Current Anthropology* 39(5):653–681.

Rossen, Jack, and Tom D. Dillehay
2000   La colonización y el asentamiento del norte del Peru: innovación, tecnología y adaptación en el Valle de Zaña. *Boletín de Arqueología PUCP* 3:121–139.

Rossen, Jack, Tom D. Dillehay, and Donald Ugent
1996   Ancient Cultigens or Modern Intrusions? Evaluating Plant Remains in an Andean Case Study. *Journal of Archaeological Science* 23:391–407.

Rowley-Conwy, P.
2001   Time, Change and the Archaeology of Hunter-Gatherers: How Original Is the "Original Affluent Society"? In *Hunter-Gatherers: An Interdisciplinary Perspective,* edited by Catherine Panter-Brick, Robert H. Layton, and Peter Rowley-Conwy, pp. 39–72. Cambridge University Press, Cambridge.

Sage, Rowan F., Meirong Li, and Russell K. Monson
1999   The Taxonomic Distribution of C4 Photosynthesis. In *C4 Plant Biology,* edited by Rowan F. Sage and Russell K. Monson, pp. 551–584. Academic Press, New York.

Salgado, Hector
- 1987 Investigaciones arqueologicas en el curso medio del Rio Calima, Cordillera Occidental, Colombia. *Boletín de Arqueología* 1(2):3–15.

Sampson, Garth C.
- 1988 *Stylistic Boundary among Mobile Hunter-Foragers.* Smithsonian Institution Press, Washington, D.C.

Sanoja, Mario
- 1989 Origins of Cultivation around the Gulf of Paria, Northeastern Venezuela. *National Geographic Research* 5(4):446–458.

Sanoja, Mario, and I. Vargas
- 1983 New Light on the Prehistory of Eastern Venezuela. *Advances in World Archaeology* 2:205–244.

Sarmiento, Guillermo
- 1983 The Savannas of Tropical America. In *Ecosystems of the World 13: Tropical Savannas,* edited by Francois Bourliére, pp. 245–288. Elsevier Scientific, Amsterdam.
- 1984 *The Ecology of Neotropical Savannas.* Harvard University Press, Cambridge, Massachusetts.

Sassaman, Kenneth E.
- 1993 *Early Pottery in the Southeast: Tradition and Innovation in Cooking Technology.* University of Alabama Press, Tuscaloosa.
- 1995 The Social Contradictions of Traditional and Innovative Cooking Technologies in the Prehistoric American Southeast. In *The Emergence of Pottery,* edited by William K. Barnett and John W. Hoopes, pp. 223–240. Smithsonian Institution Press, Washington, D.C.
- 1998 Distribution, Timing, and Technology of Early Pottery in the Southeastern United States. *Revista de Arqueología Americana* 14:101–133.

Scarry, C. Margaret
- 2003 Patterns of Wild Plant Utilization in the Prehistoric Eastern Woodlands. In *People and Plants in Ancient North America,* edited by Paul E. Minnis, pp. 50–104. Smithsonian Institution Press, Washington, D.C.

Scheinsohn, Vivian
- 2003 Hunter-Gatherer Archaeology in South America. *Annual Review of Anthropology* 32:339–361.

Schultes, Richard Evans, and Robert F. Raffauf
- 1990 *The Healing Forest: Medicinal and Toxic Plants of the Northwest Amazonia.* Dioscorides Press, Portland, Oregon.

Shady, Ruth, and Carlos Leyva (editors)
- 2003 *La ciudad sagrada de Caral-Supe: los orígenes de la civilización Andina y la formación del estado prístino en el antiguo Perú.* Instituto Nacional de Cultura, Lima.

Shott, Michael
- 1986 Technological Organization and Settlement Mobility: An Ethnographic Examination. *Journal of Anthropological Research* 42(1):15–51.

Simoes, Mario F.
  1981   Coletores-pescadores ceramistas do littoral do Salgado (Pará): nota preliminar. *Boletim do Museu Paraense Emilio Goeldi, Nova Serie* 78:1–33.

Simon, Mary L.
  2000   Regional Variations in Plant Use Strategies in the Midwest during the Late Woodland. In *Late Woodland Societies: Tradition and Transformation across the Midcontinent*, edited by Thomas E. Emerson, Dale L. McElrath, and Andrew C. Fortier, pp. 37–75. University of Nebraska Press, Lincoln.

Skibo, James M., Michael B. Schiffer, and Kenneth C. Reid
  1989   Organic-Tempered Pottery: An Experimental Study. *American Antiquity* 54(1):122–146.

Smalley, John, and Michael Blake
  2003   Sweet Beginnings: Stalk Sugar and the Domestication of Maize. *Current Anthropology* 44(5):675–703.

Smith, Bruce D.
  1987   The Independent Domestication of Indigenous Seed-Bearing Plants in Eastern North America. In *Emergent Horticultural Economies of the Eastern Woodlands*, edited by William F. Keegan, pp. 3–48. Center for Archaeological Investigations, Occasional Papers No. 7, Southern Illinois University, Carbondale.
  1992   Prehistoric Plant Husbandry in Eastern North America. In *The Origins of Agriculture*, edited by C. Wesley Cowan and Patty Jo Watson, pp. 101–119. Smithsonian Institution Press, Washington, D.C.
  1995   *The Emergence of Agriculture*. Scientific American Library, New York.
  1997   Reconsidering the Ocampo Caves and the Era of Incipient Cultivation in Mesoamerica. *Latin American Antiquity* 8:342–383.
  2001   Low-Level Food Production. *Journal of Archaeological Research* 9(1):1–43.

Smith, Bruce D., and C. Wesley Cowan
  2003   Domesticated Crop Plants and the Evolution of Food Production Economies in Eastern North America. In *People and Plants in Ancient North America*, edited by Paul E. Minnis, pp. 105–125. Smithsonian Institution Press, Washington, D.C.

Smith, Craig S.
  2003   Hunter-Gatherer Mobility, Storage, and Houses in a Marginal Environment: An Example from the Mid-Holocene of Wyoming. *Journal of Anthropological Archaeology* 22:162–189.

Snarkis, Michael J.
  1992   Wealth and Hierarchy in the Archaeology of Eastern and Central Costa Rica. In *Wealth and Hierarchy in the Intermediate Area*, edited by Frederick W. Lange, pp. 141–164. Dumbarton Oaks Research Library and Collection, Washington, D.C.

Solbrig, O. T.
  1993   Ecological Constraints to Savanna Land Use. In *The World's Savannas*, edited by M. D. Young and O. T. Solbrig, pp. 21–47. Parthenon, Paris.

References Cited

Spencer, Charles S., and Kent V. Flannery
1986 Spatial Variation of Debris at Guilá Naquitz: A Descriptive Approach. In *Guilá Naquitz: Archaic Foraging and Early Agriculture in Oaxaca, Mexico,* edited by Kent V. Flannery, pp. 331–369. Academic Press, New York.

Spjut, Richard W.
1994 *A Systematic Treatment of Fruit Types.* Memoirs of the New York Botanical Garden Vol. 70, The New York Botanical Garden, New York.

Stahl, Ann B.
1989 Plant-Food Processing: Implications for Dietary Quality. In *Foraging and Farming: The Evolution of Plant Exploitation,* edited by D. R. Harris and G. C. Hillman, pp. 171–194. Unwin Hyman, Boston.

Staller, John E.
2001 Reassessing the Development and Chronological Relationships of the Formative of Coastal Ecuador. *Journal of World Prehistory* 15(2):193–256.

Staller, John E., and Robert G. Thompson
2002 A Multidisciplinary Approach to Understanding the Initial Introduction of Maize into Coastal Ecuador. *Journal of Archaeological Science* 29:33–50.

Stark, Barbara L.
1986 Origins of Food Production in the New World. In *American Archaeology Past and Future,* edited by D. J. Meltser, D. D. Fowler, and J. A. Sabloff, pp. 277–321. Smithsonian Institution Press, Washington, D.C.

Steward, Julian H.
1938 *Basin-Plateau Aboriginal Sociopolitical Groups.* Bureau of American Ethnology Bulletin 120, Washington, D.C.

Stoltman, James B.
1972 The Late Archaic in the Savannah River Region. *The Florida Anthropologist* 25(2):37–62.

Stothert, Karen E.
1985 The Preceramic Las Vegas Culture of Coastal Ecuador. *American Antiquity* 50(3):613–637.
1988 *La prehistoria temprana de la península de Santa Elena, Ecuador: cultura Las Vegas.* Miscelánea Antropológica Ecuatoriana, Serie Monográfica 10, Guayaquil, Ecuador.

Struever, Stuart
1968 Flotation Techniques for the Recovery of Small-Scale Archaeological Remains. *American Antiquity* 33:353–362.

Terrell, John Edward, John P. Hart, Sibel Barut, Nicoletta Cellinese, Antonio Curet, Tim Denham, Chapurukha M. Kusimba, Kyle Latinis, Rahul Oka, Joel Palka, Mary E. D. Pohl, Kevin O. Pope, Patrick Ryan Williams, Helen Haines, and John E. Staller
2003 Domesticated Landscapes: The Subsistence Ecology of Plant and Animal Domestication. *Journal of Archaeological Method and Theory* 10(4):323–368.

Testart, A.
1982 The Significance of Food Storage among Hunter-Gatherers: Residence Patterns, Population Densities, and Social Inequalities. *Current Anthropology* 23:523–537.

Thomas, David Hurst
  1983 *The Archaeology of Monitor Valley, 1. Epistemology.* Anthropological Papers of the American Museum of Natural History, Vol. 58, Part 1, New York.

Tindale, Norman B.
  1977 Adaptive Significance of the Panara or Grass Seed Culture of Australia. In *Stone Tools as Cultural Markers,* edited by R. V. Wright, pp. 345–349. Australian Institute of Aboriginal Studies, Canberra.

Torrence, Robin
  1989 Tools as Optimal Solutions. In *Time, Energy, and Stone Tools,* edited by Robin Torrence. Cambridge University Press, Cambridge.

Tovar Pinzón, Hermes
  n.d. *Relaciones y visitas a los Andes.* Colcultura, Bogotá.

Turner, B. L. II, Robert Q. Hanham, and Anthony V. Portararo
  1977 Population Pressure and Agriculture Intensity. *Annals of the Association of American Geographers* 67(3):384–396.

Tykot, R. H.
  2002 Contribution of Stable Isotope Analysis to Understanding Dietary Variation among the Maya. In *Archaeological Chemistry: Materials, Methods and Meaning,* edited by K. Jakes, pp. 214–230. American Chemical Society Symposium Series 831, Washington, D.C.

Tykot, R. H., and J. E. Staller
  2002 The Importance of Early Maize Agriculture in Coastal Ecuador: New Data from La Emerenciana. *Current Anthropology* 43:666–677.

Tykot, R. H., N.J. van der Merwe, and N. Hammond
  1996 Stable Isotope Analysis of Bone Collagen and Apatite in the Reconstruction of Human Diet: A Case Study from Cuello, Belize. In *Archaeological Chemistry: Organic, Inorganic, and Biochemical Analysis,* edited by M. V. Orna, pp. 355–365. ACS Symposium Series 625, American Chemical Society, Washington, D.C.

Ubelaker, D. H.
  1984 Prehistoric Human Biology of Ecuador: Possible Temporal Trends and Cultural Correlations. In *Paleopathology and the Origins of Agriculture,* edited by Mark N. Cohen and George J. Armelagos, pp. 491–513. Academic Press, Orlando, Florida.

Van der Hammen, Thomas
  1974 The Pleistocene Changes of Vegetation and Climate in Tropical South America. *Journal of Biogeography* 1:3–26.
  1983 The Paleoecology and Paleogeography of Savannas. In *Ecosystems of the World 13: Tropical Savannas,* edited by Francois Bourliére, pp. 19–35. Elsevier Scientific, Amsterdam.
  1984 Datos sobre la historia de clima, vegetación y glaciación de la Sierra Nevada de Santa Marta. In *La Sierra Nevada de Santa Marta (Colombia) Transecto Buritaca–La Cumbra,* edited by Thomas Van der Hammen and Pedro M. Ruiz, pp. 561–573. J. Cramer, Berlin.

1991   Paleoecologia y estratigrafia de yacimientos preceramicos de Colombia. *Revista de Arqueología Americana* 3:57–77.

Van der Hammen, Thomas, J. F. Duivenvoorden, J. M. Lips, L. E. Urrego, and N. Espejo

1991   Fluctuaciones de nivel del agua del río y de la velocidad de sedimentación durante los ultimos 13000 años en el area del Medio Caquetá (Amazonia Colombiana). *Colombia Amazonica* 5(1):91–118.

Van der Merwe, N.J., J. A. Lee-Thorp, and J. S. Raymond

1993   Light, Stable Isotopes, and the Subsistence Base of Formative Cultures in Valdivia, Ecuador. In *Prehistoric Human Bone: Archaeology at the Molecular Level,* edited by J. B. Lambert and G. Grupe, pp. 63–97. Springer-Verlag, Berlin.

Vierra, Bradley J.

1975   Structure versus Function in the Archaeological Record. Unpublished Ph.D. dissertation, Department of Anthropology, University of New Mexico, Albuquerque.

Villalba, O. Marcelo

1988   *Cotocollao: una aldea formativa del Valle de Quito.* Museo Banco Central del Ecuador, Quito, Ecuador.

Vitelli, Karen D.

1989   Were Pots First Made for Foods? Doubts from Franchthi. *World Archaeology* 21(1):17–29.

Vogel, J. C., and Nikolaas van der Merwe

1977   Isotopic Evidence for Early Maize Cultivation in New York State. *American Antiquity* 42(2):238–242.

Wagner, G.

1982   Testing Flotation Recovery Rates. *American Antiquity* 47:127–132.

1986   The Corn and Cultivated Beans of the Fort Ancient Indians. *The Missouri Archaeologist* 47:107–135.

Wagner, U., R. Gebhard, E. Murad, J. Riederer, I. Shimada, C. Ulbert, F. E. Wagner, and A. M. Wipperns

1994   Condiciones de cocción y características de composición de la cerámica formativa: perspectiva arqueométrica. In *Tecnología y organización de la producción cerámica prehispanica en Los Andes,* edited by Izumi Shimada, pp. 121–156. Pontificia Universidad Católica del Perú: Fondo Editorial, Lima.

Walsh, R. P. D.

1981   The Nature of Climatic Seasonality. In *Climatic Seasonality in the Tropics,* edited by Robert Chambers, Richard Longhurst, and Arnold Pacey, pp. 11–29. Frances Printer, London.

Wandsnider, Luann

1997   The Roasted and the Boiled: Food Consumption and Heat Treatment with Special Emphasis on Pit-Hearth Cooking. *Journal of Anthropological Archaeology* 16:1–48.

Wang, R. L., A. Stec, J. Hey, L. Lukens, and J. Doebley
- 1999 The Limits of Selection during Maize Domestication. *Nature* 398:236–239.

Watson, Patty Jo
- 1974 *Archaeology of the Mammoth Cave Area.* Academic Press, New York.
- 1991 Origins of Food Production in Western Asia and Eastern North America. In *Quaternary Landscapes,* edited by Linda C. K. Shane and Edward J. Cushing, pp. 1–37. University of Minnesota Press, Minneapolis.

Wedel, Dale L.
- 1986 Some Thoughts on the Potential of Fire-Cracked Rock Studies in Archaeology. *The Wyoming Archaeologist* 29(3-4):159–164.

Wetterstrom, Wilma
- 1993 Foraging and Farming in Egypt: The Transition from Hunting and Gathering to Horticulture in the Nile Valley. In *The Archaeology of Africa: Food, Metals and Towns,* edited by Thurstan Shaw, Paul Sinclair, Bassey Andah, and Alex Okpoko, pp. 165–226. Routledge, New York.

Whallon, Robert, Jr.
- 1974 Spatial Analysis of Occupation Floors II: The Application of Nearest Neighbor Analysis. *American Antiquity* 39(1):16–34.
- 1986 A Spatial Analysis of Four Occupation Floors at Guilá Naquitz. In *Guilá Naquitz: Archaic Foraging and Early Agriculture in Oaxaca, Mexico,* edited by Kent V. Flannery, pp. 369–384. Academic Press, New York.

Widmer, Randolf
- 1988 *The Evolution of the Calusa, a Non-Agricultural Chiefdom on the Southwest Florida Coast.* University of Alabama Press, Tuscaloosa.
- 2002 The Woodland Archaeology of South Florida. In *The Woodland Southeast,* edited by D. G. Anderson and R. C. Mainfort, Jr., pp. 373–397. University of Alabama Press, Tuscaloosa.

Wiessner, Polly
- 1982 Risk, Reciprocity and Social Influences on !Kung San Economics. In *Politics and History in Band Societies,* edited by Eleanor Leacock and Richard Lee, pp. 61–84. Cambridge University Press, New York.

Wijmstra, T. A.
- 1967 A Pollen Diagram from the Upper Holocene of the Lower Magdalena Valley. *Leidse Geologische Mededelingen* 39:261–267.

Willey, Gordon R., and Charles R. McGimsey
- 1954 *The Monagrillo Culture of Panama.* Papers of the Peabody Museum of Archaeology and Ethnology, Vol. 49, No. 2, Harvard University Press, Cambridge, Massachusetts.

Williams, Denis
- 1997 Early Pottery in the Amazon: A Correction. *American Antiquity* 62(2):342–352.

Wilson, E.
- 1971 Competitive and Aggressive Behavior. In *Man and Beast: Comparative Social*

References Cited

        Behavior, edited by J. Eisenberg, W. Dillon, and S. Ripley, pp. 180–217. Smithsonian Institution Press, Washington, D.C.

Wilson, H. D.
- 1990   *Quinua* and Relatives (*Chenopodium* sect. *Chenopodium* subsect. *Cellulata*). In *New Perspectives on the Origin and Evolution of New World Domesticated Plants,* edited by Peter K. Bretting, pp. 92–110. *Economic Botany* 44 (Supplement).

Wilson, Samuel M., and Don J. Melnick
- 1990   Modelling Randomness in Locational Archaeology. *Journal of Archaeological Science* 17:403–412.

Winterhalder, Bruce
- 1986   Diet Choice, Risk, and Food Sharing in a Stochastic Environment. *Journal of Anthropological Archaeology* 5(4):369–392.
- 1990   Open Field, Common Pot: Harvest Variability and Risk Avoidance in Agricultural and Foraging Societies. In *Risk and Uncertainty in Tribal and Peasant Economies,* edited by Elisabeth Cashdan, pp. 67–87. Westview Press, Boulder, Colorado.
- 1996   Social Foraging and Behavioral Ecology of Intragroup Resource Transfers. *Evolutionary Anthropology* 5:46–57.
- 2001   The Behavioural Ecology of Hunter-Gatherers. In *Hunter-Gatherers: An Interdisciplinary Perspective,* edited by Catherine Panter-Brick, Robert H. Layton, and Peter Rowley-Conwy, pp. 12–38. Cambridge University Press, Cambridge.

Winterhalder, Bruce, and Carol Goland
- 1997   An Evolutionary Ecology Perspective on Diet Choice, Risk, and Plant Domestication. In *People, Plants, and Landscapes: Studies in Paleoethnobotany,* edited by Kristen J. Gremillion, pp. 123–160. University of Alabama Press, Tuscaloosa.

Wippern, Anna-Maria
- 1988   Evidencia estratigráfica en el desarrollo de la ceramica temprana de la Costa Caribe de Colombia. Paper presented at the 73th Congress of Americanists, Amsterdam.

Wittenberger, J.
- 1981   *Animal Social Behavior.* Wadsworth, California.

Woodburn, James
- 1982   Egalitarian Societies. *Man* 17(3):431–451.
- 1991   African Hunter-Gatherer Social Organization: Is It Best Understood as a Product of Encapsulation? In *Hunters and Gatherers: History, Evolution and Social Change,* edited by Tim Ingold, David Riches, and James Woodburn, pp. 31–63. Berg, New York.

Yarnell, Richard A.
- 1986   A Survey of Prehistoric Crop Plants in Eastern North America. *The Missouri Archaeologist* (47):47–59.

Zeidler, James A.
- 1986 La evolución local de asentamientos formativos en el Litoral Ecuatoriano: el caso de Real Alto. In *Arqueología de la Costa Ecuatoriana: Nuevos Enfoques,* edited by Jorge Marcos. Biblioteca Ecuatoriana de Arqueología, Quito, Ecuador.

Zevallos, Carlos, Walton Galinat, Donald W. Lathrap, Earl Leng, Jorge Marcos, and Kathleen Klumpp
- 1977 The San Pablo Corn Kernel and Its Friends. *Science* 196:385–389.

Zigmond, Maurice L.
- 1986 Kawaiisu. In *Great Basin,* edited by Warren L. D'Azevedo, pp. 398–411. Handbook of North American Indians, Vol. 11, Smithsonian Institution Press, Washington, D.C.

Zohary, D.
- 1989 Domestication of the Southwest Asian Neolithic Crop Assemblages of Cereals, Pulses, and Flax: The Evidence from the Living Plants. In *Foraging and Farming: The Evolution of Plant Exploitation,* edited by D. R. Harris and G. C. Hillman, pp. 358–373. Unwin Hyman, Boston.

Zohary, D., and M. Hopf
- 1988 *Domestication of Plants in the Old World.* Clarendon, Oxford.

Zvelebil, M., and P. Rowley-Conwy
- 1986 Foragers and Farmers in Atlantic Europe. In *Hunters in Transition. Mesolithic Societies of Temperate Eurasia and Their Transition to Farming,* edited by M. Zvelebil, pp. 67–93. Cambridge University Press, Cambridge.

Index

Accelerator mass spectrometry (AMS), 6, 129, 178
Achiote, 112
Achira (*Canna* sp.), 25
Adaptation, 2, 9, 20, 27, 32, 34, 41, 84, 111, 115, 131, 157
Africa, 61, 67, 107, 127, 128
Agave (*Agave* sp.), 57, 98
Agriculture, 24, 26, 33–34, 38–40, 42, 44, 46, 129, 146, 150, 153, 157, 164
Aguadulce Shelter, 27
Alabama, 43
Aldenderfer, Mark, 47
Algarrobo (*Prosopis juliflora*), 112, 156. *See also* Mesquite (*Prosopis*)
Altamaha River, 43
Amazon, xvii, xviii, 19, 24, 113, 129, 132
Amazon River, 46
American Bottom, 107, 152
Ampullariidae, 135, 136
Anacardiaceae, 10, 112
Andean High-Elevation Complex, 116
Andes, 24, 116, 119, 123, 132
Annonaceae, 10, 112
Anthropic soil, ix, 29, 31, 52, 60
Araracuara, 24, 129
Archaic/Formative period, 72, 106, 110, 113
Archaic period, 43, 44, 80, 98, 102, 106, 107, 152, 176
Argentina, 116
Arrowroot (*Maranta arundinacea*), (*Maranta* sp.), 25, 27, 108, 111, 126–27, 134, 143, 145, 155, 164
Asia, 39
Aspero, 47
Assemblage redundancy, 48, 61–64, 68, 147–48
Augering, ix, 29, 51–52, 54, 68, 165, 167–69
Australia, 34, 61, 67, 107
Ayacucho Caves, 116

Ayahuasca (*Banisteriopsis caapi*), 132
Axes, 7, 21, 25, 27, 46, 86, 151, 177

Balsas River, 127, 129
Banco de la Republica, xv, xvii, xx
Barlovento Period, 22–24, 116, 177
Barranca T-408 site, 21
Barranquilla, xvii
Barra pottery, 47
Base camps, 2, 35–36, 48, 61–65, 68, 70, 86, 111, 143, 146–48, 153, 158
Basin of Mexico, 129, 133
Bastardia viscolor, 15, 124
Beads, 2, 59, 111, 138–41, 149, 163–64
Beans (*Phaseolus lunatus*), 14, 112
Beans (*Phaseolus* spp.), 9, 14, 127
Beans (*Vigna unguiculata*), 9, 14, 127
Berggren, Greta, 115
Binford, Lewis, xix, 35–38, 39–40, 60, 63–64, 67–68, 87, 147–48, 153, 175
Bogotá, xix, 2, 19, 116, 119
Bolivia, 116, 132
Bollo limpio, 130, 145
Bottle gourds (*Lagenaria* sp.), 46–47, 105, 112
Brazil, 1, 19, 24, 46, 132, 175
Bromeliaceae, 11, 135
Brown, James A., 105
Bucarelia site, 21
Budares, 129
Burials, 68
Bushmen, 34

Caches, 36, 70, 89, 101
Caesalpiniaceae (Caesalpinoideae), 11, 12, 113, 118, 133, 142
Caimito (*Chrysophyllum cainito* L.), 17, 133
Calathea, 126
California, 34, 107, 152
Calima project, 24, 129

C. ambrosioides. See *Chenopodium* sp. (Chenopodiaceae)
Canal del Dique, 7, 21, 131
Canapote, 22, 23, 43
Canavalia sp. (jack bean), 25
Caribbean, 2, 19, 27, 129, 131, 177
Carmen de Bolívar, xvi, 18
Carnegie Museum of Natural History, Invertebrate Section, Pittsburgh, 135
Cartagena, xii, xvi–xviii, 2–3, 10
Cartagena de Indias. *See* Cartagena
Cartesian metric system, 29
Caryophyllaceae, 131
Cashdan, Elizabeth, 87
Cassia grandis, 12, 113
Cauca, 126
Cauca River, 7
Celts. *See* Shell hoes
Central America, 20, 28, 86, 129, 133
Cerro Maco, 87, 111, 149
Cerro Mangote, 27
Chiapas, 47
Chenopodium sp. (Chenopodiaceae), Quinua (*Chenopodium quinoa*), 12, 116, 117, 130
Chibcha, 119
Chicle (*Achras zapota*), 133
Chiefdom, 47
Chilca Caves, 130
Childe, V. Gordon, 42
Chile, 116
C. hircinum. See *Chenopodium* sp. (Chenopodiaceae)
Chiriquí region, 27
Chlorophora tinctoria, 113
Chocho (*Lupinus mutabilis*), 130
Chysobalanus icaco, 113
Cienaga Grande of Santa Marta, 19
Clark, John E., 47
Cloud forests, 111, 126, 135, 149
Collectors, 28, 36, 46, 80, 98, 103, 147, 156, 175–76
Colombia, iii, ix, xiii, xv–xviii, xix, 1–3, 7–9, 19–24, 28, 32, 43, 46, 73, 79, 113, 116, 123–24, 129, 131–35, 140, 142, 148, 159–60, 176
Comite Cultural y Civico de San Jacinto, xv
Common bean, 130. *See also* Beans (*Phaseolus lunatus*); Beans (*Phaseolus* spp.); Beans (*Vigna unguiculata*)

Competition, 41
Conquest, 176
Cordillera de la Costa National Park "Henry Pittier", 135
Costa Rica, 46
Cotocollao, 25–26, 130
Cotton (*Gossypium barbadense*), (*Gossypium* sp.), xvi, 15, 25, 112, 114, 124
Coxcatlán Cave, 129
C. quinoa (*quinua*). See *Chenopodium* sp. (Chenopodiaceae)
C3 plants, 1, 97, 106, 111, 119, 130, 143, 145
Cucurbitaceae, 12–13, 25. *See also* Squash
Cueva de Los Ladrones, 130
Cueva de los Vampiros, 126
Cueva San Agustín, 47
Cultivation, 34, 38, 40–41, 112, 146, 150–51, 154, 156, 165
Curated technology, 84–86, 100, 101, 106, 151, 177
Cyperaceae, 13, 110, 114, 117, 132, 142. See also *Cyperus* (Cyperaceae)
Cyperus (Cyperaceae), 25, 109, 117, 119, 131, 132, 134. *See also* Cyperaceae; *Cyperus odoratus*; *Cyperus rotundus* L.; Nut-grass (*Cyperus rotundus*)
Cyperus odoratus, 110, 114, 132. See also *Cyperus* (Cyperaceae)
Cyperus odoratus L. See *Cyperus odoratus*
Cyperus rotundus L., 132. See also *Cyperus* (Cyperaceae)

Department of Bolívar, 7, 123
Department of Boyacá, 116
Department of Sucre, xv
Depresíon Momposina (Mompos Depression), 7
Detoxification, 41
Diffusionism, 46
Dioscorea spp., 13, 27, 113
DNA, 1, 119
Domestication, 20, 38–41, 116, 146, 150–52, 154–56
Drymaeus sp., 109, 135, 137, 144
Dussan, Alicia, xix, 176
Dussan de Reichel, Alicia. *See* Dussan, Alicia
Dyson-Hudson, Rada, 87

Early Woodland, 44, 105
Earth ovens, ix, 2, 6, 21, 25–26, 30, 32, 56–

Index

59, 68, 99–100, 105–6, 111, 126–27, 130–31, 134, 143, 145, 152, 155, 157, 158, 164, 177
Eastern Agricultural Complex, 132
Ecuador, 3, 24, 25, 26, 27, 28, 32, 46–47, 116, 127, 129–30, 132, 134
Edge ground cobble, 25, 27, 88
Edge-trimmed tool tradition, 25
E. geniculata [L.] R. et S., 133
Egypt, 132
El Abra, 176
El Bongal, 21
Eleocharis sp., 117, 119, 131, 133–34
El Guamo, 21
El Paraiso, 47
El Pital, 24, 129
El Venado site, 116
Environment, 2, 6–7, 19, 25, 28, 32, 35–37, 39–41, 48, 50, 52, 60, 69, 85–86, 108–11, 115–16, 123, 126, 130, 135, 138, 142, 144, 146–50, 153, 156, 163, 166
Epipaleolithic, 132
Escobar, Pablo, xvii
Ethnobotanical study, 115
Ethnographic, 33, 37, 42, 67, 99, 107, 113, 133, 134
Eupatorium (Asteraceae), 11, 109, 117, 119, 131, 134
Euphorbiaceae, 13, 113
Europe, 131–32
Expedient technology, 21, 83–84, 85, 86, 87–88, 106, 151

Fabaceae (Papilionoideae), 14, 118, 133
Factor analysis, 64–65
Fayette County, Kentucky, x, 120
Feasting, 157–58
Feature, definition of 63, excavation of, 6, 29, 30, 31, 48, 50, 56, 57, 58, 59, 60, 64, 65, 66, 67, 68, 90, 91, 92, 93, 96, 97, 98, 99, 103, 104, 105, 108, 115, 126, 131, 134
Fermentation, 2, 41, 101, 106, 130, 145, 157–58, 164
Fermented beverage. *See* Fermentation
Fiber-tempered pottery, xi, 1, 2, 3, 7, 21, 32–33, 42–45, 46, 47, 70, 100, 144, 158–62, 176
Field camp, 36
Fire-cracked rocks, ix, x, xiii, xiv, 26, 47, 57–59, 68, 70, 72, 80–83, 87, 89, 93, 96–106, 152, 158, 176
Fire-pits, x, 56–57, 59, 66–68, 70, 72, 81, 87, 89, 93, 96, 98–99, 101–2, 104, 106, 131, 148, 177
Flannery, Kent V., 39, 87, 89, 102, 154
Florida, 43–44, 46, 177
Flotation, 31, 115
Food production, 1, 24, 26–28, 33, 38–41, 46, 48, 86, 146, 150–57, 164, 176
Foragers, 24, 36, 147, 153, 175
Ford, R. I., 39
Formative, ix, 4, 22, 25, 110, 130
14C-dated. *See* Radiocarbon dating
Fungi, 119

Genipa americana, 113
Gentry, Alwyn H., 123
Georgia, 43
Geo Shih, 154
Gift, 40, 49, 158
Gosser, Dennis, 47
Gossypium. See Cotton (*Gossypium barbadense*)
Gourds. *See* Bottle gourds (*Lagenaria* sp.)
Grasses (Poaceae), x, xiv, 7, 9, 20, 32, 40, 57, 70, 72, 78, 89, 97–98, 100, 106–8, 113–14, 115, 119, 126–28, 130, 134, 142–43, 145, 152, 156, 164. *See also* Poaceae
Great Basin, 107, 152
Grog-tempered pottery, 1, 22, 43
Ground stone, 25, 27, 41, 48, 72, 85–87, 89, 96–97, 106, 130, 143, 148, 151, 156, 157, 164
Guajaro, 22–23
Guandala, 26
Guayas province, 25
Guilá Naquitz (rockshelter), 127, 129, 154–55
Gulf Coastal Plain, 42–43, 45
Gulf Coast of Mexico, 129
Gum arabic or gum acacia (*Acacia senegal* or *A. arabica*), 133
Guttiferae, 15, 112
G/wi San, 35

Hammerstones, xiii, 71–72, 81, 83, 88, 90, 96–97
Harrington, H. D., 115
Harris, David R., 39–40, 109, 142
Harvest (*la cosecha*), 112

Hearths, 57, 67, 100
Heliconia, 126
Highbee Tavern site, x, 120
Historical ecology, 2, 20
Holldobler, Bert, 87
Holocene, 19–20
Horticulture, 24, 28, 34
Huaca de los Idolos, 47
Huaca de los Sacrificios, 47
Huaca Prieta, 25, 47
Hunter-gatherers, 2, 25, 28, 32, 34–36, 37, 41–42, 44–47, 48, 56, 60, 61, 63, 65, 82–83, 85, 98, 101, 107, 111, 146, 151, 153, 155–57, 163–64, 175
Hyriidae, 135, 136

Identity, 2, 48, 157–58, 163
Inga densiflora, 16, 112
Instituto Colombiano de Antropología e Historia, xx
Intensification, 34, 38–41, 48–49, 146, 152–54, 157–58, 177
Inuit, 35
Ipomoea sp., 113. See also Sweet potato
Isely, Duane, 115
Isotope analysis, 1, 119

Junin basin, 116

Kelly, Robert L., 86–87
Kentucky, xix, 120, 178
Kilns, 6, 29, 145, 164
Kinship, 34, 40, 45, 49
Knotweed (*Polygonum erectum*), 132
Kofán, 132
Kramer, Karen, 89
Kua San, 107
!Kung, 67

La Galgada, 47
Lake Ayauch, 24
Lake Moriru (Brazil), 19–20
Lake Valencia (Venezuela), 19
Landscape, 33, 36, 50, 138, 145–46, 148–52, 154–57, 163–64
La Palestina site, 21
Las Vegas tradition (10,000B7000 B.P.), 25–26, 129
Latin American, xv, 42
Lauraceae, 15, 112–13

Lee, Richard, 175
Leguminosae, 109, 114, 117, 118, 119, 131, 133, 142
Levant, 89, 107, 152
Lidita (flint), 83–84, 87–88
Limolite silica, 83–84, 87–88
Lipid analysis, 1
Llanos of Colombia, 19, 148
Llanos of Venezuela, 148
Location, 36
Logistic mobility, 35–38, 40–41, 42, 43, 48, 61, 62–63, 64, 65, 67, 146–49, 151, 156, 163–64
Loma Alta, 25–26, 134
Loma Torremonte site, 133
Los Gavilanes, 130

Macaví Period, 131
Machalilla Period, 26
MacNeish, Richard S., 39
Magdalena River, 7, 20–21, 131, 133
Magdalena Valley. See Magdalena River
Maíz de sereno (maize of the mists), 112
Maize (*Zea mays*), x, 1, 17, 22, 24–28, 39, 72, 86, 106, 112–14, 119–22, 123, 124–25, 126, 127–30, 145–46, 154, 156, 178
Maize mush (*choclo*), 126
Malachra rudis, 15, 109, 114, 124
Malambo, 22
Mallow family (Malvaceae), 15, 109, 118, 114, 119, 123–24, 134
Malvastrum americanum, 123
Malvastrum (Malvaceae), 109, 118–19, 123–24, 126, 134, 142
Manabí province, 25
Manioc (*Manihot esculenta*), 13, 22, 27, 112–13, 127, 129
Manos, 6, 25, 26–27, 32, 71–72, 81, 92–93, 106, 129–30, 134, 145, 151
Marantaceae, 111, 126, 134, 145, 164
Masa (humid mush), 130
Mauss, Marcel, 40, 158
Mesoamerica, 46, 85, 89, 129, 133
Mesquite (*Prosopis*), 133
Metate/Mano technology. See Metates
Metates, x, xiii, 6–7, 21, 25–27, 32, 71–72, 78–80, 88–94, 96–97, 106, 126, 129–30, 134, 145, 151, 177
Mexico, 46, 127, 129, 133
Middle Orinoco, 24

Index

Middle range theory, 61
Midwest (United States), 42, 44
Mimosaceae, 15–16, 112–13, 118, 133, 135
Mimosoideae, 133
Mina phase, 46
Mississippi, 43
Missouri River, 44
Missouri, University of, 119
Mobility, xiii, 1–2, 21, 22, 32–37, 38, 40–42, 48, 52, 60–64, 69–70, 82–87, 98, 106, 111, 135, 138, 145–51, 153, 155, 175, 177
Mollusks, x, xiv, xviii, 2, 20, 46, 56, 59, 61, 108, 111, 114, 126, 134, 136, 138, 142–45, 146, 152, 155, 163–64
Momil, 22, 129
Monagrillo site, 27–28
Monsú, 21–22, 23, 24, 43, 70, 101, 103, 105, 116, 131, 176–77
Montes de Maria, 7
Montgomery, F. H., 115
Moraceae, 113
Morse, Douglass H., 87
Mortars, x, xiii, 71–72, 81, 88, 94–96, 151, 177
Municipio de San Juan de Nepomuseno, 21
Municipio de Zambrano, 21
Museo Nacional de Colombia, Bogotá, 72, 73, 79, 159–60
Museo de Oro, Banco de la Republica, xv, xvii, 2, 74–77
Mycetopodidae, 135–36
Myrtaceae, 112–13, 116

Natufian Period, 89
Nearest-neighbor, 65, 66, 67, 68
Nebo Hill site, 44
Neocyclotus, xi, xiv, 111, 126, 135, 138–40, 143, 164
Neocyclotus cfr. *dysoni*, xi, xiv, 136, 138, 141
New World, 1–3, 20, 24, 32, 144, 146
Níspero (*Manilkara zapota* (L.) P. von Royen. Syn: *Achras zapota* L.), 18, 133–34
Norr, Lynette, 130
North America, 85–86, 105, 107, 131–32
Northwest Coast Indians, 34
Nunamiut, 61
Nutcrackers, x, 7, 21, 46, 72, 88, 95, 151, 177
Nut-grass (*Cyperus rotundus*), 132. See also *Cyperus* (Cyperaceae)
Nutting stones. *See* Nutcrackers

Oaxaca, 46, 107
Oca (*Oxalis tuberosa*), 130
Oceania, 107
O'Connell, James F., 63
Ocos pottery, 47
Ocotea, 112
Old World, 131–33
Opercula. *See* Operculum
Operculum, xi, 2, 59, 111, 135, 139–41, 149, 163–64
Orange series, 42–43
Organización de Campesinos "Hacienda Cataluña", xvii
Orthalicus maracaibensis, 109, 135, 137, 144
Orthalicus undatus (Bruguiére), 135, 137

Pachamachay Cave, 124, 130
Paleoindian, 176
Paleolithic, 132
Palmae, 16, 25, 27, 111, 113, 126, 135, 156, 177
Palynological. *See* Pollen
Panama, 24, 26–28, 46, 127, 130, 134
Panama Canal, 19
Panauluaca Cave, 116
Panela, 126
Papa (*Solanum tuberosum*), 130
Papaya, 8, 112
Pará, 46
Paraguay, 116
Parenchyma, xi, 119–21, 123–25
Parita region, 27
Parodiz, Juan, xviii, 135
Parry, William 86–87
Passion fruit, 8, 112
Patchy resources, 42, 86, 153
Pavonia, 124
Pearsall, Deborah M., 115
Pearson's correlation, 102, 104–5, 135, 138
Peñones del Río site, 21
Pepper, 9, 112
Persea americana, 112
Perez-Arbelaez, E., 123
Peru, 25, 39, 46, 47, 116, 124, 130, 132
Peten, 19
Petroglyphs, 163
Phyllanthus acidus, 13, 113
Phytoliths, xix, 24–25, 27, 108, 111, 126, 129–30, 145
Pianka, Eric R, 87
Pinder, David, 65

Pleistocene, 9, 20
Poaceae, 16–17, 109–10, 118, 119. *See also* Grasses (Poaceae)
Pohl, Richard W., 115
Point bar, 52, 56, 67–68, 110, 127, 134, 148, 163
Pollen, 9, 19, 24–25, 27, 108–9, 129–30, 135, 142, 144, 146
Polygonaceae, 17, 112, 118–19, 131
Polygonum, 110, 118–19, 131–32, 142
Polyporous spp., 119
Pomacea cornucopia (Reeve), xiv, 136, 138–39
Pomacea elegans (d'Orbigny), xiv, 136, 138–39
Pomacea spp., xi, xiv, 70, 135, 138–42
Portulacaceae, 17, 118–19, 130–31
Portulaca meracioides, 17, 110, 114
Portulaca oleracea, 131
Portulaca sp., 110, 114, 118–19, 130–31, 134, 142–43, 164
Pottery. *See* Fiber-tempered pottery, Grog-tempered pottery, Sand-tempered pottery, Shell-tempered pottery.
Pox and Espiridión complex, 46
Preceramic, 20, 24, 25, 26, 27, 28, 47, 129, 130, 132, 134
Precipitation, 9, 18, 19, 20, 50, 109, 135, 163
Predictability, 151
Prestige, 2, 157–58
Preucel, Robert W., Jr., 175
Prickly pear (*Opuntia* sp.), 57
Prosobranchia, 135–37
Prosopis juliflora. See Algarrobo (*Prosopis juliflora*)
Puerto Chacho, x, 1, 21–23, 32, 70, 72, 101, 103
Puerto Hormiga, xi, xv, 1–2, 21–23, 32, 43, 70, 72, 101, 103, 105, 160, 176–77
Puerto Nare T-46 site, 21
Pulmonates, 135, 137
Purrón pottery, 46
Purslane. See *Portulaca* sp.

Qarunian, 132
Quarries, 84
Quebrada de Las Pircas sites, 116
Quebrada de San Jacinto, 153

Radiocarbon dating, xiii, 3, 6, 21–23, 31, 46, 115, 177
Real Alto, 25–26, 129

Redundancy of features, 48, 62, 63, 64, 65, 68, 147
Reichel-Dolmatoff, Gerardo, xv, xix, 2, 94, 176–77
Reid, Kenneth C., 101
Residential camps, 36–37, 48, 62
Residential mobility, 35–37, 42, 62, 67, 147–48
Rhizomes, 89, 106, 132, 177
Río Chila, 47
Risk, 35, 39–41, 47, 56, 148
Risk-management theories. *See* Risk
Rituals, 47, 132, 134, 143, 146, 164
Roosevelt, Anna Curtenius, 24, 175
Root crops, 22, 24, 27–28
Rosaceae, 17, 113
Rosenberg, Michael, 155
Rubiaceae, 17, 113

Sago, 177
Sahara, 107
Salgado (Pará) (Brazil), 46
Salinas de Chao, 47
San Andrés, 129
Sand-tempered pottery, 1, 7, 21, 22, 24, 43, 46, 158, 175
San Jacinto 1, Colombia, South America: acknowledgements, i, iii, vii, ix–xi, xiii, xvi, xix, xxi; location, environment, and excavation, 1–7, 10, 19–22, 28–32; theoretical framework, 33, 39, 42; strata and features, 50–52, 56–57, 59, 61, 62–65, 67–69; pottery and lithics, 70–71, 73–76, 80–82, 87–89, 92–94, 97–98, 100–102, 105–7; ecofactual remains, 108–11, 114–15, 119–22, 124–27, 130–34, 139–43; conclusions in perspective, 144–59, 163–64; notes, 176, 178
San Jacinto (stream), 2
San Jacinto (town), v, xv–xviii, 2–3, 5, 7, 10, 18–20, 50, 87, 110, 112–15, 124, 126–27, 130, 134, 140, 143–44, 149, 153, 163, 177
San Jacinto 2, xi, 1, 6–7, 21–23, 101, 111, 140, 145, 159, 161–62
San Jorge River, 7
San Juan de Bedout site, 21
San Juan de Nepomuceno, Bolívar, Colombia, xiii, xvi–xvii, 8, 21
San Marcos, 23
San Marcos Cave, 129

Index

Sanoja, Mario, 24
San Pablo site, 25
Santa Elena, 26
Santa Elena Peninsula, 25
Santa Marta, xvii, 19
Santarem, Brazil, 1, 46, 175
Santee River, 43
Sapodilla. See *Níspero (Manilkara zapota* (L.) P. von Royen. Syn: *Achras zapota* L.)
Sapotaceae, 17–18, 25, 109, 113–14, 118–19, 131, 133–34, 142–43, 164
Sarmiento, Guillermo, 7
Sassaman, Kenneth, 45
Savanna, 2, 7, 9, 19, 20, 22, 32, 39–41, 48, 109, 111, 134, 142, 144, 145, 149
Savannah River, 42–43
Savannas of Bolívar, 7, 20, 111, 113
Scanning electron microscopy (SEM), x, xi, 1, 108, 119–25
Scheduling, 40–41, 85–86, 151, 153, 154, 155, 157
Scirpus/Cyperus, 25, 132
Seasonality, 2, 7, 9, 19–20, 22, 28, 31–32, 34, 35, 37, 40–41, 48, 50–52, 56, 59–60, 62, 63–65, 67–68, 107–16, 123, 127, 129, 131, 138, 140–48, 149, 150–56, 157, 163–64, 177
Secoyas, 132
Sedentism, 20, 24, 28, 33, 34, 35, 38–40, 42–43, 46–48, 63, 85, 146, 149–50, 155, 157
Sedges (*Cyperus* spp.). See *Cyperus* (Cyperaceae)
Seed crops, 27
SEM. *See* Scanning electron microscopy.
Senna, 133
Serranía, 140
Serranía de San Jacinto, ix, 7, 9, 19, 21, 155
Sharanahuas, 132
Shell hoes, 24, 177
Shell middens, 21–22, 42–43, 46, 70, 109, 135, 176
Shell mound. *See* Shell middens
Shell-tempered pottery, 22, 43, 46, 175
Sida (Malvaceae), 109–10, 118–19, 123–24, 126, 134, 142
Sida rhombifolia L., 15, 110, 126
Sierra Nevada de Santa Marta, 19, 135
Sincelejo, xv
Sinú culture, 7
Sionas, 132

Sitio Sierra, 27
Smith, Bruce D., 39, 87
Soapstone, 45
Social hierarchy, 35
Social storage, 40
Soconusco, Chiapas, 47
Sotol (*Dasylirion texanum*), 57
South African, 175
South America, 3, 20, 25, 28, 32, 110, 113, 116, 119, 129–31, 133, 144, 163, 176
South Carolina, 43
Southeast (United States), 1, 42, 44, 45
Spatial incongruity, 37
Spatial-temporal territoriality, 40, 42, 86–87, 111, 146, 149, 155–57, 163
Special-purpose camps, 2, 36, 48, 61–63, 64, 65, 67, 68, 89, 107, 115, 144, 146–49, 154, 158, 163
Special-purpose locations. *See* special-purpose camps
Special-purpose sites. *See* special-purpose camps
Spencer, Charles, 102
Squash, 112
Stallings Island, 42
Stallings series, 42–43
Starch grains, 25, 27
Stark, Barbara L., 39
Stations, 36, 107
Sterculiaceae, 18, 113
Storage, 25–26, 34–36, 37–38, 65, 100, 143, 145–46, 152, 158, 164
Stratigraphy, 3, 6, 31, 50–52, 54–55, 68, 72, 96, 135, 144, 157, 176
Strombus gigas celts. *See* Shell hoes
Sub-Sahara, 107
Subsistence, 24–26, 28, 34–35, 46, 56, 65, 70, 84–87, 100, 106–7, 130, 151, 153, 177
Sweet potato, 9, 112. *See also* Ipomoea sp.

Tamaulipas, 129
Taperinha, 24, 46
Tehuacán Valley, 46, 129
Temple of the Crossed Hands, Kotosh, 47
Temporal incongruity, 37
Tennessee Valley, 43
Teosinte, xi, 120, 121, 122, 123, 125, 127, 145. See also *Zea mays* ssp. *mexicana* x *Zea mays* ssp. *mays; Zea mays* ssp. *mexicana; Zea mays* ssp. *parviglumis*

Tequendama, 176
Terrell, John Edward, 39
Terremote, 133
Territoriality, 2, 34, 42, 48, 69, 86, 111, 143–44, 146, 149–50, 153–58, 163
Testart, A. 34–36
Thiaridae, 135, 136
Thomas, David Hurst, 89
Thom's Creek series, 42–43
Tierras Largas phase, 47
Tobacco, xvi, 112
Tocaima, 123
Tombigbee Valley, 43
Totumos (*Crescentia cujete*), 11, 105
Transhumance, 39
Tree snails, *Drymaeus* sp. See *Drymaeus* sp.
Tree snails, *Orthalicus* spp. See *Orthalicus maracaibensis*
Trilinear theory, 39
Tukanos, 132

United States, 1, 42–44, 133
Unpredictability, 40, 48–49, 175
Uruguay, 116

Valdivia I, III, 26
Valdivia Period (5500–4400 B.P.), 3, 25–26, 32

Valdivia tradition. *See* Valdivia Period (5500–4400 B.P.)
Valle, 126
Valley of Oaxaca, Mexico, 127, 129
Van der Hammen, Thomas, 19
Venezuela, 19, 24, 28, 116, 133, 135
Veranillo de San Juan, 50
Verdolaga (*Portulaca* sp.). See *Portulaca* sp.
Virgulatus (Férussac). See *Drymaeus* sp.

Wadi Kubbaniya, 132
Watson, Patti Jo, 39
Whallon, Robert, Jr, 65
Wilson, Edward O., 87
Wheeler series, 42–43

Yams (*Dioscorea* sp.). See *Dioscorea* spp.

Zea mays. See Maize (*Zea mays*)
Zea mays L. *See* Maize (*Zea mays*)
Zea mays ssp. *mexicana*, 127, 129. *See also* Teosinte
Zea mays ssp. *mexicana* x *Zea mays* ssp. *mays*, 121, 123, 125. *See also* Teosinte
Zea mays ssp. *parviglumis*, 127. *See also* Teosinte
Zoomorphic, 6, 70, 73, 101, 106, 162, 163